COMPUTER PROGRAMMING
AND
IT

AF518472

COMPUTER PROGRAMMING

AND

IT

By

Er. ASHISH SHARMA

B.E., M. Tech (Comp. Sc.), Ph.D. (Purs.)

Object Oriented Programming in Java

Head of the Department

Presidency College of Engineering

(A Part of Maharishi Arvind Group of Institution)

Kota

Rajasthan

UNIVERSITY SCIENCE PRESS

(An Imprint of Laxmi Publications Pvt. Ltd.)

BANGALORE • CHENNAI • COCHIN • GUWAHATI • HYDERABAD
JALANDHAR • KOLKATA • LUCKNOW • MUMBAI • RANCHI

NEW DELHI • BOSTON, USA

Copyright © 2013 by Laxmi Publications Pvt. Ltd. All rights reserved. No part of this publication may be reproduced, stored in a retrieval system, or transmitted in any form or by any means, electronic, mechanical, photocopying, recording or otherwise without the prior written permission of the publisher.

Published by :

UNIVERSITY SCIENCE PRESS

(An Imprint of Laxmi Publications Pvt. Ltd.)
113, Golden House, Daryaganj,
New Delhi-110002

Phone : 011-43 53 25 00
Fax : 011-43 53 25 28

www.laxmipublications.com
info@laxmipublications.com

First Edition : 2013

OFFICES

✆ **Bangalore**	080-26 75 69 30	✆ **Chennai**	044-24 34 47 26
✆ **Cochin**	0484-237 70 04, 405 13 03	✆ **Guwahati**	0361-251 36 69, 251 38 81
✆ **Hyderabad**	040-24 65 23 33	✆ **Jalandhar**	0181-222 12 72
✆ **Kolkata**	033-22 27 43 84	✆ **Lucknow**	0522-220 99 16
✆ **Mumbai**	022-24 91 54 15, 24 92 78 69	✆ **Ranchi**	0651-2204464, 221 47 64

UCP-9623-195-COMPUTER PROGRAM & IT-SHA C—

Typesetted at : Shubham Composer, New Delhi. *Printed at: Mehra Offset Press Delhi*

Contents

PREFACE

Computer Programming and IT is the entry-level subject in First year B.Tech/B.E/ MCA/MBA/ DIPLOMA and other courses. It is required of all students who are in engineering "common core curriculum", which also includes two parts—first is basic fundamental of computers and second is programming in C language. Most of the students have had little or no prior formal training in computation, although many have played with computers a bit and a few have had extensive programming or hardware-design experience.

Our design of this introductory computer-science subject reflects two major concerns. First, we want to establish the idea that a basic of computer is not just a way of getting a computer to perform operations but rather that it is a novel formal medium for expressing ideas about methodology. Thus, theory must be written for people to read, and only incidentally for machines to execute. Second, we believe that the programming part level is not the syntax of particular programming-language constructs, nor clever algorithms for computing particular functions efficiently, nor even the mathematical analysis of algorithms and the foundations of computing, but rather the techniques used to control the intellectual complexity of large software systems.

Our goal is that students who complete this subject should have a good feel for the elements of style and the aesthetics of programming. They should have command of the major techniques for controlling complexity in a large system. They should know what not to read, and what they need not understand at any moment. They should feel secure about modifying a program, retaining the spirit and style of the original author.

These skills are by no means unique to computer programming. The techniques we teach and draw upon are common to all of engineering design. We control complexity by building abstractions that hide details when appropriate.

Underlying our approach to this subject is our conviction that "computer science" is not a science and that its significance has little to do with computers. The computer revolution is a revolution in the way we think and in the way we express what we think.

—Author

ACKNOWLEDGEMENTS

We would like to thank the many people who have helped us develop this book and this curriculum.

We owe a great debt to Mrs. Bharti Parashar (Chairperson), Shri Sanjay Parashar (Director), Dr. Bharat Parashar (Director), Dr. (Prof.) A. K. Arora (Principal), Dr. (Prof.) R.D. Sharma (Principal), Maharishi Arvind Group of Institutes, Jaipur and Kota; Dr. (Prof.) A.K. Mathur (Rajasthan Technical University), Dr. (Prof.) A. K. Diwedi (Rajasthan Technical University), Dr. (Prof.) Akhil Garg (Principal),Vyas Engineering College, Jodhpur.

It is difficult to identify all the people who have contributed to the development of our curriculum. We thank all the lecturers, recitation instructors, and tutors who have worked with us over the past fifteen years and put in many extra hours on our subject, especially Mr. Arun Singh Chauhan, Harjindra, Shaukin Dhakar, Sumit, Hari Om Pancholi, Yatendra Jaimen. We would like to specially acknowledge the outstanding teaching contributions of many other peoples for their contributions to the exposition of nondeterministic evaluation in chapter 4.

Many people have put in significant effort presenting this material at other universities. Some of the people we have worked closely with us, Rajasthan Technical University of Rajasthan. We are exceptionally proud of our colleagues who have received major teaching awards for their adaptations of this subject at other universities.

We would like to thank the talented instructors who have designed continuing education courses.

We appreciate the work of those who contributed to making this a real book. Finally, we would like to acknowledge the support of the organizations.

—Author

SYLLABUS

COMPUTER PROGRAMMING AND IT

Class B. Tech. 1st Semester	Evolution
Schedule per week	Examination Time = Three (3) Hours
Lectures : 3	Maximum Marks = 100
Tutorial : -	[Mid-term (20) & End-term (80)]

Units	Contents of the Subject
I	• Introduction: Stored Program Architecture of Computers, Evolution of Processors (In terms of word length & Speed only), Storage Device- Primary Memory and Secondary Storage, Working Principle of Primary Storage devices- RAM, ROM, PROM, EPROM, EEPROM, Random, Direct, Sequential access methods. • Language Translators—Concept of High-Level, Assembly and Low Level programming languages. Working of Assembler, Interpreter and compiler. Representing Algorithms through flow chart, pseudo code, step by step etc.
II	• Number System: Data Representation, Concept of radix and representation of numbers in radix r with special cases of r=2, 8, 10 and 16 with conversion from radix r_1 to radix r_2. r's and (r–l)'s complement. Representation of Integer in sign-magnitude, signed l's and 2's complement. Floating point representation. Concept of bias and normalization. Representation of alphabets. • Binary Codes: Binary arithmetic, Addition and subtraction of Integers and floating point numbers. Multiplication of Integers. Gray code, BCD 8421 and 2421, Excess-3 and Excess-3 gray codes.
III	• Programming in C: Structure of C Program, Concept of Preprocessor, Macro Substitution, Intermediate code, Object Code, Executable Code. Compilation Process. Basic Data types, Importance of braces ({ }) in C Program, enumerated data type, Identifiers, Scope of Variable, Storage Class, Constants, Expressions in C, Type Casting, Control Statements, printf(), scanf (), reading single character. Command Line Arguments.
IV	• Arrays in C, Pointers, Using pointers to represent arrays, Dynamic Memory allocation, Structures, using typedef, Arrays of Structures & pointers, File Handling (Opening in different modes & closing of file, fscanf & fprintf only).
V	• Functions in C, Passing Parameters (By value & Reference), using returned data, Passing arrays, structures, array of structures, pointer to structures etc., passing characters and strings, The void pointer.

1

INTRODUCTION

WHAT IS A COMPUTER?

The word computer is derived from the word 'COMPUTE'. It is a machine which can perform arithmetical operations at higher speed. However, the modern days computer offers much more than the idea worked behind the invention of computer.

A computer can be defined as an electronic device which processes the information supplied (inputs) and produces the desired result (output) according to the given instruction (programs or software).

Computer : C → Calculate ; O → Operate ; M → Memorize ; P → Print ; U → Update ; T → Tabulate ; E → Edit ; R → Response.

Characteristics of a Computer

Computer is the most valuable invention of this century and it has made our life easier and fast. We should know about the unique characteristics of this under machine.

Following are the main characteristics of a computer:

1. *Speed* : A computer is a high speed device. It can perform a task in seconds for which manual man power may require a year or even more.
2. *Accuracy* : A computer maintains high degree of accuracy provided there is no human mistake *i.e.*, faulty programming or inaccurate datas.
3. *Consistency* : A computer can work for hours without lack of concentration, tiredness or emotional feelings.
4. *Versatility* : The most wonderful feature of a computer is its versatility. It can change over to various types of jobs within a very short span of time.
5. *Remembrance Power* : Human brains are volatile and remember only important information which may be lost as the time passes. A computer has permanent storage device where each and every piece of information can be retained for a long period.
6. *Lack of I.Q.* : Unlike human beings computer lacks I.Q. power. This is human being only who decides what a computer has to do. Human intelligence behind the performance of a computer.
7. *No Feelings* : Since computer is a machine it is free from emotional and sentimental feelings.

Types of Computers

There used to be two fundamentally different types of computers : analog and digital. (Hybrid computers combine elements of both types). In our everyday use, the term "computer" refers to digital computers, with a typical example being the common personal computer (PC). Digital computers are essentially simple machines that can understand and manipulate only series of elementary symbols : 0's and 1's (yes or no, true or false). The real power of a digital computer lies in the blinding speed with which it can check and manipulate these symbols, outperforming any human being. In computer lingo a bit (binary digit) is the term one uses to represent a 0 or a 1. A nibble is a series of four bits, a byte is a series of eight bits and word is used to represent multiple bytes. The trick is to arrange these series of 0's and 1's in such a manner that they represent whatever needs to be symbolized. For example, one could assign these 0's and 1's to represent a special code to instruct the machine what to do next and with what data. These designated sequences of 0's and 1's are called computer instructions. It is these instructions, when arranged in a structured sequence, *i.e.*, a computer program, that distinguish the digital computer from a fast calculator. The sequence in which these instructions are executed can be altered depending on the outcome of the actions of previous instructions within the machine or input from the outside world. Instructions arrange and shuffle the bits, nibbles and bytes in such a manner that the computer can perform complex calculations and then, minutes later, help us with word processing or enable us to record variables from a monitoring device we use during anethesia.

Today's computers are of three main types : mainframes, minicomputers and microcomputers. They differ in size, speed of operation, amount of data that can be stored and the number of simultaneous users. Mainframes allow many simultaneous users, handle typically huge databases and can perform complex mathematical operations. We find them mainly in industry, research and university computing centers. Minicomputers can support a smaller number of simultaneous users, typically 50 to 100. These machines are primarily used by larger businesses to handle accounting, billing, and inventory records.

The microcomputer is essentially a personal or desktop computer. These desktop PCs, which dwarf the capabilities of the huge early computers, are used extensively in the home (entertainment, communication, personal databases and spreadsheets) and in all types of businesses (word processing, accounting, inventory control, research).

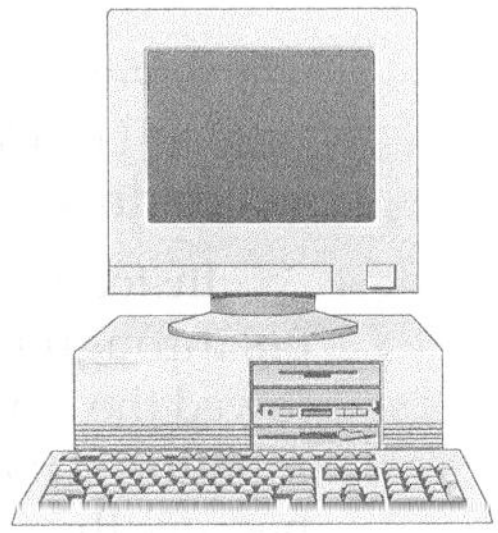

Fig. 1.1

THE FIVE GENERATIONS OF COMPUTERS

The history of computer development is often referred to in reference to the different generations or computing devices. Each generation of computer is characterized by a major technological development that fundamentally changed the way computers operate, resulting in increasingly smaller, cheaper, more powerful and more efficient and reliable devices. Read about each generation and the developments that led to the current devices that we use today.

First Generation—1940-1956 : Vacuum Tubes

The first generation computers used vacuum tubes for circuitry and magnetic drums for memory and were often enormous, taking up entire rooms. They were very expensive to operate and in addition to using a great deal of electricity, generated a lot of heat, which was often the cause of malfunctions. First generation computers relied on machine language to perform operations and they could only solve one problem at a time. Input was based on punched cards and paper tape and output was displayed on printouts.

The UNIVAC and ENIAC computers are examples of first-generation computing devices. The UNIVAC was the first commercial computer delivered to a business client, the U.S. Census Bureau in 1951.

Second Generation—1956–1963 : Transistors

Transistors replaced vacuum tubes and ushered in the second generation of computers. The transistor was invented in 1947 but did not see widespread use in computers until the late 50s. The transistor was far superior to the vacuum tube, allowing computers to become smaller, faster, cheaper, more energy-efficient and more reliable than their first-generation predecessors. Though the transistor still generated a great deal of heat that subjected the computer to damage, it was a vast improvement over the vacuum tube. Second-generation computers still relied on punched cards for input and printouts for ouptut.

Second-generation computers moved from cryptic binary machine language to symbolic, or assembly, languages, which allowed programmers to specify instructions in words. High-level programming languages were also being developed at this time, such as early versions of COBOL and FORTRAN. These were also the first computers that stored their instructions in their memory, which moved from a magnetic drum to magnetic core technology.

The first computers of this generation were developed for the atomic energy industry.

Third Generation—1964–1971 : Integrated Circuits

The development of the integrated circuit was the hallmark of the third generation of computers. Transistors were miniaturized and placed on silicon chips, called semiconductors, which drastically increased the speed and efficiency of computers.

Instead of punched cards and printouts, users interacted with third generation computers through keyboards and monitors and interfaced with an operating system, which allowed the device to run many different applications at one time with a central program that monitored the memory. Computers for the first time became accessible to a mass audience because they were smaller and cheaper than their predecessors.

Fourth Generation—1971–Present : Microprocessors

The microprocessor brought the fourth generation of computers, as thousands of integrated circuits were built into a single silicon chip. What in the first generation filled an entire room could now fit in the palm of the hand. The Intel 4004 chip, developed in 1971, located all the components of the computer-from the central processing unit and memory to input/output controls on a single chip.

In 1981 IBM introduced its first computer for the home user and in 1984 Apple introduced the Macintosh. Microprocessors also moved out of the realm of desktop computers and into many areas of life as more and more everyday products began to use microprocessors.

As these small computers became more powerful, they could be linked together to form networks, which eventually led to the development of the Internet. Fourth generation computers also saw the development of GUIs, the mouse and handheld devices.

Fifth Generation—Present and Beyond : Artificial Intelligence

Fifth generation computing devices, based on artificial intelligence, are still in development, though there are some applications, such as voice recognition, that are being used today. The use of parallel processing and superconductors is helping to make artificial intelligence a reality. Quantum computation and molecular and nanotechnology will radically change the face of computers in years to come. The goal of fifth-generation computing it to develop devices that respond to natural language input and are capable of learning and self-organization.

SUMMARY

1. A computer is normally considered to be a calculating device, which can perform arithmetic operations at enormous speed. It is also known as a data processor. Since it not only computers in the usual sense, but also performs other functions with the data.
2. The activity of processing data using a computer is called data processing. Data is the raw material used as input to data processing and information is the processed data obtained as the output of data processing.
3. Computers are characterized by their being automatic, speed and accuracy of computing, diligence, versatility power of remembering and lack of intelligence and feelings.
4. Dr. John Von Neumann introduced the "stored program" concept, which considerably influenced or the development of modern digital computers. Due to this feature, we often refer to modern digital computers as stored program digital computers.
5. 'Generation' in a computer talk is a step in technology. It provides a framework for the growth of the computer industry. Originally, it was used to distinguish between various hardware technologies, but now it has been extended to include both hardware and software.
6. Until today, there are five computer generations, namely, first, second, third, fourth and fifth generations.

REVIEW EXERCISES

1. What is computer? Why is it known as a data processor?
2. List out and explain some of the important characteristics of a computer.
3. List out the various computer generations along with the key characteristics of the computers of each generation.
4. What are the advantages of transistors over vacuum tubes?
5. Why were first and second generations computers more difficult and costlier to produce commercially then the computers of subsequent generations?
6. Name the secondary storage media popularly used in the computers of first, second, third, fourth and fifth generations.
7. Name some of the representative computer system of each of the five computer generations.

2

Basic Computer Organization

A block diagram of the basic computer organization is shown in figure. In this figure, the solid lines indicate the flow of instruction and data and the dotted lines represent the control exercised by the control unit. It displays the five major building blocks (functional units) of a digital computer system. These five units correspond to the five basic operations, performed by all computer systems. The functions of each of these units are described below.

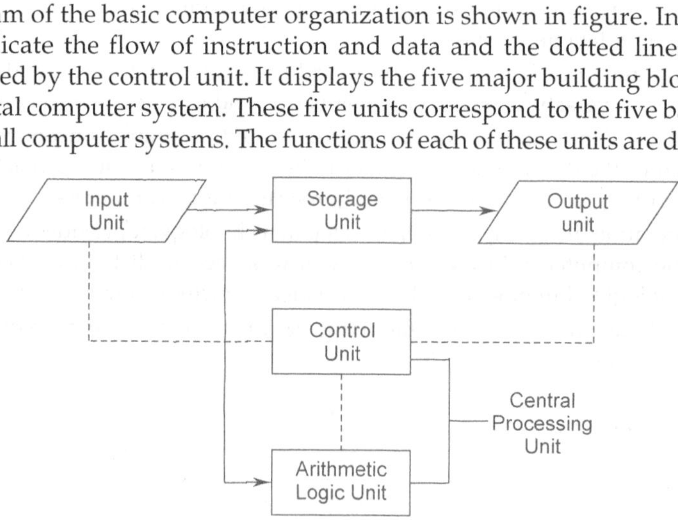

Fig. 2.1

INPUT UNIT

Data and instruction must enter the computer system, before any computation can be performed on the supplied data. The task is performed by the input unit, which links the external environment with the computer system. Data and instructions enter input units in forms, which depend upon the particular device used. For example, data are entered from a keyboard in manner similar to typing and this differs from the way in which data are entered through a scanner, which is another type of input device. However, regardless of the form in which they receive their inputs, all input devices must transform the input data into the binary codes, which the primary memory of a computer is designed to accept. This transformation is accomplished by units called input interfaces. Input interfaces are designed to match the unique physical or electrical characteristics of input devices, to the requirements of the computer system.

In short, the following functions are performed by an input unit :

1. It accepts (or reads) the instructions and data from the outside world.
2. It converts these instructions and data in computer acceptable form.
3. It supplies the converted instructions and data to the computer system for further processing.

OUTPUT UNIT

The job of a output unit is just the reverse of that of an input unit. It supplies the information obtained from data processing, to the outside world. Hence, it links the computer with the external environment. As computers work with binary code, the results produced are also in the binary form, hence, before supplying the results to the outside world, they must be converted to human acceptable (readable) form. The task is accomplished by units called output interfaces. Output interfaces are designed to match the unique physical or electrical characteristics of output devices (terminals, printers, etc.), to the requirements of the external environment.

In short, the following functions are performed by an output unit :

1. It accepts the results produced by the computer, which are in coded form and hence, cannot be easily understood by us.
2. It converts these coded results to human acceptable (readable) form.
3. It supplies the converted results to the outside world.

STORAGE UNIT

The data and instructions, which are entered into the computer system through input units, have to be stored inside the computer, before the actual processing starts. Similarly, the results produced by the computer after processing, must also be kept somewhere inside the computer system, before being passed on to the output units. Moreover, the intermediate results produced by the computer, must also be preserved for ongoing processing. The storage unit of a computer system is designed to cater to all these needs. It provides space for storing data and instructions, space for intermediate results and space for the final results.

In short, the specific functions of the storage unit are to hold (store)

1. The data and informations required for processing (received from input devices).
2. Intermediate results of processing.
3. Final results of processing, before these results are released to an output device.

The storage unit of all computers is comprised of the following two types of storage :

1. **Primary storage.** The primary storage, also known as main memory, is used to hold pieces of program instructions and data, intermediate results of processing and recently produced results of information are represented electronically in the main memory chip's circuitry and while it remains in the main memory, the central processing unit can access it directly at a very fast speed. However, the primary storage can hold information only while the computer system is on. As soon as the computer system is switched off or reset, the information held in the primary storage disappears. Moreover, the primary storage normally has limited storage capacity, because it is very

expensive. The primary storage of modern computer systems is made up of semiconductor devices.

2. **Secondary storage.** The secondary storage, also known as auxiliary storage, is used to take care of the limitations of the primary storage. That is, it is used to supplement the limited storage capacity and the volatile characteristic of primary storage. This is because secondary storage is much cheaper than primary storage and it can retain information even when the computer system is switched off or reset. The secondary storage is normally used to hold the program instructions, data and information of those jobs, on which the computer system is not working on currently, but needs to hold them for processing later. The most commonly used secondary storage medium is the magnetic disk.

ARITHMETIC LOGIC UNIT

The arithmetic logic unit (ALU) of a computer system is the place, where the actual execution of the instructions takes place, during the processing operation. To be more precise, calculations are performed and all comparisons (decisions) are made in the ALU. The data and instructions, stored in the primary storage before processing, are transferred as and when needed to the ALU, where processing takes places. No processing is done in the primary storage unit. Intermediate results generated in the ALU are temporarily transferred back to the primary storage, until needed later. Hence, data may move from primary storage to ALU, and back again to storage, many times, before the processing is over.

The type and number of arithmetic and logic operations, which a computer can perform, is determined by the engineering design of the ALU. However, almost all ALUs are designed to perform the four basic arithmetic operations (add, subtract, multiply and divide), and logic operations or comparisons, such as less than equal to.

CONTROL UNIT

How does the input device know that it is time for it to feed data into the storage unit ? How does the ALU know, what should be done with the data once they are received ? Moreover, how is it that only the final results are sent to the output device and not the intermediate results ? All this is possible due to the control unit of the computer system. Although, it does not perform any actual processing on the data, the control unit acts as a central nervous system, for the other components of the computer system. It manages and coordinates the entire computer system. It obtains instructions from the program stored in main memory, interprets the instructions and issues signals, which cause other units of the system to execute them.

CENTRAL PROCESSING UNIT

The control unit and the arithmetic logic unit of a computer system are jointly known as the Central Processing Unit (CPU). The CPU is the brain of a computer system. In a human body, all major decisions are taken by the brain and the other parts of the body function as directed by the brain. Similarly, in a computer system, all major calculations and comparisons are made inside the CPU and the CPU is responsible for activating and controlling the operations of other units of the computer system.

THE SYSTEM CONCEPT

You might have observed that we have been referring to a computer as a system (computer system). What can be the reason behind this ? To know the answer, let us first understand the definition of a system.

How Do Computers Work ?

Computer Basics

To accomplish a task using a computer, you need a combination of hardware, software and input.

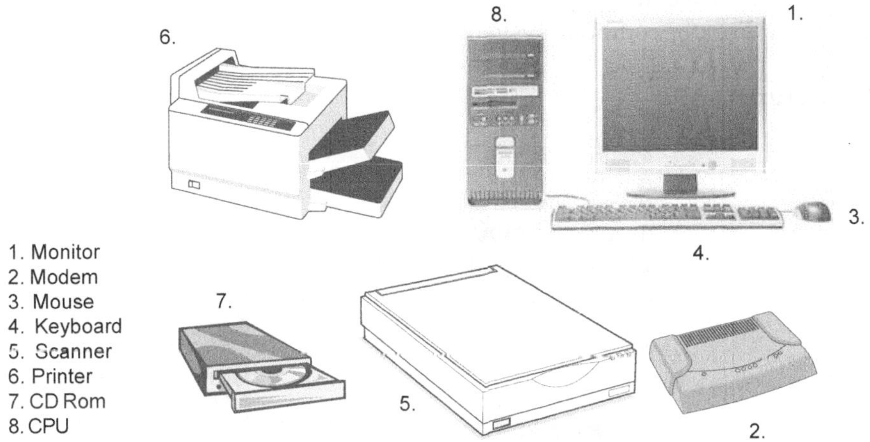

Fig. 2.2

Hardware consists of devices, like the computer itself, the monitor, keyboard, printer, mouse and speakers. Inside your computer there are more bits of hardware, including the motherboard, where you would find the main processing chips that make up the **Central Processing Unit** (CPU). The hardware processes the commands it receives from the software, and performs tasks or calculations.

Software is the name given to the programs that you install on the computer to perform certain types of activities. There is operating system software, such as the Apple OS for a Macintosh, or Windows 95 or Windows 98 for a PC. There is also application software, like the games we play or the tools we use to compose letters or do math problems.

Keyboard

Click on an area below to learn about the keys in that area of the keyboard.

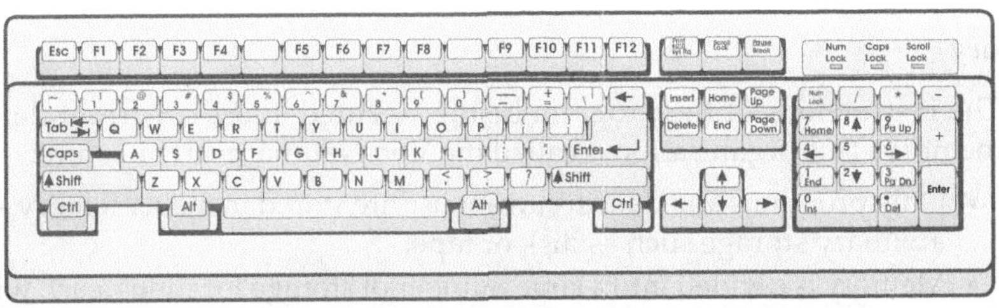

Fig. 2.3

STRUCTURE OF A COMPUTER SYSTEM

Content

1. Overall structure
2. The central processing unit
3. Memory
4. Buses
5. The clock
6. The fetch-execute cycle
7. Instruction fetch
8. Instruction execute
9. Operation of the computer system.

1. Overall Structure

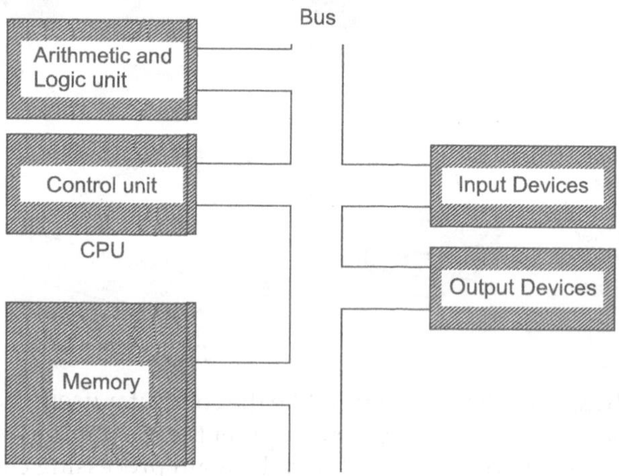

Fig. 2.4

2. The Central Processing Unit (CPU)

The CPU contains the circuitry that actually carries out the instructions.

- There are two major parts : the control unit and the arithmetic and logic unit.
- The control unit interprets the instructions and controls the flow of execution.
- The ALU performs additions, shifts, comparisons, etc.
- The CPU also contains a small amount of fast working memory.

3. Memory

The instructions of the program being executed and the current data are both stored in memory. This organisation is called the Von Neumann architecture.

- Only programs and data in current use are stored in main memory — the rest is stored in auxiliary storage such as disk or tape.
- Memory is divided into a large number of storage locations, each with a unique address.
- Data moves between memory, the CPU and the input/output devices.

4. Buses

Buses carry information around the system. Most computer system buses consist of three parts : the data bus, the address bus and the control bus.

- The data bus carries data and instructions between the CPU, memory and input/output.
- The address bus carries the address of the desired memory location when memory is being accessed.
- The control bus carries control and synchronisation signals between the various parts of the system.

5. The Clock

The computer carries out operations one at a time, in regular sequence.

This sequence is ordered by the system clock, which sends a pulse to each component in the system at regular intervals.

- The clock synchronises almost all operations within the computer.
- The clock frequency is one of the factors which determines the speed of the computer.

6. The Fetch-Execute Cycle

To execute a program the computer follows the same cycle over and over again.

```
REPEAT  forever
BEGIN
    read an instruction from memory
    execute the instruction
END.
```

This is called the fetch-execute cycle.

7. Instruction Fetch

- A program counter in the control unit stores the address of the next instruction to be executed.
- This instruction is copied from memory to an instruction register in the control unit.
- The instruction is passed to the instruction decoding circuitry.
- The program counter is incremented to point to the next instruction in memory.

8. Instruction Execute

An instruction consists of several parts.

The first is the opcode - a binary code which specifies the type of the instruction : input data, add two numbers, etc.

Following are the operands — the data on which the operation is to be carried out.

- The opcode of the instruction is decoded.
- Data may be read from input or memory.
- The ALU may carry out some operation.
- Data may be written to output or memory.

Principles of computer systems (C) Willi Geiger 2 November 1995.

willi@bournemouth.ac.uk

Computers and How They Work

Why is it important to know how a computer works ? Easy, if you don't, it will be hard to control. Computers were never built to control us even though that is how it appears. Their creation was just another tool, God gave man to use to benefit society. What can you do to learn more about computers ? I have an easy answer. Just read and use computers more. They are not that hard and with time you too can become the master over this tool.

Computers, the ones we know and love have not been around all that long. The first home personal computer was not sold until 1977. We have come a long way since then. Did you know that in 1983 there were approximately 2 million personal computers in use in the United States. However, just 10 years later in 1993 the number had jumped to more than 90 million.

Computers, today are small, fast, reliable and extremely useful. Back in 1977 that really was not the case. However, they both operated in basically the same way. They both receive data, stored data, processed data and then output data similar that the way our own brain functions. This article deals with those four functions : Memory, Processing, Input and Output.

Memory

Lets look at computer memory first. The function of storage in a computer comes in many different sizes, types and shapes. However, there are two basic categories : short-term and long-term. A typical computer contains numerous types of memory including RAM, ROM, virtual, cache and various long-term storage devices. Each type of computer memory serves a specific function and purpose.

Computer memory is measured in bytes. A single byte is made up of a sereis of 1's and 0's. Normally traveling in pairs of eight. These eight 0's and 1's are the way of the computer communicates and stores information. With each keystroke or character a byte of memory is used. In another article you will learn more about bits and how the computer thinks.

Measuring Memory

Term/Byte	*Abbreviation*	*Value*
Kilo	K, KB	1,024 bytes
Mega	M, MB, Meg	1,048,576 bytes (Million)
Giga	G, GB, Giga	1,073,741,824 bytes (Billion)
Tera	T, TB, Tera	1,099,511,628,000 bytes (Trillion)

Here is another way of looking at the measurement of memory :

Measuring Bytes

8 bits = 1 byte
1000 bytes = 1 kilobyte
1000 kilobytes = 1 megabyte
1000 megabytes = 1 gigabyte
1000 gigabytes = 1 terabyte

ROM

ROM, or **read-only memory** is permanent, long-term, **nonvolatile** memory. Nonvolatile means is doesn't disappear when the computer is shut off. It also cannot be erased or changed in anyway. However, there are types of ROM called PROM that can be altered. The

P stands for programmable. ROM's purpose is to store the basic input/output system (BIOS) that controls the start-up, or boot process.

RAM

RAM, or **random-access memory** unlike ROM works only when the computer is turned on. This memory is vital to the computer because it controls the moment by moment processes of the computer. The first thing that goes into RAM is the OS (operating system) which is most cases is Windows 95. Next for the RAM might be a game, or the Internet browser, or some type of software that you want to use.

Early personal computer only needed about 64K of RAM. Today that number is drastically higher. With photos, sounds and even movies going into RAM, the amount need is now in the millions. The computer I am currently using has 80 MB or 80,000K of RAM.

Multitasking has put more demand on RAM in the past few years. Multitasking is the ability to run more than one program at the same time. For instance, many people like to run Netscape Communicator along with their word processing software. This means you need lots of RAM to hold both programs.

Other types of temporary memory are cache (pronounced "cash") and virtual memory. Both of these types of memory supplement the computer's primary RAM and perform the same function as RAM.

Storage Devices

RAM and ROM may be very important parts of the computer ; however, without storage devices like hard drives and disk drives your computer would not be near as useful.

Here are the most common forms of Storage Devices found on your home computer :

Floppy disk or Floppy	*Hard disk (drive) or HD*
A round plastic surface that is coated with magnetic film. They come in 3½ size. They hold about 720K to 1440K of information. They are used to install new software, save, share and/or copy files. Floppy drives are given letters. Commonly the floppy is A, a 2nd floppy is B and the hard drive is C.	A stack of round metal platters called disks encased in a metal air tight shell. They commonly range in sizes from 1 to 10 gigabytes (1000 MB=1 GB). The hard drive's function is to store all the files and software the computer will ever use. Any file or software program used by RAM most likely will come from the disk drive.

CD-ROM (Compact disk, read-only memory)	*DVD-ROM (digital video disk, read-only memory)*
CD's function much like hard drive in that they store large amounts of memory. What separates them is their mobility and optical storage technology. Their storage capacity is also very limited compared to hard drives. They can only hold up to approximately 650 MB of information. The other big difference is that you have to have a special drive to write to CD's. Otherwise they can only be read from.	DVD's are similar to CD in that they are written and read by laser. Hard drives use magnetic currents store data. However CD's and DVD's use light (laser) to write and read data on a disk. These long and short pits are then stored or etched on the surface of the disk. They can only be read by laser technology. The new DVD technology increased the amount of memory a regular CD can hold. DVD's can range in sizes from 4.34 GB (1000 MB = 1 GB) to 7.95 GB.

Processing

If someone had to find the brains of the computer they would most certainly say its the microprocessor. The microprocessor is often referred to as the CPU (Central Processing Unit). The microprocessor is a chip the size of a postage stamp. The processor is the one part of the computer that is most important to the computer. The microprocessor controls how data is sorted and directs the flow of data.

Pentium II Processor

Fig. 2.5

To a great extent a computer is defined by the power of its microprocessor. Chips with higher processing speed and more recent design offer the greatest performance and access to new technologies. Most microprocessors made for PCs are made by Intel or by companies that clone Intel chips, such as Advanced Micro Devices (AMD) and Cyrix.

The early Intel chip came in models called 286, 386, and 486. The 586 chip was given the name Pentium. The series of Pentiums were given the following names : Pentium Pro, Pentium with MMX, and Pentium II. The newer processors hold more transistors and thus more computing power on a single chip.

Fig. 2.6

Microprocessor

Processor	*No. of Transistors*	*Bus Width*
80286	134,000	16 bit
80386	275,000	32 bit
80486	1,600,000	32 bit
Pentium	3,300,000	64 bit external/32 bit internal
Pentium Pro	5,500,000	64 bit
Pentium w/ MMX	4,500,000	64 bit external/32 bit internal
Pentium II	7,500,000	64 bit

Input

One of the best features of a computer is the ability to give the computer commands and feed it information. Without an input device this would not be possible. Input devices can be built into the computer, like the keyboard in a laptop, or it can be connected to the computer by a cable. The most common input device is the keyboard. There are lots of others such as : mice, trackballs, touch pads, touch screens, pens, joy sticks, scanners, bar code readers, video and digital cameras, and microphones. In addition, storage devices such as disk drives can serve as input devices.

Output

Input is important but equally important is the ability to read what the computer is doing. The computer output devices are used to serve the user. The most common output device is the monitor, or screen. However most computer come with speakers and a printer which are excellent output devices. Storage devices such as disk drives and diskettes also serve as output devices when it is necessary to write new or updated data files to disk or tape.

You provide the input. When you type a command or click on an icon, you are telling the computer what to do. That is called input.

How They Work Together

First, you provide input when you turn on the computer. Then the system software tells the CPU to start up certain programs and to turn on some hardware devices so that they are ready for more input from you. This whole process is called booting up.

The next step happens when you choose a program you want to use. You click on the icon or enter a command to start the program. Let's use the example of an Internet browser. Once the program has started, it is ready for your instructions. You either enter an address (called a URL, which stands for Uniform Resource Locator), or click on an address you've saved already. In either case, the computer now knows what you want it to do. The browser software then goes out to find that address, starting up other hardware devices, such as a modem, when it needs them. If it is able to find the correct address, the browser will then tell your computer to send the information from the web page over the phone wire or cable to your computer. Eventually, you see the web site you were looking for.

Fig. 2.7

If you decide you want to print the page, you click on the printer icon. Again, you have provided input to tell the computer what to do. The browser software determines whether you have a printer attached to your computer and whether it is turned on. It may remind you to turn on the printer, then send the information about the web page from your computer over the cable to the printer, where it is printed out.

WHAT IS SOFTWARE?

A computer cannot do anything on its own. It must be instructed to do desired job. Hence, it is necessary to specify a sequene of instructions, which a computer must perform to solve a problem. Such a sequence of instructions, written in a language, which can be understood by a computer, is called a computer program. It is the program, which controls the activity of processing by the computer and the computer performs precisely what the program wants it to do. When a computer is using program, we say, it is running or executing that program.

The term **software** refers to the set of computer programs, procedures and associated documents (flowcharts, manuals, etc.), which describe the programs and how they are to be used. To be precise, software means a collection of programs, whose objective is to enhance the capabilities of the hardware.

A software package is a group of programs, which solve a specific problem or perform a specific type of job. For example, a word-processing package may contain programs for text editing, text formatting, drawing graphics, spelling checking, etc. Hence, a multipurpose computer system has several software packages, one each for every type of job it can perform.

RELATIONSHIP BETWEEN HARDWARE AND SOFTWARE

In order for a computer to produce useful output, its hardware and software must work together. Nothing useful can be done with the computer hardware on its own and software cannot be utilized without supporting hardware.

To take an analogy, a cassette player and the cassettes purchased from market are hardware. However, the songs recorded on the cassettes are its software. To listen to a particular song, first of all that song has to be recorded on one of the cassettes, which should then be mounted on the cassette player and played. Similarly, to get a particular job done by a computer, the corresponding software should be loaded in the hardware, before processing starts.

The following important points regarding the relationship between hardware and software are brought out by this analogy :

1. Both hardware and software are necessary for a computer to do useful job. Both are complementary to each other.
2. The same hardware can be loaded with different software to make a computer system perform different types of jobs, just as different songs can be played using the same cassette player.
3. Except for upgrades (like increasing the main memory and hard disk capacities, or adding speakers, modems, etc.), hardware is normally a one-time expense, whereas software is a continuing expense. Just as we buy new cassettes for the newly released songs, or for songs whose cassettes we do not have, similarly one buys new software to be run on the same hardware, as and when need arises or funds become available.

TYPES OF SOFTWARE

Although, the range of software available today is vast and varied, most software can be divided into two major categories:

1. System software, and
2. Application software.

System Software

System software is a set of one or more programs, designed to control the operation and extend the processing capability of a computer system. In general, a computer's system performs one or more of the following functions:

1. Supports the development of other application software.
2. Supports the execution of other application software.
3. Monitors the effective use of various hardware resources, such as CPU, memory, peripherals, etc.

4. Communicates with and controls the operation of peripheral devices, such as printer, disk, tape, etc.

Hence, system software makes the operation of a computer system more effective and efficient. It helps the hardware components work together and provides support for the development and execution of application software (programs). The programs included in a system software package are called system programs and the programmers who prepare system are referred to as system programmers.

Some of the most commonly known types of system software as:

1. *Operating Systems.* Every computer has a operating system software, which takes care of the effective and efficient utilization of all the hardware and software components of the computer system. Operating system has been discussed in later Chapter.
2. *Programming Language Translators.* Programming language translators are system software, which transform the instructions prepared by programmers in a programming language, into a from, which can be interpreted and executed by a computer system. Programming language translators have been discussed in later Chapter.
3. *Communications Software.* In a network environment (where multiple computers are interconnected together by communications network), communications software enables transfer of data and programs from one computer system to another.
4. *Utility Programs.* Utility programs (also known as utilities) are a set of programs, which help users in system maintenance tasks and in performing tasks of routine nature. Some of the tasks commonly performed by utility programs include formatting of hard disks or floppy disks, taking backup of files stored on hard disk on to a tape or floppy disk, sorting of the records stored in a file in a particular order based on some key field(s), etc.

Applications Software

Application software is a set of one or more programs, designed to solve a specific problem, or do a specific task. For example, an applications software for payroll processing pay slips as the major output and an application software for processing examination results produces mark sheets as the major output along with some other statistical reports. Similarly, a program written by a scientist to solve his/her particular research problem is also an application software. The programs included in an application software package are called application programs and the programmers who prepare application software are referred to as application programmers.

There are literally millions of application software available for a wide range of applications, ranging form simple applications, such as word processing, inventory management, preparation of tax returns, banking, hospital administration, insurance, publishing, to complex scientific and engineering applications, such as weather forecasting, space shuttle launching, oil and natural gas exploration, design of complex structures like airctafts, ships, bridges, sky-rise buildings, etc. With so many applications available, it is not possible to categorize them all and to cover them here. Some of the most commonly known application software are :

1. *Word-Processing Software.* A word-processing software enables us to make use of a computer system for creating, editing, viewing, formatting, storing, retrieving and printing documents (written material, such as letters, reports, books, etc.).

2. *Spreadsheet Software.* A spreadsheet software is a numeric data analysis tool, which allows us to create a kind of computerized ledger. A manual ledger is a book having rows and columns, which accountants use for keeping a record of financial transactions and for preparing financial statements.
3. *Database Software.* A database is a collection of related data stored and treated as a unit for information retrieval purposes. A database software is a set of one or more programs, which enable us to create a database, maintain it (add, delete and update its records), organize its data in desired fashion (for example, sort its records alphabetically namewise) and to selectively retrieve useful information from it (for example, get the telephone number of the person named Kashyap Rana from the address database, or get the names of all currently enrolled students from the student database whose birthdays fall today).
4. *Graphics Software.* A graphics software enables us to use a computer system for creating, editing, viewing, storing, retrieving and printing designs, drawings, pictures, graphs and anything else that can be drawn in the traditional manner.
5. *Personal Assistance Software.* A personal assistance software allows us to use personal computers for storing and retrieving our personal information, and planning and managing our schedules, contacts,financial and inventory of important items.
6. *Education Software.* Education software allows a computer system to be used as a teaching and learning tool. A few examples of such applications are those that teach young children to do (*a*) mathematics ; (*b*) recognize alphabets ; and (*c*) read whole words and sentences.
7. *Entertainment Software.* Entertainment software allows a computer systems to be used as an entertainment tool. A good example of such an application is computer video games.

LOGICAL SYSTEM ARCHITECTURE

The logical architecture of a computer system is shown in Figure 2.8. The architecture basically depicts the relationship among the hardware, system software, application software and users of a computer system. As shown in the figure, at the center of any computer system is the hardware, which comprises of the physical devices/components of the computer system. Surrounding the hardware is the system software layer, which constitutes the operating and programming environment of the computer system. That is, the software at this layer is designed to hide the hardware details of the system from application programmers, and to coordinate the operations of the various hardware devices for optimizing the performance of tall the devices. Surrounding the system software is the application software layer, which consists of a wide consists of a wide range of software, which are designed to do a specific task, or solve a specific problem. The final layer is the layer of users who normally interact with the system via the user interface provided by the application software. Different application software usually provide different user interfaces. Hence, how a particular user interacts with the computer system, depends on which application he/she is using.

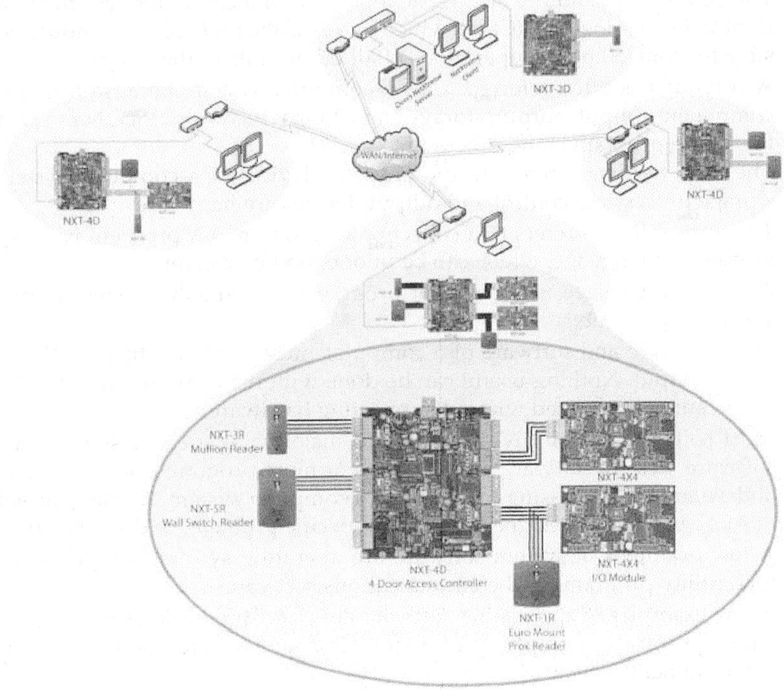

Fig. 2.8

SUMMARY

1. All computer systems perform the following five basic operations, fir converting raw input data into useful information – inputting, storing, processing, outputting and controlling.
2. The input unit allows data and instructions to be fed to the computer system from the outside world, in computer acceptable form.
3. The input interfaces transform the input data and instructions fed to the computer, through its input devices, into the binary codes, which are acceptable to the computer.
4. The output unit allows the computer system to supply the information, obtained from data processing, to the outside world, in human acceptable (readable) form.
5. The output interfaces transform the information, obtained from data processing, from binary form to human acceptable (readable) form.
6. The storage unit of a computer system hold the data and instructions to be processed and the intermediate and final results of processing. The two types of storage are – primary and secondary storage. As compared to primary storage, secondary storage is slower in operation, larger in capacity, cheaper in price and can retain information even when the computer system is switched off or reset.
7. During data processing, the actual execution of the instructions takes place in the Arithmetic Logic Unit (ALU) of a computer system.
8. The control unit of a computer system manages and coordinates the operations of all the other components of the computer system.

9. The control unit and the arithmetic logic unit of a computer system are jointly known as the Central Processing Unit (CPU), which serves as the brain of the computer system and is responsible for controlling the operations of all other units of the system.
10. A computer is often referred to as a computer system, because it is made up of integrated components (input, output, storage and CPU), which work together to perform the steps called for, in the program being executed.
11. The term hardware refers to the physical devices of a computer system. Hence, the input, storage processing, control and output devices are hardware.
12. The term software refers to a collection of programs. A program is a sequence of instruction written in a language, which can be understood by a computer.
13. A software package is a group of programs, which solve a specific problem, or perform a specific type of job.
14. The hardware and software of a computer must work together for the computer to produce useful output. Nothing useful can be done with the computer hardware on its own and software cannot be utilized without supporting hardware.
15. Most software can be divided into two major categories—system software and application software. System software is a set of one or more programs, designed to control the operation and extend the processing capability of a computer system. Application software is a set of one or more programs, designed to solve a specific problem, or do a specific task.
16. A few examples of system software are operating systems, programming language translators, utility programs and communications software.
17. A few examples of application software are word-processing software, spreadsheet, software, database software, graphics software, personal assistance software, education software and entertainment software.
18. A user can acquire a desired software in one or more of the following ways :
    - By using pre-written software
    - By ordering customized software
    - By developing customized software
    - By downloading public-domain software

    Each of these ways of acquiring software has its own advantages and limitations.
19. Developing a software and putting it to use is a complex process, which involves the following steps :
    - Analyzing the problem at hand and planning the program(s) to solve the problem.
    - Coding the program(s).
    - Testing, debugging and documenting the program(s).
    - Implementing the program(s).
    - Evaluating and maintaining the program(s).
20. Firmware is software substituted for hardware, and stored in read-only memory.

REVIEW EXERCISES

1. What are the five basic operations performed by any computer system?
2. Draw a block diagram to illustrate the basic organization of a computer system, and explain the functions of the various units.
3. What is an input interface? How does it differ from an output interface?
4. How many types of storage are normally there in the storage unit of a computer system? Justify the need for each storage type.
5. Differentiate between the characteristics of primary and secondary storage of a computer system.
6. What are the basic components of the CPU of a computer system? Describe the roles of each of the components in the functioning of a computer system.

7. List out of the logical steps taken by a computer system, along with the roles of its units in each step, while transforming input data to useful information, for presentation to the user.
8. What is a system? Why is a computer often referred to as a computer system?
9. Define the terms hardware and software.
10. What is a computer program?
11. What is meant by running/executing a computer program?
12. What is a software package?
13. Hardware and software of a computer system are like two sides of a coin. Discuss.
14. Give an analogy to bring out of the relationship between hardware and software of a computer system.
15. Hardware is normally a one-time expense whereas software is a continuing expense. Elaborate.
16. How many type of software are there? Give three examples of each.
17. Define and distinguish between application software and system software.
18. Define the following terms:
    (*a*) System software (*b*) System program (*c*) System programmer
    (*d*) Application software (*e*) Application program (*f*) Application programmer
19. List out some of the key functions performed by the system software of a computer system.
20. Explain the importance of system software for a computer system.
21. What is a utility program? List out some of the tasks commonly performed by utility programs.
22. What is a communications software?
23. What is an education software? Give a few examples such software.
24. What is an entertainment software? Give a few examples of such software.
25. Explain the relationship among the hardware, system software, application software and users of a computer system.
26. How does a normal users interact with the hardware of a computer? Describe the various in-between layers.
27. What are different ways of acquiring software? List out their relative advantages and limitations.
28. List out the relative advantages and disadvantages of creating a customized software in-house by an organization, versus getting it created by another organization.
29. What is a turnkey solution?
30. What is shareware? What are the advantages and limitations of using a shareware?
31. List out the steps typically followed in developing a software and putting it to use.
32. Write short notes on:
    (*a*) Hardware (*b*) Software (*c*) Firmware
33. Write short notes on :
    (*a*) Types of software
    (*b*) Acquiring software
    (*c*) Relationship between hardware and software.
34. Write short notes on :
    (*a*) System software
    (*b*) Application software
    (*c*) Relationship among the hardware, system software, application software and users of a computer.
35. What is firmware and what is its importance to the computer system architect?
36. Why is firmware gaining popularity?
37. Differentiate among hardware, software and firmware.

3

INPUT-OUTPUT DEVICES

A computer system can be useful, only when it is able to communicate with its external environment (its users). As shown in Figure 3.1, the input-output devices (abbreviated I/O devices) provide the means of communication between the computer and the outer world. They are also known as peripheral devices, because they surround the CPU and the memory of a computer system. Input devices are used to enter data form the outside world into primary storage, and output devices supply the results of processing from the primary storage to the users. A wide variety of I/O devices are now available. For a particular application, one type may be more desirable than another. There are some devices, which are used for both input and output functions. The goal of this chapter is to familiarize you with the various types of I/O devices available for computer systems.

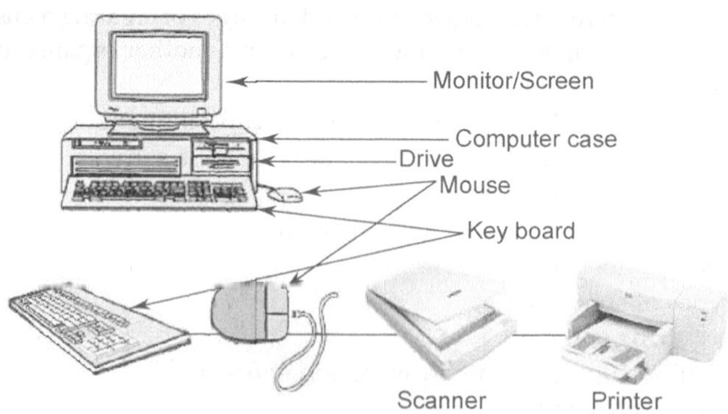

Fig. 3.1 *Input-output devices*

It is important to note that even the fastest of the I/O devices is very slow, when compared to the speed of primary storage and CPU. The main reason for this is that the speed of I/O devices in most cases depends upon mechanical movement, and the potential for improvement of such devices if limited. It has been difficult to produce I/O devices, which can match the processor and memory speeds, and there is a constant demand for faster and faster I/O devices.

INPUT DEVICES

An input device is an electromechanical device, which accepts data from the outside world, and translates them into a form, which the computer can interpret. Several input devices are available today. They can be broadly classified into the following categories:

1. Keyboard devices
2. Point-and-draw devices
3. Data scanning devices
4. Digitizer
5. Electronic cards based devices
6. Voice recognition devices
7. Vision based devices

The various types of input devices alongwith their typical applications are described below.

Keyboard Devices

Keyboard devices are the most commonly used input devices today. The allow data entry into a computer system by pressing a set of keys (labeled buttons), which are neatly mounted on a keyboard, which is connected to the computer system. The most popular keyboard used today is the 101-keys QWERTY keyboard. It is shown in Figure 3.2.

Fig. 3.2 *Keyboard*

Point-and-Draw Devices

Interaction with computers was initially restricted mainly to text mode. However, it was soon realized that interacting with computers in text-mode is cumbersome and time-consuming. Hence, a new type of interface, called Graphical User Interface (GUI), was devised for interacting with computers. As shown in Figure 3.3 a GUI provides a screen full of graphic icons (small images on the screen) or menus to the user, and allows the user to make a rapid selection from the displayed icons or menus to give instructions to the computer. With such a user interface, the basic requirement is to have an input device, which can be used to rapidly point to and select a particular graphic icon or menu item form the multiple options displayed on the screen. The keyboard was found to be very inconvenient and unsuitable for this requirement. Hence, research efforts to find a suitable input device to meet this requirement, gave birth to several input devices like mouse, track ball, joystick, light pen and touch screen. Later it was realized that many of these devices, like mouse and light pen, could also be very effectively used to create graphic elements on the screen, such as lines, curves, and freehand shapes. With this new ability, these devices came to be known as point-and-draw devices. These input devices have made computers as much more easily usable tool, and have established the computer as a versatile tool for graphic designers. Some of the most commonly used point-and-draw devices are described as follows.

Fig. 3.3 *Point and draw devices*

Mouse

As of today, mouse is the most popular point-and-draw device. It has become a must-have input device on personal computers and workstations, which have a GUI-based user interface. As shown in Figure 3.4, a mouse is a small hand-held device, which can comfortably fit in a user's palm. It rolls on a small bearing, and has one or more buttons on the top. When a user rolls the mouse across a flat surface, such as on top of the table on which the computer is placed, the graphics cursor moves on the screen of the video display terminal in the direction of the mouse's movement. The graphics cursor, which is used to point and draw, is displayed on the screen as a variety of symbols, such as an arrow (☞), a wrist with a pointing finger (↗), etc. Depending on the application, the text and graphics cursor may be displayed on the screen at the same time.

Fig. 3.4 *Mouse*

Since all movements of the mouse are reproduced by the graphics cursor on the screen, you can move the graphics cursor at a menu item or an icon by moving the mouse. For example, move the mouse away from you to move the cursor up on the screen, move the mouse towards you to move the cursor down on the screen, move the mouse right to move the cursor right on the screen, and move the mouse left to move the cursor left on the screen. In this way, the mouse can be used for quick positioning of the graphics cursor on the desired menu item or an icon. When positioned at a menu item or an icon, the graphics cursor is said to point to that menu item or icon. With a click of the mouse's button, the system can then be notified of this choice. Note that, notifying the system of a particular choice, out of the various options provided by the software, is much easier with a mouse than processing various key combinations. With the proper software, a mouse can also be used to draw pictures on the screen and edit text.

Trackball

A trackball is a pointing device, which is similar to a mouse. As shown in Figure 3.5 the ball, which is placed in the base of a mouse, is placed on the top along with the buttons, in case of a trackball. To move the graphics cursor around this screen, the ball is rolled with the fingers. Because the whole device is not moved for moving the graphics cursor, a trackball requires less space than a mouse for operation. Since it need not be moved for moving the graphics cursor, it is often attached to or built into the keyboard. Trackballs built into the keyboard are commonly used in laptop (notebook) computers, because a mouse is not practical for laptop users in a small space. Because the ball is fixed on the top, some people find it helpful to think of a trackball as an upside-down mouse.

A trackball comes in various shapes and forms with the same functionality. The three commonly used shapes are a ball, a button, and a square. In case of a ball, the ball is rolled with the help of fingers to move the graphics cursor. In case of a button, the button is pushed with a finger in the desired direction of the graphics cursor movement. In case of a square plastic, the finger is placed on top of it, and moved in the desired direction of the graphics cursor movement.

Fig. 3.5 *Trackball*

Joystick

A joystick is a pointing device, which works on the same principle as a trackball. To make the movement of the spherical ball easier, the spherical ball, which moves in a socket, has a stick mounted on it (see Figure 3.6). Instead of using the fingers in case of a trackball, the user of a joystick moves the spherical ball with the help of the stick with his/her hand. The stick can be moved forward or backward, left or right, to move and position the graphics cursor at the desired position. Potentiometers are used to sense the movements. On most joysticks, a button on the top is provided to select the option, which is currently pointed to by the cursor. The button is clicked to make this selection. Typical uses of a joystick include video games, flight simulators, training simulators, and for controlling industrial robots.

Fig. 3.6 *Joystick*

Electronic Pen

Another point-and-draw device is an electronic pen. In a pen-based system, you hold the pen in your hand, and directly point with it on the screen to select menu items or icons : or directly draw graphics on the screen with it : or write it on a special pad for direct input of the written information to the system.

Touch Screen

Touch screen is the most simple, intuitive, and easiest to learn of all input devices. A touch screen enables the users to choose from available options by simply touching with their finger the desired icon or menu item displayed on the computer's screen.

Touch screens are the most preferred human-computer interface devices used in information kiosks. An information kiosk is an unattended system, which is used to store information of public interest, and allows common people to access the stored information as per their requirement. For example, information kiosks may be located.

1. At an airport or a railway station to provide information to arriving passengers about hotels, restaurants, tourists spots, *etc.*, in the city.
2. In large museums or zoos to guide the visitors to the locations of various attractions and facilities, and to caution them against things, which they are not supposed to do while inside.

Data Scanning Devices

Data scanning devices are input devices, which are used for direct data entry into the computer system form source documents. Some of the data scanning devices are also capable of recognizing marks or characters. Data scanning devices typically have the following characteristics:

1. They eliminate some of the duplication of human effort required to get data into the computer. Human beings do not have to manually enter the data.
2. The reduction in human intervention improves data accuracy, and can increase the timeliness of the information processed.
3. Since scanners are direct data entry devices, they demand high quality of input documents. Documents that are poorly typed or have strikeovers or erasures are normally rejected.
4. With these devices, form design and ink specification may become more critical than is the case when people key in the data from the forms.

Data scanning devices are of many types. Some of the commonly used ones are described below.

Image Scanner

An image scanner is an input device, which translates paper documents into an electronic format, which can be stored in a computer. The input documents may be typed text, pictures, graphics, or even handwritten material. This input device has been found to be very useful in preserving paper documents in electronic form. The copy of a document stored a computer in this manner will never deteriorate in quality or become yellow with age, and can be displayed or printed, whenever desired. If the computer in which the scanned document is stored has the right kind of software (called image-processing software), the store images can be altered and manipulated in interesting ways.

Image scanners come in various shapes and sizes. The two commonly used types are:

1. *Flatbed scanner.* As shown in Figure 3.7, a flatbed scanner is like a copy machine, which consists of a box having a glass plate on its top and a lid that covers the glass plate. The documents to be scanned is placed upside down on the glass plate. The light source is situated below the glass plate, and moves horizontally from left to right when activated. After scanning one line, the light beam moves up a little, and scans the next line. The process is repeated for all the lines. It takes about 20 seconds to scan a document of size 21 cm × 28 cm.

Fig. 3.7 *Flatbed scanner*

2. *Hand-held scanner.* As shown in Figure 3.8, a hand-held scanner has a set of light emitting diodes encased in a small case, which can be conveniently held in hand during operation. To scan a document, the scanner is slowly dragged from one end of the document to its other end, with its light on. The scanner has to be dragged very steadily and carefully over the document, otherwise the conversion of the document into its equivalent bitmap will not be correct. Due to this reason, hand-held scanners are used only in cases where high accuracy is not needed. They are also used when the volume of documents to be scanned is low. They are also much cheaper as compared to flatbed scanners.

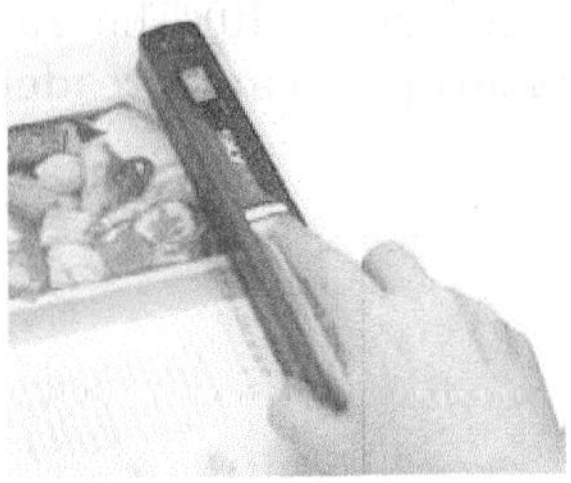

Fig. 3.8 *Hand-held scanner*

Optical Character Recognition (OCR) Device

When image scanners are used for inputting text documents (typed or handwritten), they have the following two limitations:

1. Since the input document is stored as an image, instead of text, it is not possible to do any word processing of the document (the computer cannot interpret the stored document as letters, numbers and special characters).
2. The storage required for storing the document as an image is much more than that required for storing the same document as a text. For example, a page of printed text, having 2000 characters, can be stored as 2000 bytes using the ASCII representation. A bitmap image representation of the same document will require 10 to 15 times more storage, depending on the resolution (granularity) of grid points.

The OCR technology is used to overcome these limitations. In this case, the scanner is equipped with a character recognition software (called OCR software), which converts the bitmap images of characters to equivalent ASCII codes. That is, the scanner first characters the bitmap image of the document, and then the OCR software translates the array of grid points into ASCII text, which the computer can interpret as letters, numbers and special characters.

OCR software is extremely complex, because it is difficult to make a computer recognize an unlimited number of typefaces and fonts. Hence, these software are designed to recognize texts, which are written using standard types fonts (called OCR fonts). Two such standard fonts are OCR-A (American standard) and OCR-B (European standard). Figure 3.9 shows OCR-A fonts. Note that, if the documents contains italics or bold face letters, or fonts other than that for which the OCR software has been designed, the OCR software will not work effectively.

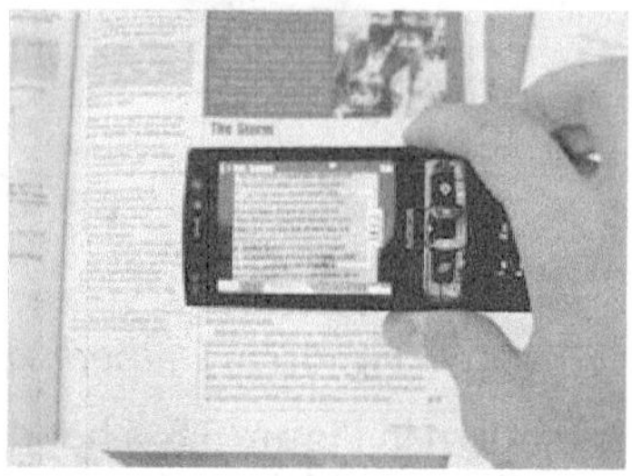

Fig. 3.9 *Optical character recognition*

Optical Mark Reader (OMR)

These scanners are capable of recognizing a pre-specified type of mark by pencil or pen. For example, many students might have appeared in objective type tests, in which they had to mark their answers to question on a special pre-printed test scoring sheet by darkening a small square, circular, or oval shaped box by a pencil, to indicate their correct choice out of the various given options (see Figure 3.10). These answer sheets are directly fed to a computer for grading with the use of an optical mark reader.

Fig. 3.10 *Optical mark reader*

The actual technique use by an OMR device for recognition of marks involves focusing a light on the page being scanned, and detecting the reflected light pattern from the marks. Pencil marks made with a soft lead pencil (high graphite content) reflect the light, enabling the reader to determine which responses are marked.

Bar-Code Reader

Data coded in the form of small lines (known as bars) are known as bar codes. Bar codes represent alphanumeric data by a combination of adjacent vertical lines (bars) by varying their width and the spacing between them. They are particularly used for unique identification of all types of goods, books, postal packages, badges, tags, etc.

A bar-code reader is a device, which is used for reading (decoding) bar-coded data. It may be a hand-held scanner, or may be embedded in a stationary scanner. It scans a bar-code image, and converts it into an alphanumeric value, which is then fed to the computer to which the bar-code reader is connected, just as through the alphanumeric value had been typed on a keyboard.

A bar-code reader uses a laser-beam scanning technology. The laser beam is stroked across the pattern of bars of a bar code. Different bar codes, having different patterns of bars, reflect the beam in different ways, which is sensed by a light-sensitive detector. Reflected light patterns are converted into electric pulses, and then transmitted to recognition logic circuits, which convert it into an alphanumeric value.

Just as there are a variety of internal bit encoding systems, there are a variety of bar-coding systems. The most widely known bar-coding system is the Universal Product Code (UPC), which now appears on almost all retail packages in USA. The UPC, originally used for supermarket items, is now being printed on other consumer goods also. The UPC bar-code patterns are decoded as 10 digits. The first five of these digits identify the manufacturer of supplier of the product, and the next five digits identify a specific product of the manufacturer (see Figure 3.11).

Bar code readers are commonly found in supermarkets and department stores. When a customer picks up a product for purchasing, and brings it to the cash counter for payment, the sales person at the counter uses a bar-code reader to scan the bar code printed on the product. The bar-code reader converts the bar code into an alphanumeric value, and feeds it to the computer, which looks up the price of the product, possibly updates inventory and sales records, and uses the price and description information to prepare a purchase bill for the customer. Postal delivery services also use bar codes to identify and track each packet. For example, federal express of USA uses a unique bar-coding system, and their employees can usually tell a customer, within a matter of minutes, the current location of any packet.

Fig. 3.11 *Bar-code reader – 1*

Magnetic-ink Character Recognition (MICR)

MICR is similar to OCR, and is used by the banking industry for faster processing of the large volume of cheques being handled every day by this industry. Banks, which employ MICR technology, use a special type of cheque.

The bank's identification code (name, branch, etc.) account number, and the cheque number are pre-printed (encoded) by using characters form a special character set on all these cheques with a special ink, which contains magnetizable particles of iron oxide, before the cheques are given to the customers for use. A sample cheque, which employs MICR technology, is shown in Figure 3.12.

Fig. 3.12 *Magnetic-ink character recognition*

When a customer presents a filled-in cheque at a bank, a bank employee manually enters (keys in) the amount written on the cheque, in the lower right corner of the cheque by using an MICR inscriber, which prints the amount with the magnetic ink. The data of the transaction is automatically recorded for all cheques processed that day. This cheque is then processed by using an MICR reader-sorter, which can recognize magnetic ink characters. The MICR reader-sorter reads the data on the cheques, and sorts the cheques for distribution to other banks, or for further processing.

The most commonly used character set by MICR devices is known as E13B font, which consists of the numbers 0 to 9, and four special characters, as shown in Figure 3.13. Coded data in the form of these fonts are transferred from cheques to the computer by an MICR reader-sorter. As the cheques enter the reading unit, they pass through a magnetic field, which causes the particles in the ink to become magnetized. Read heads then interpret these characters by examining their shapes. The sorter is used to sort the cheques into different pockets, according to their identification code numbers.

MICR technology speeds up data input for the banking industry, because cheques can be directly fed into the input device, and automatically processed thereafter. Besides enabling faster processing of cheques, this technology also ensures accuracy of data entry, because most of the information is pre-printed of the cheque, and is directly fed to the computer. However, MICR has not been adopted by other industries, because the currently supported character set has only 14 symbols (10 digits and 4 special characters). No alphabetic characters are available.

Fig. 3.13 *Graphic or digitizer tablet*

Digitizer

A digitizer is an input device, which is used for converting (digitizing) pictures, maps and drawings into digital form for storage in computers. For example, the x and y coordinates of points in a drawing may be stored in digital form. The enables recreation of the drawing form the stored information, and easy incorporation of changes in the drawing, as and when required.

As shown in Figure 3.14, a digitizer consists of a digitizing tablet (also known as graphic tablet) associated with a stylus. The digitizing tablet is a flat surface, which contains hundreds of fine copper wires forming a gird. Each copper wire receives electric pulses. The digitizing tablet can be spread over a working table, and is connected to a computer. The stylus is like a pen, or a lens-like cursor with a cross hair and button. The stylus is connected to the tablet, and can be pressed down at a point on the tablet to input the (x, y) coordinates of the point. When the stylus is moved on the tablet, the cursor on the computer's screen moves simultaneously to a corresponding position on the screen to provide visual feedback to the operator. This enables the operator to draw sketches directly, or to input sketched drawings very easily. Inputting drawings or developing sketches by using a digitizer is further simplified by the fact that poorly sketched lines, arcs and other graphical objects are automatically input as mathematically precise objects, like straight lines and smooth curves.

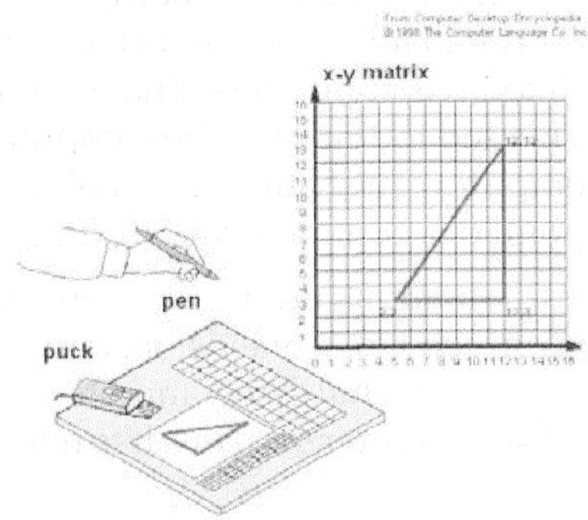

Fig. 3.14 *Digitizer tablet*

Digitizers are commonly used in the area of Computer Aided Design (CAD) by architects and engineers to design cars, buildings, medical devices, robots, mechanical parts etc. They are also used in the area of Geographical Information System (GIS) for digitizing of maps, which are available in paper form.

OUTPUT DEVICES

An output device is an electromechanical device, which accepts data form a computer and translates them into a form, which is sutiable for use by the outside world (the users). Several output devices are available today. They can be broadly classified into the following categories:

1. Monitors
2. Printers
3. Plotters
4. Screen image projector
5. Voice response systems

The various types of output devices along with their typical applications are described below.

Output devices generate computer output, which can be broadly classified into the following two types :

1. *Soft-copy output.* A soft-copy output is an output, which is not produced on a paper or some material, which can be touched and carried for being shown to others. They are temporary in nature, and vanish after use. For example, output displayed on a terminal screen, or spoken out by a voice response system are soft-copy output.
2. *Hard-copy output.* A hard-copy output is an output, which is produced on a paper or some material, which can be touched and carried for being shown to others. They are permanent in nature, and can be kept in paper files, or can be looked later, when the person is not using the computer. For example, output produced by printers or plotters on paper are hard-copy output.

Monitors

Monitors are by far the most popular output devices used today for producing soft-copy output. They display the generated output on a television like screen (see Figure 3.15). A monitor is usually associated with a keyboard, and together they form a Video Display Terminal (VDT). A VDT (often referred to as just terminal) is the most popular input/output (I/O) device used with today's computers. That is, it serves as both an input and an output device. The keyboard is used for input to the computer, and the monitor is used to display the output from the computer. The name "terminal" comes from the fact that a terminal is at the terminal, or end, point of a communication path.

The two basic types of monitors used today are Cathode-Ray-Tube (CRT) and flat-panel. The CRT monitors look much like a television, and are used with non-portable computer systems. On the other hand, the flat-panel monitors are thinner and lighter, and are commonly used with portable computer systems, like notebook computers.

Fig. 3.15 *Monitor CRT*

Printers

Printers are the most commonly used output devices today for producing hard-copy output. The various types of printers in use today are described below.

Dot-Matrix Printers

Dot-matrix printers are character printers, which print one character at a time. They form characters and all kinds of images as a pattern of dots. Figure 3.16 shows how various types of characters can be formed as a pattern of dots. A dot-matrix printer has a print head, which can move horizontally (left to right and right to left) across the paper. The print head contains an array of pins, which can be activated independent of each other to extend and strike against an inked ribbon to form a pattern of dots on the paper. To print a character, the printer activates the appropriate set of pins as the print head moves horizontally. For faster printing, many dot matrix printers are designed to print both while the print head moves form left to right, and while it moves from right to left, on return. Figure 3.17 shows a dot-matrix printer.

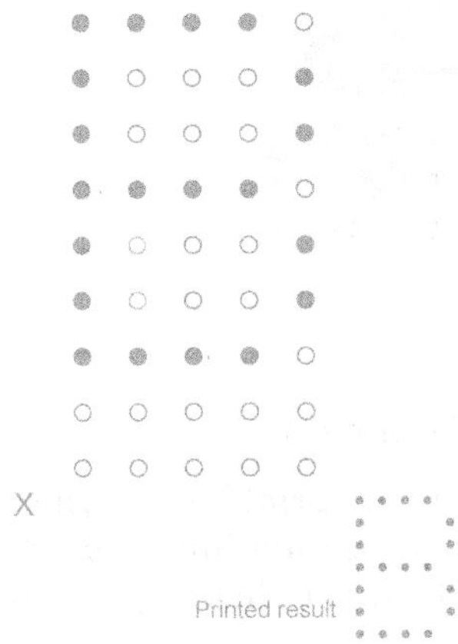

Fig. 3.16

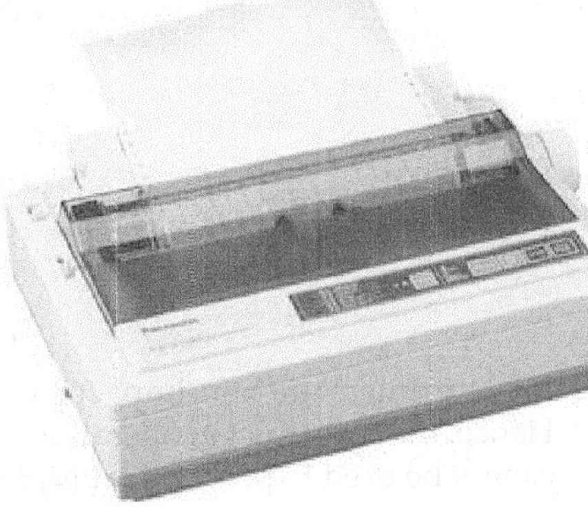

Fig. 3.17 *Dot matrix printer*

Since dot matrix printers printed output as patterns of dots, they can print any shape of character, which a programmer can describe. This allows the printer to print many special characters, different sizes of print, and the ability to print graphics such as charts and graphs.

Dot-matrix printers are impact printers, because they print by hammering the pins on the inked ribbon to leave ink impressions on the paper. Hence, they can be used to produce multiple copies by using carbon paper on its equivalent. However, due to impact printing, dot-matrix printers are noisy as compared to non-impact printers.

Dot-matrix printers are normally slow with speeds usually ranging between 30 to 600 characters per second. However, they are cheap in terms of both initial cost and of operation. Hence, they are preferred by individuals and organizations for generating printed outputs, if the speed and quality of printing are not important factors. They are also used for applications, which require multicopy output, such as shipping forms and invoices, which rely or impact for generating multiple copies.

Inkjet Printers

Inkjet printers are character printers, which form characters and all kinds of images by spraying small drops of ink on to the paper. The print head of an inkjet printer contains up to 64 tiny nozzles, which can be selectively heated up in a few microseconds by an integrated circuit register. When the register heats up, the ink near it vaporizes, and is ejected through the nozzle, and makes a dot on the paper placed in front of the print head. To print a character, the printer selectively heats the appropriate set of nozzles as the print head moves horizontally. As inkjet printer is shown in Figure 3.18.

Inkjet printers produce higher quality output than dot-matrix printers, because they form characters by very tiny ink dots. A high-resolution inkjet printer has as many as 64 nozzles within height of 7 mm, providing print resolution of around 360 dots per inch.

Since inkjet printers produce printed output as patterns of tiny dots, they can print any shape of characters, which a programmer can describe. This allows the printer to print many special characters, different sizes of print, and the ability to print graphics, such as charts and graphs.

Fig. 3.18 *Inkjet printers*

Inkjet printers are non-impact printers, because they print by spraying ink on the paper. Hence, they are quiet in operation. However, like other non-impact printers, inkjet printers cannot be used to produce multiple copies of a document in a single printing.

Inkjet printers are slower than dot-matrix printers with speeds usually ranging between 40 to 300 characters per second. Typically, an inkjet printer is more expensive than a dot-matrix printer. They are preferred by individuals and organizations for generating printed outputs, if the speed of printing is not an important factor.

Drum Printers

Drum printers are the line printers, which print one line at a time. The print mechanism of a drum printer is shown in Figure 3.19. It consists of a solid cylindrical drum with characters embossed (raised characters) on its surface in the form of circular bands. Each band consists of all the printing characters supported by the printer in its character set, and the total number of bands in equal to the maximum number of characters (print positions) that can be printed on a line. Hence, a drum printer with 132 characters per line, and supporting a character set of 96 characters, will have altogether 12,672 (132×96) characters embossed on its surface.

In addition to the drum, the printer has a set of hammers mounted in front of the drum in a manner that an inked ribbon and paper can be placed between the hammers and the drum. The total number of hammers is equal to the total number of bands on the drum, that is, one hammer is located opposite to each band of the drum.

The drum rotates at a high speed, and a character at a print position is printed by activating the appropriate hammer, when the character embossed on the band at the print position passes below it. Hence, the drum would have to complete one full revolution to print each line of output. This means that all characters on a line are not printed at exactly the same time, but the time required to print an entire line is so fast that is appears as if one line is printed at a time.

The drum of a drum printer is expensive and cannot be changed often. Hence, drum printers can only print a predefined set of characters, in a predefined style, which is embossed on the drum. Due to this reason, drum printers do not have the ability to print any shape of characters, different sizes of print, and graphics, such as charts and graphs.

Drum printers are impact printers, because they print by hammering the paper and the inked ribbon against the characters embossed on the drum. Hence, they can be used to produce multiple copies by using carbon paper or its equivalent. However, due to impact printing, drum printers are noisy in operation, and often use a cover to reduce the noise level. Typical speeds to drum printers are in the range of 300 to 2000 lines per minute.

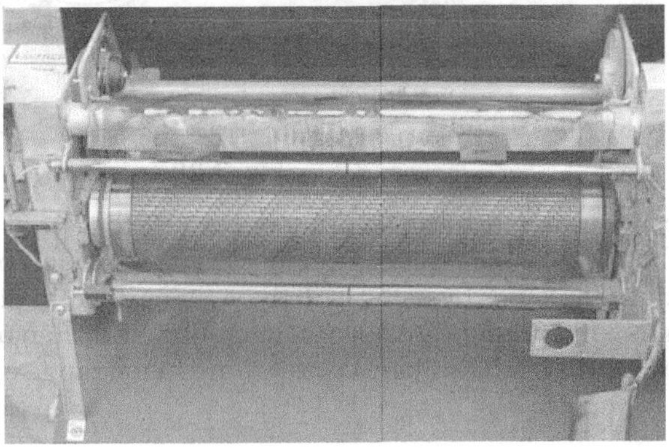

Fig. 3.19 *Drum printers*

Chain/Band Printers

Chain/band printers are line printers, which print one line at a time. The print mechanism of a chain/band printer is shown in Figure 3.20. It consists of a metallic chain/band on which all the characters of the character set supported by the printer are embossed. A standard character set may have 48, 64 or 96 characters. In order to enhance the printing speed, the characters in the character set are embossed several times on the chain/band. For example, the chain/band of a 64 character set printer may have 4 sets of 64 characters each embossed on it. In this case, the chain/band will have altogether 256 (64×4) characters embossed on it.

In addition to the chain/band, the printer has a set of hammers mounted in front of the chain/band in a manner that an inked ribbon and paper can be placed between the hammers and the chain/band. The total number of hammers is equal to the total number of print positions. Therefore, if there are 132 print positions, the printer will have 132 hammers.

The chain/band rotates at a high speed, and a character at a print position is printed by activating the appropriate hammer, when the character embossed on the chain/band passes below it. Since the character set is repeated several times on the chain/band, it is not necessary to wait for the chain/band to make a complete revolution to position the desired character in the correct print position.

Unlike the drum of a drum printer, the chain/band of a chain/band printer can be easily changed. This allows the use of different fonts (styles of characters) and different scripts (languages) to be used with the same printer. However, just like drum printers, chain/band printers can only print pre-defined sets of characters, which are embossed on the chain/band used with the printer. Due to this reason, chain/band printers do not have the ability to print any shape of characters, different sizes of print, and graphics, such as charts and graphs.

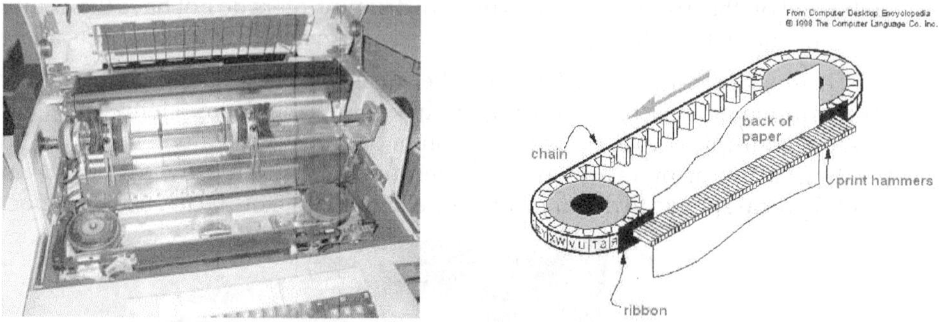

Band Printer *Chain Printer*

Fig. 3.20

Chain/band printers are impact printers, because they print by hammering the paper and the inked ribbon against the characters embossed on the chain/band. Hence, they can be used to produce multiple copies by using carbon paper or its equivalent. However, due to impact printing, chain/band printers are noisy in operation, and often use a cover to reduce the noise level. Typical speeds of chain/band printers are in the range of 400 to 300 lines per minute.

Laser Printers

Laser printers are page printers, which print one page at a time. The main components of a laser printer are a laser beam source, a multi-sided mirror, a photoconductive drum and toner (tiny particles of oppositely charged ink). To print a page of output, the laser beam is focused on the electro statically charged drum by the spinning multi-sided mirror. The mirror focuses the laser beam on the surface of the drum in a manner to create the patterns of characters/images to be printed on the page. As the drum is photocondcutive, a difference in electric charge is created on those parts of the drum surface, which are exposed to the laser beam. As a result, the toner, which is composed of oppositely charged ink particles, sticks to the drum in the places, where the laser beam has charged the drum's surface. The toner is then permanently fused on the paper with head and pressure to generate the printed output. The drum is then rotated and cleaned with a rubber blade to remove the toner sticking to its surface to prepare the drum for the next page printing. A laser printer is shown in Figure 3.21.

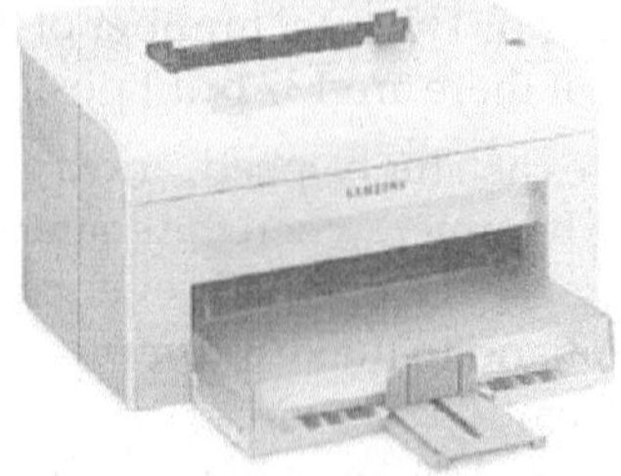

Fig. 3.21 *Laser printer*

Laser printers produce very high quality output, because they form characters by very tiny ink particles. The most common laser printers have resolution of 600 dpi (dots per inch), whereas some high-end laser printers have resolution of 1200 dpi. Because of their high resolution, these printers give excellent graphics art quality.

Since laser printers produce printed output as patterns generated by the laser beam, they can print any shape of characters, which a programmer can describe. This allows the printer to print many special characters, different sizes of print, and the ability to print graphics, such as charts and graphs.

Laser printers are non-impact printers, because they do not have hammers striking on an inked ribbon or paper. Hence, they are very quiet in operation. However, like other non-impact printers, laser printers cannot be used to produce multiple copies of a document in a single printing.

Laser printers are faster in printing speed than other printers discussed before. Low speed laser printers can print 4 to 12 pages per minute. Very high-speed laser printers are also available, which can print 500 to 1000 pages per minute. That is fast enough to print this entire book in about one minute. Because of their better print quality and printing speed, laser printers are more expensive than other printers.

Plotters

We saw above that dot matrix, inkjet and laser printers are capable of producing graphics output. However, many engineering design applications, like architectural plan of a building, design of mechanical components of an aircraft or a car, etc., often require high-quality, perfectly-proportioned graphic output on large sheets. The various types of printers discussed above are not suitable for meeting this output requirement of such applications. A special type of output device, called plotters, is used for this purpose. Plotters are ideal output device for architects, engineers, city planners, and others who need to routinely generate high-precision, hard-copy, graphic output of widely varying sizes. The two commonly used types of plotters are drum plotter and flatbed plotter. They are briefly described below.

Drum Plotter

In a drum plotter the paper, on which the design has to be made is placed over a drum, which can rotate in both clockwise and anti-clockwise directions to produce vertical motion. The mechanism also consists of one or more penholders mounted perpendicular to the drum's surface. The pen(s) clamped in the holder(s) can move left to right, or right to left to produce horizontal motion. The movements of the drum and the pen(s) are controlled by the graph-plotting program. That is, under computer control, the drum and the pen(s) move simultaneously to draw the designs and graphs on the sheet placed on the drum. The plotter can also annotate the designs and graphs so drawn by using the pen to draw characters of various sizes. Since each pen is program selectable, pens having ink of different colors can be mounted in different holders to produce multi-colored designs. Figure 3.22 shows a drum plotter.

Fig. 3.22 *Drum plotter*

Flatbed Plotter

A flatbed plotter a design or graph on a sheet of paper, which that is spread and fixed over a rectangular flatbed table. In this type of plotter, normally the paper does not move, and the pen holding mechanism a designed to provide all types of motions necessary to draw complex designs and graphs. That is, under computer control, the pen(s) move in the required manner to draw the designs and graphs on the sheet placed on the flatbed table. The plotter can also annotate the designs and graphs so drawn by using the pen to draw characters of various sizes. Here also, provision is there to mount more than one pen in the pen(s) holding mechanism. Since each pen's is program selectable, pens having ink of different colors can be mounted in different holders to produce each pen is program selectable, pens having ink of different colors can be mounted in different holders to produce multi-colored designs. The plot size is restricted by the area of the bed. Some may be as small as A4 size (8″ × 11″), while some very large beds used in the design of cars, ships, aircrafts, buildings, highways, etc. can be up to ft. by 50 ft. Some plotters are also designed to etch plastic or metal plates. In this case, the plastic or metal sheet is spread on the bed, and the drawing pen has a sharp-edged needle. Figure 3.23 shows a flatbed plotter.

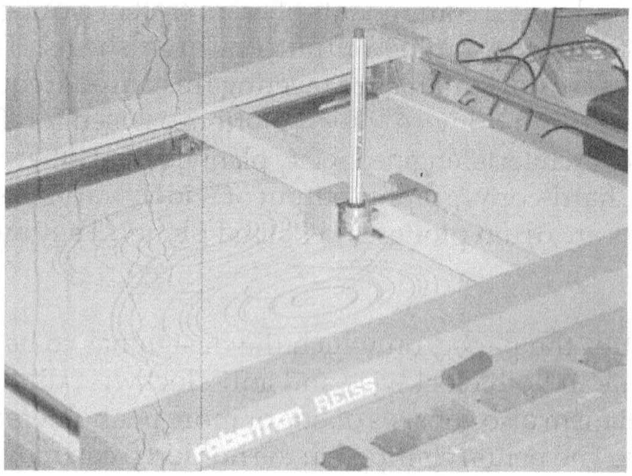

Fig. 3.23 *Flatbed Plotter*

Screen Image Projector

Screen image projector is an output device, which is used to project information from a computer on to a large screen (sch as a cloth screen or a wall), so that it can be simultaneously viewed by a large group of people. This output device is very useful for making presentations to a group of people with the direct use of a computer. Before such an output device was available, the contents of a presentations were prepared using a computer, the presentation material was then printed on a printer, the printout was next reproduced on overhead projector transparency sheets by using a copy machine, and finally, the presentation was made by using an overhead projector. Special marker pens had to be used for marking certain portions of the contents on the transparency sheets during the presentation. A screen image projector greatly simplifies this job. It can be directly plugged to a computer system, and the presenter can make a presentation to a group of people by projecting the presentation material one after another on a large screen with the help of computer's keyboard or mouse. With this facility, the presenter can also directly point to, mark, or edit certain portions of the contents of the displayed material during the presentation to make the presentation more understandable. Additionally, a full-fledged multimedia presentation with audio, video, image and animation can be prepared made by using this facility to make the presentation more lively and interesting, and also to greatly simplify the job of the presenter.

Screen image projectors have become a common presentation equipment today. They are commonly used with portable notebook computers to quickly setup a modern presentation facility at any place with great ease. Like monitors, screen image projectors provide a temporary, soft-copy output.

Voice Response Systems

Just as voice recognition system allows a user to talk to a computer, similarly, a voice response system enables a computer to talk to a user. A voice response system has an audio-response device, which produces audio output. Obviously, the output is temporary, soft-copy output. Voice response systems are of two types-voice reproduction system and speech synthesizer. They are briefly described below.

Voice Reproduction System

A voice reproduction system produces audio output by selecting an appropriate audio output from a set of pre-recorded audio responses. The set of pre-recorded audio responses may include words, phrases or sentences spoken by human beings ; music or alarms generated by musical instruments; or any other type of sound. The actual analog recordings of the pre-recorded sounds are first converted into digital data and then permanently stored on the computer's disk, or in its memory chip. When audio output is to be produced, the computer selects the appropriate sound form the set of pre-recorded sounds, the selected sound is converted back into analog form, which is then routed to a speaker to produce the audio output.

Voice reproduction systems are very useful in a wide range of applications. Their typical uses include:

1. Audio help for guiding how to operate a system. For example, banking industry use voice reproduction systems in Automatic Teller Machines to provide systematic guidance to customers on how to transact with the bank by using an ATM.
2. Automatic answering machines. For examples, telephone enquiries for new telephone numbers in place of an old number, or vacancy status of a particular flight or train if often taken care of by an automatic answering machine.
3. Video games are made exciting and interesting by playing an event-based sound from a set of pre-recorded sounds.
4. Talking alarm clocks. For example, every hour the clock speaks out what is the time by selecting the appropriate voice message corresponding to that hour from the set of pre-recorded voice messages. Else the clock may speak "its time to wake up" at the time set for alarm.
5. Talking toys and home appliances also employ a voice reproduction system.
6. Often, personal computers with audio facility are used for automated multimedia presentations during exhibitions.

A speech synthesizer converts text information into spoken sentences. To produce speech, these devices combine basic sound units, called phonemes. From a given text information, sequence of words are combined into phonemes, amplified, and output through the speaker attached to the system. Speech synthesizers are still in their infancy, because currently, they can produce only limited unique sounds with only limited vocal infections and phrasing. However, they are very useful in a wide range of applications. Their typical uses include:

1. For reading out text information to blind persons. For example, a recently published book may be scanned using a scanner, converted into text using OCR software, and read out to blind persons using a speech synthesizer. This will allow blind persons to know the latest information published in a book, as soon as it is printed, rather than wait for the book to appear in Braille.
2. For allowing those persons, who cannot speak, to communicate effectively. For example, the person simply types the information, and the speech synthesizer converts it into spoken words.
3. For translation systems, which convert an entered text into spoken words in a selected language. For example, a foreigner coming to India may enter a text, which he/she wants to communicate to an Indian, and the speech synthesizer converts it into spoken words of the selected Indian language.

SUMMARY

1. The *input-output devices* (abbreviated I/O devices) provide the means of communication between the computer and the outer world. They are also known as peripheral devices.
2. An input device is an electromechanical device, which accepts data from the outside world and translates them into a form, which the computer can interpret.
3. An output device is an electromechanical device, which accepts data from a computer and translates them into a form, which is suitable for use by the outside world (the users).
4. Keyboard devices are the most commonly used input devices today. They allow data entry into a computer system by pressing a set of keys (labeled buttons), which are neatly mounted on a keyboard, which is connected to the computer system.
5. A *graphical user interface* (GUI) provides a screen full of graphic icons (small images on the screen) or menus to the user, and allows the user to make a rapid selection form the displayed icons or menus to give instructions to the computer.
6. Point-and-draw devices are input devices, which can be used to rapidly point to and select a particular graphic icon or menu item form the multiple options displayed on the screen. Many of these devices can also be very effectively used to create graphic elements on the screen, such as lines, curves and freehand shapes. Some of the commonly used point-and-draw devices are mouse, trackball, joystick, electronic pen and touch screen.
7. Data scanning devices are input devices, which are used for direct data entry into the computer system from source documents. Some of the data scanning devices are also capable of recognizing marks or characters.
8. An image scanner is an input device, which translates paper documents into an electronic format, which can be stored in a computer. The input documents may be typed text, pictures, grahics, or even handwritten material.
9. An *optical character recognition* (OCR) device is a scanner equipped with a character recognition software. It is used for inputting text documents and storing them in a form, which is suitable for doing word processing of the documents. That is, the computer can interpret the stored document as letters, numbers and special characters.

10. An *optical mark reader (OMR)* is a scanner, which is capable of recognizing a pre-specified type of mark made by pencil or pen. Any input data, which is of a choice or selection nature can be recorded for OMR input.
11. *Bar codes* represent alphanumeric data by a combination of adjacent vertical lines (called bars) by varying their width and the spacing between them. A *bar-code reader* is a scanner, which is used for reading (decoding) bar-coded data.
12. *Magnetic-ink character recognition (MICR)* technology is used by the banking industry for faster processing of the large volume of cheques. This technology also ensures accuracy of data entry, because most of the information is pre-printed on the cheque and is directly fed to the computer.
13. A *digitizer* is an input device, which is used for converting (digitizing) pictures, maps and drawings into digital form for storage in computers. This enables re-creation of the drawing from the stored information whenever required, as well as easy incorporation of changes in the drawing as and when required.
14. *Electronic cards* are small plastic cards having encoded data, which are appropriate for the application for which they are used. An *electronic-card reader*, which is normally connected to a computer, is used to read the data encoded on an electronic card, and transfer it to the computer for further processing.
15. *Voice recognition devices* are input devices, which allow a person to input data to a computer system by speaking to it.
16. *A vision-input system* allows a computer to accept input just by seeing an object. The input data in this case is normally an object's shape and features in the form on the image.
17. Computer output generated by devices are of two types—soft-copy output and hard-copy output. *Soft-copy outputs* are temporary in nature, and vanish after use. *Hard-copy outputs* are permanent in nature, and can be kept in paper files, or can be looked at a later time, when the person is not using the computer.
18. *Monitors* are by far the most popular output device used today for producing soft-copy output. They display the generated output on a television like screen.
19. A monitor and a keyboard are usually associated together to form a *video display terminal (VDT)*, which is often referred to as just *terminal*. A terminal serves as both an input and an output device, and is the most popular input/output (I/O) device used with today's computers.
20. *Printers* are the most commonly used output devices used today for producing hard-copy output.
21. *Dot-matrix printers* are character printers, which form characters and all kinds of images as a pattern of dots.
22. *Inkjet printers* are character printers, which form characters and all kinds of images by spraying small drops of ink on to the paper.
23. *Drum printers* are line printers, which print characters by striking a set of hammers on an inked ribbon and paper placed against a solid cylindrical drum with characters embossed on its surface in the form of circular bands.
24. *Chain/band printers* are line printers, which print characters by striking a set of hammers on an inked ribbon and paper placed against a metallic chain/band on which all the characters of the character set supported by the printer are embossed.
25. *Laser printers* are page printers, which produce very high quality output by forming characters and all kinds of images with very tiny ink particles.
26. *Plotters* are ideal output device for architects, engineers, city planners, and others, who need to routinely generate high-precision, hard copy graphic output of widely varying sizes. The two commonly used types of plotters are drum potter and flatbed plotter.

27. *Screen image projector* is an output device, which is used to project information from a computer on to a large screen (such as a cloth screen or a wall), so that it can be simultaneously viewed by a large group of people.

28. *Voice response systems* enable computers to talk to their users. They are of two types—voice reproduction system and speech synthesizer. A *voice reproduction system* produces audio output by selecting an appropriate audio output from a set of pre-recorded audio responses. On the other hand, a *speech synthesizer* converts text information into spoken sentences.

REVIEW EXERCISES

1. Why are I/O devices necessary for a computer system?
2. What are peripheral devices ? Why are they so called?
3. Differentiate between an input device and an output device. Can a device be used as both an input device and an output device? If no, explain why. If yes, give an example of such a device.
4. Why are I/O devices very slow as compared to the speed of primary storage and CPU?
5. What is an input device? Name some of the commonly used print devices.
6. What are keyboard devices?
7. What are point-and-draw devices? Name some of the commonly used point-and-draw devices.
8. What is a mouse ? Explain how it is used to notify the system of a particular user choice out of a given set of choices on the monitor's screen.
9. What is trackball ? How is it different from a mouse?
10. Explain how a trackball is used to notify the system of a particular user choice out of given set of choices on the monitor's screen.
11. What is a joystick ? How is it different from a trackball?
12. Explain how an electronic pen is used as an input device.
13. What is a touch screen device?
14. Give some typical applications for which touch screen is most suitable as an input device.
15. What is an information kiosk? Give some typical uses of an information kiosk.
16. Write short notes on :
    (*a*) Mouse (*b*) Trackball (*c*) Joystick
    (*d*) Electronic Pen (*e*) Touch screen (*f*) Information kiosk
17. What are data scanning devices? How do they help in improving input data accuracy as compared to keyboard devices?
18. What is an image scanner?
19. Differentiate between a flatbed and a hand-held image scanner?
20. What are the limitations of an image scanner when it is used for inputting text documents? How does an OCR device overcome these limitations?
21. What is an OCR device? List out some of its advantages and limitations for inputting text documents?
22. What is an OMR device? What types of applications is it suitable for? Explain the technique used by it for recognition of marks.
23. What are bar codes? How does a bar-code reader read bar-coded data? Give a typical use of a bar-code reader.
24. What is the Universal Product Code (UPC)? Which input device is used for inputting data based on UPC?

25. What is an MICR device? Which industry is the primary user of MICR?
26. Explain how an MICR device helps in faster processing of bank cheques with greater accuracy.
27. What is main limitation of MICR technology?
28. What is a digitizer? What are its two main components? What are its main areas of application?
29. Explain how a digitizer can be used to convert a drawing into digital form for storage in computers.
30. What is an electronic card? Give two applications where electronic cards can be effectively used.
31. What is a voice recognition device? Why do currently available voice recognition devices have limited success?
32. Give some typical applications of voice recognition systems.
33. What is a vision-input system? Give some typical applications of vision-input systems.
34. Write short notes on :
    (*a*) Image scanner
    (*b*) Bar-code reader
    (*c*) Digitizer
    (*d*) Electronic-card reader
    (*e*) Vision-input systems
    (*f*) Optical Mark Reader (OMR)
    (*g*) Optical Character Recognition (OCR)
    (*h*) Voice recognition devices
    (*i*) Magnetic-Ink Character Recognition (MICR)
35. Write short notes on :
    (*a*) Keyboard devices
    (*b*) Point-and-draw devices
    (*c*) Data scanning devices
36. What is an output device? Name some of the commonly used output devices.
37. Differentiate between soft-copy and hard-copy outputs.
38. Name two output devices used for producing soft-copy output, and two output devices used for producing hard-copy output.
39. What is a computer terminal? Why is it so called?
40. What is a monitor device? Name the two basic types of monitors used today, along with their relative advantages and disadvantages.
41. What is a flat panel monitor? Where is it commonly used?
42. What is a printer? What are the commonly used types of printers?
43. Differentiate between impact and non-impact printer. Give their relative advantages and disadvantages. Name few printers of both types.
44. Explain the printing mechanism of dot-matrix printers.
45. List out the key features and limitations of dot-matrix printer.
46. Explain the printing mechanism of inkjet printers.
47. List out the key features and limitations of inkjet printers.
48. Explain the printing mechanism of drum printers.
49. List out the key features and limitations of drum printers.
50. Explain the printing mechanism of chain/band printers.
51. List out the key features and limitations of chain/band printers.
52. Explain the printing mechanism of laser printers.
53. List out the key features and limitations of laser printers.
54. Write short notes on:
    (*a*) Dot-matrix printers
    (*b*) Inkjet printers
    (*c*) Drum printers
    (*d*) Chain/band printers
    (*e*) Laser printers
55. What is a plotter? What types of users need it?

56. Explain the working mechanism of drum plotter.
57. Explain the working mechanism of a flatbed plotter.
58. What is a screen image projector? What is it typically used for?
59. What is a voice response system? Give some of its typical applications.
60. What is a voice reproduction system? How does it function ? Give some of its typical applications.
61. What is a speech synthesizer? How does it function? Give some of its typical applications.
62. Write short notes on:
    (*a*) Plotter
    (*b*) Screen image projector
    (*c*) Voice response systems
    (*d*) Voice reproduction system
63. Write the full forms of the following abbreviations :
    (*a*) GUI
    (*b*) CAD
    (*c*) OCR
    (*d*) OMR
    (*e*) UPC
    (*f*) MICR
    (*g*) VDT
    (*h*) CRT

4

Processor and Memory

THE MAIN MEMORY

In the discussion above, we saw that the CPU contains the necessary circuitry for data processing and controlling the other components of a system. However, one thing it does not have built into it is the place to store programs and data, which are needed during data processing. We also saw that the CPU does contain several registers for storing data and instructions, but these are very small areas, which can hold only a few bytes at a time, and are just sufficient to hold only one or two instructions and the corresponding data. If the instructions and data of a program being executed by the CPU, were to reside in secondary storage like a disk, and fetched and loaded one by one into the registers of the CPU as the program execution proceeded, this would lead to the CPU being idle most of the time, because there is a large speed mismatch between the rate at which CPU can process data and the rate at which data can be transferred from disk to CPU registers. For example, a CPU can process data at a rate of about five nanosecond/byte, and a disk reader can read data at a speed of around five microsecond/byte. Hence, within the time in which the disk can supply one byte of data, the CPU can process 1000 bytes. This would lead to a very slow overall performance, even if the computer system used a very fast CPU. To overcome this problem, there is a need to have a reasonably large storage space, which can hold the instructions and data of the program(s), on which the CPU is currently working. The time to fetch and load data from this storage space into the CPU registers must also be very small as compared to that for disk storage, to reduce the speed mismatch problem with the CPU speed. Every computer has such a storage space, which is known as primary storage, main memory, or simply memory. It is a temporary storage area, which is built into the computer hardware, and in which instructions and data of a program reside, mainly when the program is being executed by the CPU. Physically, this memory consists of some chips either on the motherboard, or on a small circuit board attached to the motherboard of a computer system. This built-in memory allows the CPU to store and retrieve data very quickly. The rate of fetching data from this memory is typically of the order of 50 nanosecond/byte. Hence, the rate of data fetching from the main memory is about 100 times faster than that from a high-speed secondary storage like disk.

Storage Evaluation Criteria

Any storage unit of a computer system is characterized and evaluated based on the following properties:

1. *Storage capacity.* It is the amount of data, which can be stored in the storage unit. A large capacity is desired. As compared to secondary storage units, primary storage units have less storage capacity.
2. *Access time.* This is the time required to locate and retrieve stored data from the storage unit, in response to a program instruction. A fast access time is preferred. As compared to secondary storage units, primary storage units have faster access time.
3. *Cost per bit of storage.* This refers to the cost of a storage unit for a given storage capacity. Obviously, a lower cost is desirable. As compared to secondary storage units, primary storage units have higher cost per bit of storage.
4. *Volatile.* If the storage unit can retain the data stored in it, even when the power is turned off or interrupted, it is called non-volatile storage. On the other hand, if the data stored are lost, when the desirable. In almost all computer systems, the primary storage units are volatile and the secondary storage units are non-volatile.
5. *Random access.* If the time taken to access a piece of data from the storage unit is independent of the location of the data in storage unit, it is called a random access storage Memory (RAM). Each separate location of RAM is as easy to access as any other location, and takes the same amount of time. In almost all computer systems, the primary storage units have random access property, and the secondary storage units have either pseudo-random access (access time is nearly same for all locations but not exactly same), or sequential access (access time directly depends on the location of the data) property.

Main Memory Organization

A primary storage or main memory of a computer system is made up of several small storage areas, called locations or cells. Each of these locations can store a fixed number of bits, called word length of that particular memory. Hence, as shown in Fig. 4.3, a given memory is divided into N words, where N generally is some power of 2. Each word or location has a built-in and unique number assigned to it. This number is called the address of the location, and is used to identify the location. Each location can hold either a data item or an instruction, and its address remains the same, regardless of its contents. The addresses normally start at 0, and the highest address equals the number of words, which can be stored in the memory minus 1. For example, if a memory has 1024 locations, the address ranges between 0 and 1023. Hence, at address 0 we find a word, at address 1 a second word, at address second a third word, and so on, up to the final word at the largest address.

RAM, ROM, PROM and EPROM

Random Access Memory (RAM)

When people talk about computer memory, they usually mean the volatile RAM memory. Physically, this memory consists of some integrated circuit chips (IC chips, shown in Fig. 2.6), either on the motherboard, or on a small circuit board attached to the motherboard. A computer's motherboard is designed in manner that its memory capacity can be easily enhanced by adding more memory chips. Hence, if you decide to have more memory than you computer currently has, you can buy more memory chips, and plug them in the empty memory slots on the motherboard. This job is normally done by the service engineers. The additional RAM chips, which plug into special sockets on the motherboard, are also known as single in-line memory modules (SIMM).

Read-Only Memory (ROM)

A special type of RAM, called read-only memory (ROM), is non-volatile memory chip, in which data is stored permanently and cannot be altered by the programmer. In fact, storing data permanently into this kind of memory is called "burning in the data", because data in such memory is stored by using fuse-links. Once a fuse-link is burnt, it is permanent. The data stored in a ROM chip can only be read and used – they cannot be changed. This is the reason why it is called read-only memory (ROM). Since ROM chips are non-volatile, the data stored inside a ROM are not lost, when the power supply is switched off, unlike the case of a volatile RAM chip. ROMs are also known as field stores, permanent stores, or dead stores.

ROMs are mainly use to store programs and data, which do not change and are frequently used. For example, the most basic computer operations are carried out by wired electronic circuits. However, several higher-level operations, which are very frequently used, require very complicated electronic circuits for their implementations.

Hence, instead of building electronic circuits for these operations, special program are written to perform them. These programs are called microprograms, because they deal with low-level machine functions, and are essentially substitutes for additional hardware. ROMs are used by computer manufacturers for storing these microprograms, so that they cannot be modified by the users.

A good example of a microprogram is the set of instructions needed to make the computer system ready for use, when its power is switched on. This microprogram, called "system boot program", contains a set of start-up instructions to check if the system hardware like memory, I/O devices, *etc.*, are functioning properly, and looks for an operating system and loads its core part in the volatile RAM of the system, to produce the initial display-screen prompt. Note that this microprogram is used every time the computer is switched on, and needs to be retained when the computer is switched off. Hence, ROM is an ideal storage for storing it.

Programmable Read-Only Memory (PROM)

There are two types of Read-Only Memory (ROM) — manufacturer-programmed and user-programmed. A manufacturer-programmed ROM is one in which data is burnt in by the manufacturer of the electronic equipment in which it used. For example, a personal computer manufacturer may store the system boot program permanently in the ROM chip used on the motherboard of all the PCs manufactured by it. Similarly, a printer manufacturer may store the printer controller software in the ROM chip used on the circuit board of all the printers manufactured by it. Manufacturer-programmed ROMs are mainly used in those cases, where the demand for such programmed ROMs is large. Note that manufacturer-programmed ROM chips are supplied by the manufacturers of electronic equipment, and it is not possible for a user to modify the programs or data stored inside the ROM chip. On the other hand, a user-programmed ROM is one in which the user can load and store "read-only" programs and data. That is, it possible for a user to "customize", a system by converting his/her own programs to microprograms, and storing them in a user-programmed ROM chip. Such a ROM is commonly known as Programmable Read-Only Memory (PROM), because a user can program it. Once the user programs are stored in a PROM chip, they can usually be executed in a fraction of the time previously required. PROMs are programmed to record information using a special device, known as PROM-programmer. However, once the chip has been programmed, the recorded information cannot be changed, *i.e.*, the PROM becomes a ROM, and it is only possible to read the stored information. PROM is also non-volatile storage, *i.e.*, the stored information remains intact, even if power is switched off.

Erasable Programmable Read-Only Memory (EPROM)

Once information is stored in a ROM chip a PROM chip, it cannot be altered. However, there is another type of memory chip, called Erasable Programmable Read-Only Memory (EPROM), which overcomes this problem. As the name implies, it is possible to erase information stored in an EPROM chip, and the chip can be reprogrammed to store new information. EPROMs are often used by R & D personnel (experimenters), who frequently change the microprograms to test the efficiency of the computer system with new programs. EPROMs are also useful in case of those applications, where one may like to store a program in a ROM, which would normally not change, but under some unforeseen conditions one may like to alter it. When an EPROM is in use, information stored in it can only be "read", and the information remains in the chip, until it is erased.

EPROM chips are of two types-one in which the stored information is erased by exposing the chip for some time to ultraviolet light, and the other one in which the stored information is erased by using high voltage electric pulses. The former is known as Ultra Violet EPROM (UVEPROM), and the latter is known as Electrically EPROM (EEPROM). It is easier to alter information stored in an EEPROM chip. Due to the ease with which stored programs can be altered, EEPROM is also known as flash memory. Flash memory is used in many new I/O and storage devices.

CACHE MEMORY

We saw that the use of main memory helps in minimizing the disk-processor speed mismatch to a large extent because the rate of data fetching by the CPU from the main memory is about 100 times faster than that from a high-speed secondary storage like disk. However, even with the use of main memory, the memory-processor speed mismatch becomes a bottleneck in the speed with which the CPU can process instructions because there is it 1 to 10 speed mismatch between the processor and the memory. That is, the rate at which data can be fetched from memory is about 10 times slower than the rate at which CPU can process data. Hence, in many situations, the performance of processors gets limited due to the slow speed of main memory. Obviously, the overall the performance of a processor can be greatly improved by minimizing the memory-processor speed mismatch. Cache memory (pronounced "cash" memory) is commonly used for minimizing the memory-processor speed mismatch. Cache memory is an extremely fast, small memory between CPU and main memory (see Figure 4.1), whose access time is closer to the processing speed of the CPU. It acts as a high-speed buffer between CPU and main memory and is used to temporarily store very active data and instructions during processing. Since the cache memory is faster than main memory, the processing speed is increased by making data and instructions needed in current processing available in the cache.

SUMMARY

1. The CPU is the brain of computer system. All major calculations and comparisons performed by a computer are carried out inside its CPU. The CPU is also responsible for activating and controlling the operations of other units of the computer system. Hence, no other single component of a computer determines its overall performance, as much as the CPU.
2. The two basic components of a CPU are the control unit and the arithmetic logic unit.
3. The control unit of the CPU acts as a central nervous system for the other components of the computer. It manages and coordinates the entire computer system, including the input and output units. It obtains instructions from the program stored in the main memory, interprets the instructions, and issues signals, which cause other units of the system to execute them.
4. The Arithmetic Logic Unit (ALU) of the CPU is the place, where the actual execution of the instructions takes place, during the data processing operation.
5. Every CPU has built-in ability to execute a set of machine instructions, called its instructions set.
6. As the instruction are interrupted and executed by the CPU, there is a movement of information between the various units of the computer system. In order to handle this process satisfactorily, and to speed up the rate of information transfer, the computer uses a number of special memory units, called registers. These registers are used to hold information on a temporary basis, and are part of the CPU (not main memory).
7. The speed of a processor is directly related to the computer's clock speed, which is the number of pulses, produced per second by the built-in electronic clock. This clock speed is measured in megahertz (or MHz).
8. The three commonly known processor architectures are CISC (Complex Instruction Set Computer), RISC (Reduced Instruction Set Computer) and EPIC (Explicitly Parallel Instruction Computing).
9. Every computer has a temporary storage area, which is built into the computer hardware, and in which instruction and data of a program reside mainly when the program is being executed by the CPU. This storage space is known as primary storage, main memory, or simply memory.
10. Any storage unit of a computer system, is characterized and evaluated based on the following properties — storage capacity, access time, cost per bit of storage, volatile, and random access.
11. A primary storage or main memory of a computer system is made up of several small storage areas, called locations or cells. Each of these locations can store a fixed number of bits, called word length of that particular memory.
12. In a word-addressable computer, each numbered address location can store a fixed number of characters (equal to its word-length in bytes). In these computers, storage space is always allocated in multiplies of word-length. On the other hand, in a character-addressable computer, each numbered address can only store a single character (A, B, 1, 2, +, –, etc.)
13. The main memory capacity of large computer systems is normally than that of small systems. This capacity is defined in terms of the number of bytes a computer system can store. Memory capacity of a computer system is normally stated in terms of kilobytes (KB), which is equal to 1024 (2^{20}) bytes of storage, or in terms of gigabytes (GB), which is equal to 1, 073, 741, 824 (2^{30}) bytes storage.
14. A computer's main memory is built of volatile RAM chips.
15. A special type of RAM, called Read-Only Memory (ROM), is a non-volatile memory chip, in which data are stored permanently and cannot be altered by the programmer. There are two types of read-only programmer. There are two types of Read-Only Memory (ROM) – manufacturer-

programmed and user-programmed. The later is commonly known as Programmable Read-Only Memory (PROM), because a user can program it.

16. Once information is stored in a ROM chip or PROM chip, it cannot be altered. However, Erasable Programmable Read-Only Memory (EPROM) chips can be reprogrammed to store new information. EPROM chips are of two types – Ultra Violet EPROM (UVEPROM) and Electrically EPROM (EEPROM). EEPROM is also known as flash memory.
17. Cache memory is an extremely fast, small memory between CPU and main memory, whose access time is closer to the processing speed of the CPU. It acts as high-speed buffer between CPU and main memory, and is used to temporarily store very active data and instruction during processing.

REVIEW EXERCISES

1. List out the main functions of CPU in a computer system.
2. What are the two main components of CPU of a computer system? List out the main functions of each of these components.
3. Describe the role of the decoder of the control unit of a CPU.
4. What is a microprocessor?
5. What is an instruction set of a computer system? Do computers made by different manufacturers generally have the same or different instruction sets?
6. Machine language programs written for one computer will generally not run on another computer with a different CPU. Explain why?
7. What is meant by a family of CPUs ? When do two CPUs belong to the same family?
8. When is a computer said to be upward compatible with another computer? How is this feature useful for the users of these computers?
9. What are registers? Name some of the commonly used registers, and briefly describe the function of each.
10. What is meant by the length of a register? What are the commonly used register-lengths in modern computer systems? Why is larger register length more desirable?
11. List out the main steps involved in the execution of an instruction by the CPU of a computer system.
12. What is meant by the clock speed of a computer system? How does it influence the overall speed of a computer system?
13. Differentiate between CISC and RISC processors.
14. List out the relative advantages and disadvantages of CISC and RISC processors.
15. List out the key properties used to characterize and evaluate storage units of computer systems.
16. Explain the difference between volatile and non-volatile memory. Give an example of each type of memory.
17. Explain the difference among random access, pseudo-random access, and sequential access storage units. Give an example of each type of storage unit.
18. Differentiate among a bit, a byte, and a word.
19. Explain the difference between an address and the contents of an address.
20. Explain the key difference between memory read and write operations.
21. Explain why is it advantageous to have more number of bits per word, instead of having more words of shorter length, in the memory architecture of a computer system?

22. Distinguish between word-addressable and character-addressable computers. Discuss their relative advantages and disadvantages.
23. How many bytes will be required to store the word 'MEMORY' in (*a*) a character-addressable computer, (*b*) a word-addressable computer having word-length of 64 bits?
24. Name some of the commonly used this for stating memory capacity. How many characters is each unit roughly equivalent to?
25. A computer has 512 MB of memory. How many characters can be stored in its memory at a time?
26. What is a ROM? Why is it so called? Give few typical uses of ROM?
27. What is a microprogram? Give an example of a microprogram, which is a good candidate for storage in the ROM of a computer system.
28. Differentiate between PROM and EPROM.
29. Differentiate between UVEPROM and EEPROM.
30. What is a flash memory? Why is to so called?

5

NUMBERS SYSTEMS

NUMBERS : FLOAT/INT

C++ supports two basic number types :

- *integers :* These are "whole" numbers like 1, 2, 3 and their negative values
- *floating point numbers :* These are numbers with a decimal point (which "floats" - called a floating point number) like 2.3, -14.5

There are variations of these numbers to get bigger or smaller versions.

- char, short, int, long for integers (from smallest to biggest)
- float, double, long double for floating point numbers. (from smallest to biggest)

Mostly you will just use "int" and "float" as appropriate.

Floating point and integer numbers have different rules for their arithmetic.

In particular dividing an integer by an integer produces an integer (called integer divide) by simply removing the part after the decimal point (called truncating to an integer).

Also integers have a way of producing the remainder of the division as a integer called the modulus operator (written as "%"). This operator does not work for floats. (see tutor page on evaluating expressions for more examples).

It is possible to mix integers and floating points numbers. Such expressions are called mixed type or mixed mode expressions. In such cases, all numbers are converted to floating point number and the result is a floating point number. Such a conversion is called implicit since it is done automatically.

You can also force a conversions to occur explicitly by using a type cast operator.

This exercise tests your understanding of mixed mode expressions.

Given the statements : (adapted from the program lab3el.cpp)

```
int g1,g2,g3,g4;
float avg;
int iavg;
```

```
        g1 = 86; g2 = 56; g3 = 75; g4 = 98; // it is OK to put more than one
statement on a line
```

Octal Number System

The octal number system has a base of eight, meaning that it has eight possible digits : 0, 1, 2, 3, 4, 5, 6, 7.

8^3	8^2	8^1	8^0		8^{-1}	8^{-2}	8^{-3}
= 512	= 64	= 8	= 1		$= \frac{1}{8}$	$= \frac{1}{64}$	$= \frac{1}{512}$
Most Significant Digit				Octal point			Least Significant Digit

Octal to Decimal Conversion

For example, $24.6_8 = 2 \times (8^1) + 4 \times (8^0) + 6 \times (8^{-1}) = 20.75_{10}$

Binary-To-Octal/Octal-To-Binary Conversion

Octal Digit	0	1	2	3	4	5	6	7
Binary Equivalent	000	001	010	011	100	101	110	111

Each Octal digit is represented by three bits of binary digit.

For example, $100\ 111\ 010_2 = (100)\ (111)\ (010)_2 = 4\ 7\ 2_8$

Repeat Division

This method uses repeated division by 8. For example, convert 177_{10} to octal and binary:

$\frac{177}{8}$ = 22+ remainder of 1 1 (Least significant Bit)

$\frac{22}{8}$ = 2+ remainder of 6 6

$\frac{2}{8}$ = 0 + remainder of 2 2 (Most significant Bit)

Result 177_{10} = 261.

Convert to Binary = 010110001_2

ASCII Codes

It is a very well-known fact that computers can manage internally only 0s (zeros) and 1s (ones). This is true, and by means of sequences of 0s and 1s the computer can express any numerical value as its binary translation, which is a very simple mathematical operation (as explained in the paper numerical bases).

Nevertheless, there is no such evident way to represent letters and other non-numeric characters with 0s and 1s. Therefore, in order to do that, computers use ASCII tables, which are tables or lists that contain all the letters in the roman alphabet plus some additional characters. In these tables each character is always represented by the same order number. For example, the ASCII code for the capital letter "A" is always represented by the order number 65, which is easily representable using 0s and 1s in binary : 65 expressed as a binary number is 1000001.

The standard ASCII table defines 128 character codes (from 0 to 127), of which, the first 32 are control codes (non-printable), and the remaining 96 character codes are representable characters :

<table>
<tr><th>*</th><th>0</th><th>1</th><th>2</th><th>3</th><th>4</th><th>5</th><th>6</th><th>7</th><th>8</th><th>9</th><th>A</th><th>B</th><th>C</th><th>D</th><th>E</th><th>F</th></tr>
<tr><td>0</td><td>NUL</td><td>SOH</td><td>STX</td><td>ETX</td><td>EOT</td><td>ENQ</td><td>ACK</td><td>BEL</td><td>BS</td><td>TAB</td><td>LF</td><td>VT</td><td>FF</td><td>CR</td><td>SO</td><td>SI</td></tr>
<tr><td>1</td><td>DLE</td><td>DC1</td><td>DC2</td><td>DC3</td><td>DC4</td><td>NAK</td><td>SYN</td><td>ETB</td><td>CAN</td><td>EM</td><td>SUB</td><td>ESC</td><td>FS</td><td>GS</td><td>RS</td><td>US</td></tr>
<tr><td>2</td><td></td><td>!</td><td>"</td><td>#</td><td>$</td><td>%</td><td>&</td><td>'</td><td>(</td><td>)</td><td>*</td><td>+</td><td>,</td><td>-</td><td>.</td><td>/</td></tr>
<tr><td>3</td><td>0</td><td>1</td><td>2</td><td>3</td><td>4</td><td>5</td><td>6</td><td>7</td><td>8</td><td>9</td><td>:</td><td>;</td><td><</td><td>=</td><td>></td><td>?</td></tr>
<tr><td>4</td><td>@</td><td>A</td><td>B</td><td>C</td><td>D</td><td>E</td><td>F</td><td>G</td><td>H</td><td>I</td><td>J</td><td>K</td><td>L</td><td>M</td><td>N</td><td>O</td></tr>
<tr><td>5</td><td>P</td><td>Q</td><td>R</td><td>S</td><td>T</td><td>U</td><td>V</td><td>W</td><td>X</td><td>Y</td><td>Z</td><td>[</td><td>\</td><td>]</td><td>^</td><td>_</td></tr>
<tr><td>6</td><td>`</td><td>a</td><td>b</td><td>c</td><td>d</td><td>e</td><td>f</td><td>g</td><td>h</td><td>i</td><td>j</td><td>k</td><td>l</td><td>m</td><td>n</td><td>o</td></tr>
<tr><td>7</td><td>p</td><td>q</td><td>r</td><td>s</td><td>t</td><td>u</td><td>v</td><td>w</td><td>x</td><td>y</td><td>z</td><td>{</td><td>|</td><td>}</td><td>~</td><td>-</td></tr>
</table>

*This panel is organized to be easily read in hexadecimal : row numbers represent the first digit and the column numbers represent the second one. For example, the "A" character is located at the 4th row and the 1st column, for that it would be represented in hexadecimal as 0 × 41 (65).

Because most systems nowadays work with 8bit bytes, which can represent 256 different values, in addition to the 128 standard ASCII codes there are other 128 that are known as extended ASCII, which are platform- and locale-dependent. So there is more than one extended ASCII character set.

The two most used extended ASCII character sets are the one known as OEM, that comes from the default character set incorporated by default in the IBM-PC and the other is the ANSI extend ASCII which is used by most recent operating systems.

The first of them, the OEM character set, is the one used by the hardware of the immense majority of PC compatible machines, and was also used under the old DOS system. It includes some foreign signs, some marked characters and pieces to represent panels.

OEM Extended ASCII

	0	1	2	3	4	5	6	7	8	9	A	B	C	D	E	F
8	Ç	ü	é	â	ä	á	å	ç	ê	ë	è	ï	î	ì	Ã	Å
9	□	æ	Æ	ô	ö	ò	û	ù	ÿ	u	ü	¢	£	¥	Æ	ƒ
A	à	ì	ó	ú	ñ	Ñ	ö	õ	¿	⌐	¬	¼	½	¡	«	»
B	■	■	■	│	┤	╡	╢	╖	╕	╣	║	╗	╝	╜	╛	┐
C	┌	┴	┬	├	─	┼	╞	├	╝	╔	╦	╩	╠	═	╬	╧
D	µ	╦	π	u	╘	F	Π	╫	╪	┘	┌	█	▄	▌	▐	▀
E	α	β	Γ	π	Σ	σ	µ	τ	Φ	θ	Ω	δ	∞	Ø	∈	∩
F	≡	±	≥	≤	⌠	⌡	÷	≈	°	−	•	√	n	2	▌	

cplusplus.com

The ANSI character set is a standard that many systems incorporate, like Windows, some UNIX platforms and many standalone applications. It includes many more local symbols and marked letters so that it can be used with no need of being redefined in many more languages :

ANSI Extended ASCII (Windows)

	O	1	2	3	4	5	6	7	8	9	A	B	C	D	E	F
8	□	□	‚	ƒ	„	…	†	‡	ˆ	‰	Š	‹	Œ	□	□	□
9	□	‘	‘	“	”	•	–	—	˜	™	š	›	œ	□	□	Ÿ
A		¡	¢	£	¤	¥		§	¨	©	ª	«	¬		®	¯
B	°	±	²	³	´	µ	¶	·	¸	¹	º	»	¼	½	¾	¿
C	À	Á	Å	Ã	Ä	Å	Æ	Ç	È	É	Ê	Ë	Ì	Í	Î	Ï
D	Ð	Ñ	Ò	Ó	Ô	Õ	Ö	×	Ø	Ù	Ú	Û	Ü	Ý	Þ	ß
E	à	á	â	ã	ä	å	æ	ç	è	é	ê	ë	ì	í	î	ï
F	ð	ñ	ò	ó	ô	õ	ö	÷	ø	ù	ú	û	ü	ý	þ	ÿ

cplusplus.com

Dec	Hx	Oct	Char		Dec	Hx	Oct	Html	Chr	Dec	Hx	Oct	Html	Chr	Dec	Hx	Oct	Html
0	0	000	NUL	(null)	32	20	40		space	64	40	100	@	@	96	60	140	&#96
1	1	001	SOH	(start of heading)	33	21	041	!	!	65	41	101	A	A	97	61	141	&#97
2	2	002	STX	(start of text)	34	22	042	"	"	66	42	102	B	B	98	62	142	&#98
3	3	003	ETX	(end of text)	35	23	043	#	#	67	43	103	C	C	99	63	143	&#99
4	4	004	EOT	(end of transmission)	36	24	044	$	$	68	44	104	D	D	100	64	144	&#10
5	5	005	ENQ	(enquiry)	37	25	045	%	%	69	45	105	E	E	101	65	145	&#10
6	6	006	ACK	(acknolwedge)	38	26	046	&	&	70	46	106	F	F	102	66	146	&#10
7	7	007	BEL	(bell)	39	27	047	'	1	71	47	107	G	G	103	67	147	&#10
8	8	010	BS	(backspace)	40	28	050	(	(	72	48	110	H	H	104	68	150	&#10
9	9	011	TAB	(horizontal tab)	41	29	051	)	)	73	49	111	I	I	105	69	151	&#10
10	A	012	LF	(NL line feed, new line)	42	2A	052	*	*	74	4A	112	J	J	106	6A	152	&#10
11	B	013	VT	(vertical tab)	43	2B	053	+	+	75	4B	113	K	K	107	6B	153	&#10
12	C	014	FF	(NP form feed, new page)	44	2C	054	,	`	76	4C	114	L	L	108	6C	154	&#10
13	D	015	CR	(carriage return)	45	2D	055	-	-	77	4D	115	M	M	109	6D	155	&#10
14	E	016	SO	(shift out)	46	2E	056	.	.	78	4E	116	N	N	110	6E	156	&#11
15	F	017	SI	(shift in)	47	2F	057	/	/	79	4F	117	O	O	111	6F	157	&#11
16	10	020	DLE	(data link escape)	48	30	060	0	0	80	50	120	P	P	112	70	160	&#11
17	11	021	DC1	(device control 1)	49	31	061	1	1	81	51	121	Q	Q	113	71	161	&#11
18	12	022	DC2	(device control 2)	50	32	062	2	2	82	52	122	R	R	114	72	162	&#11
19	13	023	DC3	(device control 3)	51	33	063	3	3	83	53	123	S	S	115	73	163	&#11
20	14	024	DC4	(device control 4)	52	34	064	4	4	84	54	124	T	T	116	74	164	&#11
21	15	025	NAK	(negative acknowledge)	53	35	065	5	5	85	55	125	U	U	117	75	165	&#11
22	16	026	SYN	(synchronous idle)	54	36	066	6	6	86	56	126	V	V	118	76	166	&#11
23	17	027	ETB	(end of trans. block)	55	37	067	7	7	87	57	127	W	W	119	77	167	&#11
24	18	030	CAN	(cancel)	56	38	070	8	8	88	58	130	X	X	120	78	170	&#12
25	19	031	EM	(end of medium)	57	39	071	9	9	89	59	131	Y	Y	121	79	171	&#12
26	1A	032	SUB	(substitute)	58	3A	072	:	:	90	5A	132	Z	Z	122	7A	172	&#12
27	1B	033	ESC	(escape)	59	3B	073	;	;	91	5B	133	[	[	123	7B	173	&#12
28	1C	034	FS	(file separator)	60	3C	074	<	<	92	5C	134	\	\	124	7C	174	&#12
29	1D	035	GS	(group separator)	61	3D	075	=	=	93	5D	135	]	]	125	7D	175	&#12
30	1E	036	RS	(record separator)	62	3E	076	>	>	94	5E	136	^	^	126	7E	176	&#12
31	1F	037	US	(unit separator)	63	3F	077	?	?	95	5F	137	_	_	127	7F	177	&#12

***Source* : www.Lookup Tab**

TABLE OF CONTENTS

Basic Concepts Behind the Binary System

To understand binary numbers, begin by recalling elementary school math. When we first learned about numbers, we were taught that, in the decimal system, things are oragnized into columns :

```
H | T | 0
1 | 9 | 3
```

such that "H" is the hundreds column, "T" is the tens column, and "O" is the ones column. So the number "193" is 1-hundreds plus 9-ten plus 3-ones.

Years later, we learned that the ones column meant 10^0, the tens column meant 10^1, the hundreds column 10^2 and so on, such that

```
10^2 | 10^1 | 10^0
  1  |   9  |   3
```

the number 193 is really {(1*10^2)+(9*10^1)+(3*10^0)}.

As you know, the decimal system uses the digits 0-9 to represent numbers. If we wanted to put a larger number in column 10^n (e.g., 10), we would have to multiply 10*10^n, which would give 10^(n+1), and be carried a column to the left. For example, putting ten in the 10^0 column is impossible, so we put a 1 in the 10^1 column, and a 0 in the 10^0 column, thus using two columns. Twelve would be 12*10^0, or 10^0(10+2), or 10^1+2*10^0, which also uses an additional column to the left (12).

The binary system works under the exact same principles as the decimal system, only it operates in base 2 rather than base 10. In other words, instead of columns being

```
10^2 | 10^1 | 10^0
```

they are

```
2^2 | 2^1 | 2^0
```

Instead of using the digits 0-9, we only use 0-1 (again, if we used anything larger it would be like multiplying 2 *2 ^n and getting 2 ^ n + 1, which would not fit in the 2 ^ n column. Therefore, it would shift you one column to the left. For example, "3" in binary cannot be put into one column. The first column we fill is the right-most column, which is 2 ^ 0, or 1. Since 3 > 1, we need to use an extra column to the left, and indicate it as "11" in binary (1 *2 ^1) + (1 *2 ^0).

Examples : What would the binary number 1011 be in decimal notation ?

Click here to see the answer.

Try converting these numbers from binary to decimal :

- 10
- 111
- 10101
- 11110

Remember:

```
2^4 | 2^3 | 2^2 | 2^1 | 2^0
    |     |     |  1  |  0
    |     |  1  |  1  |  1
 1  |  0  |  1  |  0  |  1
 1  |  1  |  1  |  1  |  0
```

Click here to see the answer

Return to Table of Contents

Binary Addition

Consider the addition of decimal numbers :

$$\begin{array}{r} 23 \\ +\ 48 \\ \hline \end{array}$$

We begin by adding 3 + 8 = 11. Since 11 is greater than 10, a one is put into the 10's column (carried), and a 1 is recorded in the one's column of the sum. Next, add {(2 + 4) + 1} (the one is from the carry) = 7, which is put in the 10's column of the sum. Thus, the answer is 71.

Binary addition works on the same principle, but the numerals are different. Begin with one-bit binary addition :

$$\begin{array}{r} 0 \\ +0 \\ \hline 0 \end{array} \qquad \begin{array}{r} 0 \\ +1 \\ \hline 1 \end{array} \qquad \begin{array}{r} 1 \\ +0 \\ \hline 1 \end{array}$$

1 + 1 carries us into the next column. In decimal form, 1 + 1 = 2. In binary, any digit higher than 1 puts us a column to the left (as would 10 in decimal notation). The decimal number "2" is written in binary notation as "10" (1 * 2 ^ 1) + (0 * 2 ^ 0). Record the 0 in the ones column, and carry the 1 to the twos column to get an answer of "10". In our vertical notation,

$$\begin{array}{r} 1 \\ +1 \\ \hline 10 \end{array}$$

The process is the same for multiple-bit binary numbers :

$$\begin{array}{r} 1010 \\ +1111 \\ \hline \end{array}$$

- Step one :
  Column 2 ^ 0 : 0 + 1 = 1.
  Record the 1.
  Temporary Result : 1; Carry : 0

- Step two :
  Column 2 ^ 1 : 1 + 1 = 10.
  Record the 0, carry the 1.
  Temporary Result : 01; Carry : 1
- Step three :
  Column 2 ^ 2 : 1 + 0 = 1 Add 1 from carry : 1 + 1 = 10.
  Record the 0, carry the 1.
  Temporary Result : 001; Carry : 1
- Step four :
  Column 2 ^ 3 : 1 + 1 = 10. Add 1 from carry : 10 + 1 = 11.
  Record the 11.
  Final result : 11001
  Alternately :

```
  11    (carry)
  1010
+ 1111
------
 11001
```

Always remember

- 0 + 0 = 0
- 1 + 0 = 1
- 1 + 1 = 10

Try a few examples of binary addition :

```
 111     101     111
+110    +111    +111
----    ----    ----
```

Click here to see the answer

Return to Table of Contents

Binary Multiplication

Multiplication in the binary system works the same way as in the decimal system :

- 1 * 1 = 1
- 1 * 0 = 0
- 0 * 1 = 0

```
  101
 * 11
 ----
  101
 1010
 ----
 1111
```

Note that multiplying by two is extremely easy. To multiply by two, just add a 0 on the end.

Return to Table of Contents

Binary Division

Follow the same rules as in decimal division. For the sake of simplicity, throw away the remainder.

For example : 111011/11

```
      10011 r 10
   11)111011
     -11
      ---
       101
       -11
       ---
        101
         11
        ---
         10
```

Return to Table of Contents

Decimal to Binary

Converting from decimal to binary notation is slightly more difficult conceptually, but can easily be done once you know how through the use of algorithms. Begin by thinking of a few examples. We can easily see that the number 3 = 2 + 1, and that this is equivalent to (1 * 2 ^ 1) + (1 * 2 ^ 0). This translates into putting a "1" in the 2 ^ 1 column and a "1" in the 2 ^ 0 column, to get "11". Almost as intuitive is the number 5 : it is obviously 4 + 1, which is the same as saying [(2 * 2) + 1], or 2 ^ 2 + 1. This can also be written as [(1 * 2 ^ 2) + (1 * 2 ^ 0)]. Looking at this in columns,

```
2^2 | 2^1 | 2^0
 1     0     1
```

or 101.

What we're doing here is finding the largest power of two within the number (2 ^ 2 = 4 is the largest power of 2 in 5), subtracting that from the number (5 – 4 = 1), and finding the largest power of 2 in the remainder (2 ^ 0 = 1 is the largest power of 2 in 1). Then we just put this into columns. This process continues until we have a remainder of 0. Let's take a look at how it works. We know that :

```
2^0=1
2^1=2
2^2=4
2^3=8
2^4=16
2^5=32
2^6=64
2^7=128
```

and so on. To convert the decimal number 75 to binary, we would find the largest power of 2 less than 75, which is 64. Thus, we would put a 1 in the 2 ^ 6 column, and subtract 64 from 75, giving us 11. The largest power of 2 in 11 is 8, or 2 ^ 3. Put 1 in the 2 ^ 3 column, and 0 in 2 ^ 4 and 2 ^ 5. Subtract 8 from 11 to get 3. Put 1 in the 2 ^ 1 column, 0 in 2 ^ 2, and subtract

2 from 3. We're left with 1, which goes in 2 ^ 0, and we subtract one to get zero. Thus, our number is 1001011.

Making this algorithm a bit more formal gives us :

1. Let D = number we wish to convert from decimal to binary
2. Repeat until D = 0
    - (a) Find the largest power of two in D. Let this equal P.
    - (b) Put a 1 in binary column P.
    - (c) Subtract P from D.
3. Put zeros in all columns which don't have ones.

This algorithm is a bit awkward. Particularly step 3, "filling in the zeros". Therefore, we should rewrite it such that we ascertain the value of each column individually, putting in 0's and 1's as we go :

1. Let D = the number we wish to convert from decimal to binary
2. Find P, such that 2 ^ P is the largest power of two smaller than D.
3. Repeat until P < 0

- If 2 ^ P <= D then
    - put 1 into column P
    - subtract 2 ^ P from D
- Else
    - put 0 into column P
- End if
- Subtract 1 from P

Now that we have an algorithm, we can use it to convert numbers from decimal to binary relatively painlessly. Let's try the number D = 55.

- Our first step is to find P. We know that 2 ^ 4 = 16, 2 ^ 5 = 32, and 2 ^ 6 = 64. Therefore, P = 5.
- 2 ^ 5 <= 55, so we put a 1 in the 2 ^ 5 column : 1-----.
- Subtracting 55–32 leaves us with 23. Subtracting 1 from P gives us 4.
- Following step 3 again, 2 ^ 4 <= 23, so we put a 1 in the 2 ^ 4 column : 11----.
- Next, subtract 16 from 23, to get 7. Subtract 1 from P gives us 3.
- 2 ^ 3 > 7, so we put a 0 in the 2 ^ 3 column : 110---
- Next, subtract 1 from P, which gives us 2.
- 2 ^ 2 <= 7, so we put a 1 in the 2 ^ 2 column: 1101--
- Subtract 4 from 7 to get 3. Subtract 1 from P to get 1.
- 2 ^ 1 <= 3, so we put a 1 in the 2 ^ 1 column : 11011-
- Subtract 2 from 3 to get 1. Subtract 1 from P to get 0.
- 2 ^ 0 <= 1, so we put a 1 in the 2 ^ 0 column : 110111
- Subtract 1 from 1 to get 0. Subtract 1 from P to get – 1.
- P is now less than zero, so we stop.

Another algorithm for converting decimal to binary

However, this is not the only approach possible. We can start at the right, rather than the left.

All binary numbers are in the form

```
a[n] * 2^n + a[n-1] * 2^(n-1) + ... + a[1]*2^1 + a[0]*2^0
```

where each a [i] is either a 1 or a 0 (the only possible digits for the binary system). The only way a number can be odd is if it has a 1 in the 2 ^ 0 column, because all powers of two greater than 0 are even numbers (2, 4, 8, 16...). This gives us the rightmost digit as a starting point.

Now we need to do the remaining digits. One idea is to "shift" them. It is also easy to see that multiplying and dividing by 2 shifts everything by one column: two in binary is 10, or (1 * 2 ^ 1). Dividing (1 * 2 ^ 1) by 2 gives us (1 * 2 ^ 0), or just a 1 in binary. Similarly, multiplying by 2 shifts in the other direction : (1 * 2 ^ 1) * 2 = (1 * 2 ^ 2) or 10 in binary. Therefore

```
{a[n]*2^n + a[n-1]*2^(n-1) + ... + a[1]*2^1 + a[0]*2^0}/2
```

is equal to

```
a[n]*2^(n-1) + a[n-1]*2^(n-2) + ... + a(1)2^0
```

Let's look at how this can help us convert from decimal to binary. Take the number 163. We know that since it is odd, there must be a 1 in the 2 ^ 0 column (a [0] = 1). We also know that it equals 162 + 1. If we put the 1 in the 2 ^ 0 column, we have 162 left, and have to decide how to translate the remaining digits.

Two's column : Dividing 162 by 2 gives 81. The number 81 in binary would also have a 1 in the 2 ^ 0 column. Since we divided the number by two, we "took out" one power of two. Similarly, the statement a [n – 1] * 2 ^ (n – 1) + a [n – 2) * 2 ^ (n – 2) + ... + a [1] * 2 ^ 0 has a power of two removed. Our "new" 2 ^ 0 column now contains a1. We learned earlier that there is a1 in the 2 ^ 0 column if the number is odd. Since 81 is odd, a [1] = 1. Practically, we can simply keep a "running total", which now stands at 11 (a [1] = 1 and a [0] = 1). Also note that a1 is essentially "remultiplied" by two just by putting it in front of a [0], so it is automatically fit into the correct column.

Four's column : Now we can subtract 1 from 81 to see what remainder we still must place (80). Dividing 80 by 2 gives 40. Therefore, there must be a 0 in the 4's column, (because what we are actually placing is a 2 ^ 0 column, and the number is not odd).

Eight's column : We can divide by two again to get 20. This is even, so we put a 0 in the 8's column. Our running total now stands at a [3] = 0, a [2] = 0, a [1] = 1, and a [0] = 1.

We can continue in this manner until there is no remainder to place.

```
Let's formalize this algorithm:
1. Let D= the number we wish to convert from decimal to binary.
2. Repeat until D = 0:
   a) If D is odd, put "1" in the leftmost open column, and subtract 1 from D.
   b) If D is even, put "0" in the leftmost open column.
   c) Divide D by 2.
   End Repeat
   For the number 163, this works as follows:
1. Let D=163
2. b) D is odd, put a 1 in the 2^0 column.
   Subtract 1 from D to get 162.
```

```
    c) Divide D=162 by 2.
    Temporary Result: 01  New D=81
    D does not equal 0, so we repeat step 2.
2. b) D is odd, put a 1 in the 2^1 column.
    Subtract 1 from D to get 80.
    c) Divide D=80 by 2.
    Temporary Result: 11  New D=40
    D does not equal 0, so we repeat step 2.
2. b) D is even, put a 0 in the 2^2 column.
    c) Divide D by 2.
    Temporary Result:011  New D=20
2. b) D is even, put a 0 in the 2^3 column.
    c) Divide D by 2.
    Temporary Result: 0011  New D=10
2. b) D is even, put a 0 in the 2^4 column.
    c) Divide D by 2.
    Temporary Result: 00011  New D=5
2. a) D is odd, put a 1 in the 2^5 column.
    Subtract 1 from D to get 4.
    c) Divide D by 2.
    Temporary Result: 100011  New D=2
2. b) D is even, put a 0 in the 2^6 column.
    c) Divide D by 2.
    Temporary Result: 0100011  New D=1
2. a) D is odd, a put a 1 in the 27 column.
    Subtract 1 from D to get D=0.
    c) Divide D by 2.
    Temporary Result: 10100011  New D=0
    D=0, so we are done, and the decimal number 163 is equivalent to the
    binary number 10100011.
```

Since we already knew how to convert from binary to decimal, we can easily verify our result. 10100011 = (1 * 2 ^ 0) + (1 * 2 ^ 1) + (1 * 2 ^ 5) + (1 * 2 ^ 7) = 1 + 2 + 32 + 128 = 163.

Return to Table of Contents

Negation in the Binary System

- Signed Magnitude
- One's Complement
- Two's Complement
- Excess 2 ^ (m – 1)

These techniques work well for non-negative integers, but how do we indicate negative numbers in the binary system ?

Before we investigate negative numbers, we note that the computer uses a fixed number of "bits" or binary digits. An 8-bit number is 8 digits long. For this section, we will work with 8 bits.

Signed Magnitude : The simplest way to indicate negation is signed magnitude. In signed magnitude, the left-most bit is not actually part of the number, but is just the equivalent of a +/– sign. "0" indicates that the number is positive, "1" indicates negative. In 8 bits, 00001100 would be 12 (break this down into (1 * 2 ^ 3) + (1 * 2 ^ 2). To indicate – 12, we would simply put a "1" rather than a "0" as the first bit : 10001100.

One's Complement : In one's complement, positive numbers are represented as usual in regular binary. However, negative numbers are represented differently. To negate a number, replace all zeros with ones, and ones with zeros — flip the bits. Thus, 12 would be 00001100, and – 12 would be 11110011. As in signed magnitude, the leftmost bit indicates the sign (1 is negative, 0 is positive). To compute the value of a negative number, flip the bits and translate as before.

Two's Complement : Begin with the number in one's complement. Add 1 if the number is negative. Twelve would be represented as 00001100, and – 12 as 11110100. To verify this, let's subtract 1 from 11110110, to get 11110011. If we flip the bits, we get 00001100, or 12 in decimal.

In this notation, "m" indicates the total number of bits. For us (working with 8 bits), it would be excess 2 ^ 7. To represent a number (positive or negative) in excess 2 ^ 7, begin by taking the number in regular binary representation. Then add 2 ^ 7 (= 128) to that number. For example, 7 would be 128 + 7 = 135, or 2 ^ 7 + 2 ^ 2 + 2 ^ 1 + 2 ^ 0, and, in binary, 10000111. We would represent – 7 as 128 – 7 = 121, and, in binary, 01111001.

Note :

- Unless you know which representation has been used, you cannot figure out the value of a number.
- A number in excess 2 ^ (m – 1) if the same as that number in two's complement with the leftmost bit flipped.

To see the advantages and disadvantages of each method, let's try working with them.

Using the regular algorithm for binary addition, add (5 + 12), (– 5 + 12), (– 12 + – 5), and (12 + – 12) in each system. Then convert back to decimal numbers.

Click here to see the answers Return to Table of Contents.

Answers:

What would the binary number 1011 be in decimal notation?

1011 = (1*2^3) + (0*2^2) + (1*2^1) + (1*2^0)

= (1*8) + (0*4) + (1*2) + (1*1)

= 11 (in decimal notation)

Go back to the question

Try converting these numbers from binary to decimal :

10 = (1*2^1) + (0*2^0) = 2 + 0 = 2

111 = (1*2^2) + (1*2^1) + (1*2^0) = 4+2+1=7

10101 = (1*2^4) + (0*2^3) + (1*2^2) + (0*2^1) + (1*2^0)=16+0+4+0+1=21

11110 = (1*2^4) + (1*2^3) + (1*2^2) + (1*2^1) + (0*2^0)=16+8+4+2+0=30

Go back to the question

Try a few examples of binary addition :

```
                  1          1
  111           111        111
 +110          +110       +110
 ----          ----       ----
    1            01       1101
    1            11          1
  101           101        101
 +111          +111       +111
 ----          ----       ----
    0            00       1100
    1             1          1
  111           111        111
 +111          +111       +111
 ----          ----       ----
    0            10       1110
```

Click here to return to the question

Using the regular algorithm for binary addition, add (5 + 12), (– 5 + 12), (– 12 + – 5), and (12 + – 12) in each system. Then convert back to decimal numbers.

```
     Signed Magnitude:
  5+12       -5+12      -12+-5     12+-12
00000101   10000101   10001100   00001100
00001100   00001100   10000101   10001100
--------   --------   --------   --------
00010001   10010001   00010000   10011000
   17        -17         16        -24
   One Complement :
00000101   11111010   11110011   00001100
00001100   00001100   11111010   11110011
--------   --------   --------   --------
00010001   00000110   11101101   11111111
   17          6        -18          0
     Two's Complement:
00000101   11111011   11110100   00001100
00001100   00001100   11111011   11110100
--------   --------   --------   --------
00010001   00000111   11101111   00000000
   17          7        -17          0
     Signed Magnitude:
10000101   01111011   01110100   00001100
10001100   10001100   01111011   01110100
--------   --------   --------   --------
00010001   00000111   11101111   01111100
  109        119        111        124
```

128	Ç	144	È	161	í	177	▒	193	┴	209	╤	225	ß	241	±
129	ü	145	æ	162	ó	178	▓	194	┬	210	╥	226	Γ	242	≥
130	é	146	Æ	163	ú	179	│	195	├	211	╙	227	π	243	≤
131	â	147	ô	164	ñ	180	┤	196	─	212	╘	228	Σ	244	⌠
132	ä	148	ö	165	Ñ	181	╡	197	┼	213	╒	229	σ	245	⌡
133	à	149	ò	166	`	182	╢	198	╞	214	╓	230	µ	246	÷
134	å	150	û	167	°	183	╖	199	╟	215	╫	231	τ	247	≈
135	ç	151	ù	168	¿	184	╕	200	╚	216	╪	232	Φ	248	°
136	ê	152	_	169	_	185	╣	201	╔	217	┘	233	Θ	249	.
137	ë	153	Ö	170	¬	186	║	202	╩	218	┌	234	Ω	250	.
138	è	154	Ü	171	½	187	╗	203	╦	219	█	235	δ	251	√
139	ï	156	£	172	¼	188	╝	204	╠	220	■	236	∞	252	_
140	î	157	¥	173	i	189	╜	205	═	221	▌	237	φ	253	²
141	ì	158	_	174	«	190	╛	206	╬	222	▐	238	³	254	■
142	Ä	159	j	175	»	191	┐	207	╧	223	■	239	∩	255	
143	Å	160	á	176	░	192	└	208	╨	224	α	240	≡		

Source: www.LookupTables.com

HEXADECIMAL NUMBER SYSTEM

The Hexadecimal Number Base System

A big problem with the binary system is verbosity. To represent the value 202 requires eight binary digits.

The decimal version requires only three decimal digits and, thus, represents numbers much more compactly than does the binary numbering system. This fact was not lost on the engineers who designed binary computer systems.

When dealing with large values, binary numbers quickly become too unwieldy. The hexadecimal (base 16) numbering system solves these problems. Hexadecimal numbers offer the two features :

- hex numbers are very compact
- it is easy to convert from hex to binary and binary to hex.

Since we'll often need to enter hexadecimal numbers into the computer system, we'll need a different mechanism for representing hexadecimal numbers since you cannot enter a subscript to denote the radix of the associated value.

The Hexadecimal system is based on the binary system using a Nibble or 4-bit boundary. In Assembly Language programming, most assemblers require the first digit of a hexadecimal number to be 0, and we place an H at the end of the number to denote the number base.

The Hexadecimal Number System

uses base 16

includes only the digits 0 through 9 and the letters A, B, C, D, E and F

In the Hexadecimal number system, the hex values greater than 9 carry the following decimal value:

Binary	*Octal*	*Decimal*	*Hex*
0000B	00Q	00	00H
0001B	01Q	01	01H
0010B	02Q	02	02H
0011B	03Q	03	03H
0100B	04Q	04	04H
0101B	05Q	05	05H
0110B	06Q	06	06H
0111B	07Q	07	07H
1000B	10Q	08	08H
1001B	11Q	09	09H
1010B	12Q	10	0AH
1011B	13Q	11	0BH
1100B	14Q	12	0CH
1101B	15Q	13	0DH
1110B	16Q	14	0EH
1111B	17Q	15	0FH
1 0000B	20Q	16	10H

This table provides all the information you'll ever need to convert from one number base into any other number base for the decimal values from 0 to 16.

To convert a hexadecimal number into a binary number, simply brake the binary number into 4-bit groups beginning with the LSB and substitute the corresponding four bits in binary for each hexadecimal digit in the number.

For example, to convert 0ABCDh into a binary value, simply convert each hexadecimal digit according to the table above. The binary equivalent is :

0ABCDH = 0000 1010 1011 1100 1101

To convert a binary number into hexadecimal format is almost as easy. The first step is to pad the binary number with leading zeros to make sure that the binary number contains multiples of four bits. For example, given the binary number 10 1100 1010, the first step would be to add two bits in the MSB position so that it contains 12 bits. The revised binary value is 0010 1100 1010.

The next step is to separate the binary value into groups of four bits, *e.g.*, 0010 1100 1010. Finally, look up these binary values in the table above and substitute the appropriate hexadecimal digits, *e.g.*, 2CA.

The weighted values for each position is as follows :

16^3	16^2	16^1	16^0
4096	256	16	1

Binary to Hex Conversion

It is easy to convert from an integer binary number to hex. This is accomplished by :

1. Break the binary number into 4-bit sections from the LSB to the MSB.
2. Convert the 4-bit binary number to its Hex equivalent.

   For example, the binary value 1010111110110010 will be written :

1010	1111	1011	0010
A	F	B	2

Hex to Binary Conversion

It is also easy to convert from an integer hex number to binary. This is accomplished by :

1. Convert the Hex number to its 4-bit binary equivalent.
2. Combine the 4-bit sections by removing the spaces.

   For example, the hex value 0AFB2 will be written :

A	F	B	2
1010	1111	1011	0010

This yields the binary number 1010111110110010 or 1010 1111 1011 0010 in our more readable format.

Hex to Decimal Conversion

To convert from Hex to Decimal, multiply the value in each position by its hex weight and add each value. Using the value from the previous example, 0AFB2H, we would expect to obtain the decimal value 44978.

A*16^3	F*16^2	B*16^1	2*16^0
10*4096	15*256	11*16	2*1
40960	3840	176	2

40960 + 3840 + 176 + 2 = 44978

Decimal to Hex Conversion

To convert decimal to hex is slightly more difficult. The typical method to convert from decimal to hex is repeated division by 16. While we may also use repeated subtraction by the weighted position value, it is more difficult for large decimal numbers.

Repeated Division By 16

For this method, divide the decimal number by 16, and write the remainder on the side as the least significant digit. This process is continued by dividing the quotient by 16 and writing the remainder until the quotient is 0. When performing the division, the remainders which will represent the hex equivalent of the decimal number are written beginning at the least significant digit (right) and each new digit is written to the next more significant digit (the left) of the previous digit. Consider the number 44978.

Division	*Quotient*	*Remainder*	*Hex Number*
44978 / 16	2811	2	2
2811 / 16	175	11	B2
175 / 16	10	15	FB2
10 / 16	0	10	0AFB2

As you can see, we are back with the original number. That is what we should expect.

When you use hex numbers in an 8085 program, the Assembler usually requires the most significant hex digit to be 0 even if this number of digits exceed the size of the register. This is an Assembler requirement and your value will be assembled correctly.

6

Computer Codes

BCD CODE

The Binary Coded Decimal (BCD) code is one of the early computer codes. It is based on the idea of converting each digit of a decimal number into its binary equivalent, rather than converting the entire decimal value into a pure binary form. This makes the conversion process easier.

The BCD equivalent of each decimal digit is shown in Fig. 6.1. Since 8 and 9 require 4 bits, all decimal digits are represented in BCD by 4 bits. For example, if 42_{10} is equal to 101010_2 in a pure binary form. Converting 42_{10} into BCD, however, produces the following result :

$$42_{10} = \frac{0100}{4} \quad \frac{0010}{4} \qquad \text{or} \qquad 01000010 \text{ in BCD}$$

Note that each decimal digit is independently converted to a 4 bit binary number, and hence, the conversion process is very easy. Also note that when 4 bits are used, altogether 16 (2^4) configurations are possible (refer to hexadecimal number system). However, from Figure 6.1 you can see that only the first 10 of these combinations are used to represent decimal digits. The remaining 6 arrangements (1010, 1011, 1100, 1101, 1110 and 1111) have decimal values from 10 to 15. These arrangements are not used in BCD coding. That is, 1010 does not represent 10_{10} in BCD. Instead,

Decimal Digits	*BCD Equivalent*
0	0000
1	0001
2	0010
3	0011
4	0100
5	0101
6	0110
7	0111
8	1000
9	1001

Fig. 6.1 *BCD equivalent of decimal digits*

$$10_{10} = \frac{0001}{1} \quad \frac{0000}{0} \quad \text{or} \quad 00010000 \text{ in BCD}$$

Similarly,

$$15_{10} = \frac{0001}{1} \quad \frac{0101}{5} \quad \text{or} \quad 00010101 \text{ in BCD}$$

In the discussion above, we have used to group of 4 bits to represent a digit (character) in BCD. 4-bit BCD coding system can be used to represent only decimal numbers, because 4 bits are insufficient to represent the various characters used by a computers. Hence, instead of using 4 bits with only 16 possible characters, computer designers commonly use 6 bits to represent characters in BCD code. In the 16-bit BCD code, the four BCD numeric place positions are retained, but two additional zone positions are added. With 6 bits, it is possible to represent 64 (2^6) different characters. This is a sufficient number to code the decimal digits (10), alphabetic letters (26), and other special characters (28). Figure 6.2 illustrates the coding of alphabetic and numeric characters in BCD.

In Chapter 5, we have seen the use of octal and hexadecimal number systems, as shortcut notations for binary. Since BCD is a 6-bit code, it can be easily divided into two 3-bit groups. Each of these 3-bits groups can be represented by 1 octal digit. Hence, octal number system is used a shortcut notation for memory dump by computers, which use BCD code for internal representation of characters. This results in a one-to-three reduction in the volume of memory dump. Figure 6.2 also shows the octal equivalent of the alphabetic and numeric characters coded in BCD.

Example 6.1. *Show the binary digits used to record the word BASE in BCD.*

Solution :

B = 110010 in BCD binary notation
A = 110001 in BCD binary notation
S = 010010 in BCD binary notation
E = 110101 in BCD binary notation

Hence, the binary digits

$$\frac{110010}{B} \quad \frac{110001}{A} \quad \frac{010010}{S} \quad \frac{110101}{E}$$

will record the word BASE in BCD.

Example 6.2. *Using octal notation, show the BCD coding for the word DIGIT.*

Solution :

D = 64 in BCD octal notation
I = 71 in BCD octal notation
G = 67 in BCD octal notation
I = 71 in BCD octal notation
T = 23 in BCD octal notation

Hence, the BCD coding for the word DIGIT in octal notation will be

$$\frac{64}{D} \quad \frac{71}{I} \quad \frac{67}{G} \quad \frac{71}{I} \quad \frac{23}{T}$$

Character	BCD code		Octal Equivalent
	Zone	Digit	
A	11	0001	61
B	11	0010	62
C	11	0011	63
D	11	0100	64
E	11	0101	65
F	11	0110	66
G	11	0111	67
H	11	1000	70
I	11	1001	71
J	10	0001	41
K	10	0010	42
L	10	0011	43
M	10	0100	44
N	10	0101	45
O	10	0110	46
P	10	0111	47
Q	10	1000	50
R	10	1001	51
S	01	0010	22
T	01	0011	23
U	01	0100	24
V	01	0101	25
W	01	0110	26
X	01	0111	27
Y	01	1000	30
Z	01	1001	31
1	00	0001	01
2	00	0010	02
3	00	0011	03
4	00	0100	04
5	00	0101	05
6	00	0110	06
7	00	0111	07
8	00	1000	10
9	00	1001	11
0	00	1010	12

Fig. 6.2 *Alphabetic and numeric characters in BCD, along with their Octal equivalent*

EBCDIC

The major problem with BCD code is that only 64 (2^6) different characters can be represented in it. This is not sufficient for providing decimal numbers (10), lower-case letters (26), capital letters (26), and a large number of other special characters (26+).

Hence, the BCD code was extended from a 6-bit code to an 8-bit code. The added 2 bits are used as additional zone bits, expanding the zone to 4 bits. The resulting code is called the Extended Binary-Coded Decimal Interchange Code (EBCDIC). In this code, it is possible to represent (256 (2^8) different characters, instead of 64 (2^6). In addition to the various character requirements mentioned above, this also allows a large variety of printable characters and several nonprintable control characters. The control characters are used to control such activities as printer vertical spacing, movement of cursor on the terminal screen, etc. All of the 256 bit combinations have not yet been assigned characters. Hence, the code can still grow, as new requirements develop.

Since EBCDIC is an 8-bit code, it can be easily divided into two 4-bit groups. Each of these 4-bit groups can be represented by 1 hexadecimal digit (refer to Chapter 5). Hence, hexadecimal number system is used as shortcut notation for memory dump by computers, which use EBCDIC for internal representation of characters. This results in a one-to-four reduction in the volume of memory dump. Figure 6.3 shows the alphabetic and numeric characters in EBCDIC, along with their hexadecimal equivalent.

Developed by IBM, EBCDIC code is used in most IBM models, and in many other computers.

Zoned and Packed Decimal Numbers

From Figure 6.3, it can be observed that in the EBCDIC code, the digit values are the same as the numeric characters – 0 through 9 (0000-1001). However, numeric values need some special consideration, because we must have a way of indicating whether the number is positive, negative, or unsigned (implies positive). Hence, when numeric value is represented in EBCDIC, a sign indicator is used in the zone position of the rightmost digit. A sign indicator of hexadecimal C is a plus sign, hexadecimal D is a minus sign, and hexadecimal F means the number is unsigned. Figure 6.4 illustrates the representation of numeric values in EBCDIC. Note that the only zoned affected by the sign is the zone of the rightmost digit. All other zones remain as F, the zone value for numeric characters in EBCDIC. Since each decimal digit has a zone with it, numbers coded in EBCDIC are called zoned decimal numbers. Numeric data input into the computer are usually zoned decimal numbers. Printers can print only those numeric characters, which are in a zoned-decimal format.

Most computers cannot perform arithmetic operation on zoned-decimal data. Hence, before any arithmetic operation can be performed, the data must be converted to a format on which arithmetic operations are possible. One such acceptable format is the packed decimal format. The following steps are used to convert a zoned decimal number to a packed decimal number :

Step 1 : The zone half and the digit half to the rightmost byte are reversed. This moves the sign to the extreme right of number.

Step 2 : All remaining zones are dropped out.

Figure 6.5 illustrates the conversion process of zoned decimal data to packed data. It may be observed that packed data requires less number of bytes (group of 8 bits) as compared to zoned data. In the zoned format, there is only one digit per byte (each digit along with the zone requires 8 bits). However, there are two digits in each bytes in the packed format (each digit requires 4 bits). If the packing process does not completely fill a byte, it is filled with a zero. For example, the zoned data F3F4F5F6 will convert to packed data 03456F. Observe that in this example, the zoned data requires 4 bytes, and the packed data requires only 3 bytes.

Character	*EBCDIC code*		*Hexadecimal*
	Zone	*Digit*	*Equivalent*
A	1100	0001	C1
B	1100	0010	C2
C	1100	0011	C3
D	1100	0100	C4
E	1100	0101	C5
F	1100	0110	C6
G	1100	0111	C7
H	1100	1000	C8
I	1100	1001	C9
J	1101	0001	D1
K	1101	0010	D2
L	1101	0011	D3
M	1101	0100	D4
N	1101	0101	D5
O	1101	0110	D6
P	1101	0111	D7
Q	1101	1000	D8
R	1101	1001	D9
S	1110	0010	E2
T	1110	0011	E3
U	1110	0100	E4
V	1110	0101	E5
W	1110	0110	E6
X	1110	0111	E7
Y	1110	1000	E8
Z	1110	1001	E9
0	1111	0000	F0
1	1111	0001	F1
2	1111	0010	F2
3	1111	0011	F3
4	1111	0100	F4
5	1111	0101	F5
6	1111	0110	F6
7	1111	0111	F7
8	1111	1000	F8
9	1111	1001	F9

Fig. 6.3 *Alphabetic and numeric characters in EBCDIC, along with their Hexadecimal equivalent*

Numeric Value	*EBCDIC*	*Sign Indicator*
345	F3F4F5	F for unsigned
+ 345	F3F4C5	C for positive
– 345	F3F4D5	D for negative

Fig. 6.4 *Numeric values in EBCDIC in Hexadecimal notation*

Numeric Value	*EBCDIC*	*Sign Indicator*
345	F3F4F5	345 F
+ 345	F3F4C5	345 C
– 345	F3F4D5	345 D
– 345	F3F4D5	03456 F

Fig. 6.5 *Zoned and packed decimal numbers*

Example 6.3. *Using binary notation, write the EBCDIC coding for the word BIT. How many bytes are required for this representation ?*

Solution :

B = 1100 0010 in EBCDIC binary notation

I = 1100 1001 in EBCDIC binary notation

T = 1110 0011 in EBCDIC binary notation

Hence, the EBCDIC coding for the word BIT in binary notation will be

$$\underset{B}{\underline{11000010}} \quad \underset{I}{\underline{11001001}} \quad \underset{T}{\underline{11100011}}$$

3 bytes will be required for this representation, because each letter requires 1 byte (or 8 bytes).

Example 6.4. *Write the EBCDIC coding for the word ZONE (use hexadecimal notation). How many bytes will be required for this representation ?*

Solution :

Z = E9 in EBCDIC hexadecimal notation

O = D6 in EBCDIC hexadecimal notation

N = D5 in EBCDIC hexadecimal notation

E = C5 in EBCDIC hexadecimal notation

Hence, the EBCDIC coding for the word ZONE in hexadecimal notation will be

$$\underset{Z}{\underline{E9}} \quad \underset{O}{\underline{D6}} \quad \underset{N}{\underline{D5}} \quad \underset{E}{\underline{C5}}$$

Each hexadecimal digit requires 4 bits, and there are altogether 8 hexadecimal digits. Therefore, 8 x 4 = 32 bits or 4 bytes (8 bits = 1 byte) will be required for this representation. We may also write directly that, since each letter requires 1 byte for its representation in EBCDIC, and there are 4 letters in the word ZONE, 4 bytes will be required for this representation.

Example 6.5. *Write the EBCDIC zoned-decimal coding for the value + 256 (use hexadecimal). How many bytes will be required for this representation ?*

Solution :

+ 256 = F2F5C6 in EBCDIC

Each hexadecimal digit requires 4 bits, and there are altogether $6 \times 4 = 24$ bits or 3 bytes (8 bits = 1 byte) will be required for this representation. We may also write directly that, since each digit requires 1 byte for its representation in the EBCDIC zoned decimal coding, and there are 3 digits in the given number, 3 bytes will be required for this representation.

Example 6.6. *Write – 128 as packed decimal number (use hexadecimal). How many bytes will be required for this representation ?*

Solution :

– 128 = F1F2D8 in EBCDIC

= 128D in packed format

Each hexadecimal digit requires 4 bits, and there are altogether 4 hexadecimal digits. Therefore, $4 \times 4 = 16$ bits or 2 bytes (1 byte = 8 bits) will be required for this representation.

ASCII

Another computer code, which is widely used, is the American Standard Code for Information Interchange (ASCII). ASCII has been adopted by several American computer manufactures as their computer's internal code. This code is popular in data communications, is used almost exclusively to represent data internally in microcomputers, and is frequently found in the larger computers produced by some vendors.

ASCII is of two types – ASCII-7 and ASCII-8. ASCII-7 is a 7-bit code, which allows 128 (2^7) different characters. The first 3 bits are used as zone bits, and the last 4 bits indicate the digit. Microcomputers using 8-bit byte (group of 8 bits for 1 byte) use the 7-bit ASCII by leaving the leftmost first bit of each byte as a zero. Figure 6.6 shows the alphabetic and numeric characters in ASCII-7 notations.

ASCII-8 is an extended version of ASCII-7. It is an 8-bit code, which allows 256 (2^8) different characters, rather than 128. The additional bit is added to zone bits. Figure shows the alphabetic and numeric characters in ASCII-8 notation. Observe that, other than the zone value differences, ASCII-7 and ASCII-8 are identical. ASCII also uses hexadecimal as its four-to-one shortcut notation for memory dump.

Example 6.7. *Write the binary coding for the word BOY in ASCII-7. How many bytes are required for this representation ?*

Solution :

B = 1000010 in ASCII-7 binary notation

O = 1001111 in ASCII-7 binary notation

Y = 1011001 in ASCII-7 binary notation

Hence, the binary coding for the world BOY in ASCII-7 will be

$$\underbrace{1000010}_{B} \quad \underbrace{1001111}_{O} \quad \underbrace{1011001}_{Y}$$

Since each character in ASCII-7 requires one byte for its representation, and there are 3 characters in the world BOY, 3 bytes will be required for this representation.

Example 6.8. *Write the hexadecimal coding for the world GIRL in ASCII-7. How many bytes are required for this representation ?*

Solution :

G = 47 in ASCII-7 hexadecimal notation

I = 49 in ASCII-7 hexadecimal notation

R = 52 in ASCII-7 hexadecimal notation

L = 4C in ASCII-7 hexadecimal notation

Hence, the hexadecimal coding for the word GIRL in ASCII-7 will be

$$\frac{47}{G} \quad \frac{49}{I} \quad \frac{52}{R} \quad \frac{4C}{L}$$

Since each character in ASCII-7 requires one byte for its representation, and there are 4 characters in the world GIRL, 4 bytes will be required for this representation.

Example 6.9. *Write the binary coding for the world SKY in ASCII-8. How many bytes are required for this representation ?*

Solution :

S = 10110011 in ASCII-8 binary notation

K = 10101011 in ASCII-8 binary notation

Y = 10111001 in ASCII-8 binary notation

Hence, the binary coding for the world SKY in ASCII-8 will be

$$\frac{10110011}{S} \quad \frac{10101011}{K} \quad \frac{10111001}{Y}$$

Since each character in ASCII-8 requires one byte for its representation, and there are 3 characters in the word SKY, 3 bytes will be required for this representation.

Character	*ASCII-7 Code*		*Hexadecimal Equivalent*
	Zone	*Digit*	
0	011	0000	30
1	011	0001	31
2	011	0010	32
3	011	0011	33
4	011	0100	34
5	011	0101	35
6	011	0110	36
7	011	0111	37
8	011	1000	38
9	011	1001	39
A	100	0001	41
B	100	0010	42
C	100	0011	43

D	100	0100	44
E	100	0101	45
F	100	0110	46
G	100	0111	47
H	100	1000	48
I	100	1001	49
J	100	1010	4A
K	100	1011	4B
L	100	1100	4C
M	100	1101	4D
N	100	1110	4E
O	100	1111	4F
P	100	0000	50
Q	100	0001	51
R	100	0010	52
S	100	0011	53
T	100	0100	54
U	100	0101	55
V	100	0110	56
W	100	0111	57
X	100	1000	58
Y	100	1001	59
Z	100	1010	5 A

Fig. 6.6 *Numeric and alphabetic characters in ASCII-7 notation, along with their Hexadecimal equivalent*

Character	*ASCII-7 Code*		*Hexadecimal Equivalent*
	Zone	*Digit*	
0	0101	0000	50
1	0101	0001	51
2	0101	0010	52
3	0101	0011	53
4	0101	0100	54
5	0101	0101	55
6	0101	0110	56
7	0101	0111	57
8	0101	1000	58
9	0101	1001	59

A	1010	0001	A1
B	1010	0010	A2
C	1010	0011	A3
D	1010	0100	A4
E	1010	0101	A5
F	1010	0110	A6
G	1010	0111	A7
H	1010	1000	A8
I	1010	1001	A9
J	1010	1010	AA
K	1010	1011	AB
L	1010	1100	AC
M	1010	1101	AD
N	1010	1110	AE
O	1010	1111	AF
P	1011	0000	B0
Q	1010	0001	B1
R	1010	0010	B2
S	1010	0011	B3
T	1010	0100	B4
U	1010	0101	B5
V	1010	0110	B6
W	1010	0111	B7
X	1010	1000	B8
Y	1010	1001	B9
Z	1010	1010	BA

Fig. 6.7 *Numeric and alphabetic characters in ASCII-8 notation, alongwith their Hexadecimal equivalent*

Example 6.10. *Write the hexadecimal coding for the STAR in ASCII-8. How many bytes are required for with representation ?*

Solution :

S = B3 in ASCII-8 hexadecimal notation
T = B4 in ASCII-8 hexadecimal notation
A = A1 in ASCII-8 hexadecimal notation
R = B2 in ASCII-8 hexadecimal notation

Hence, the hexadecimal coding for the word STAR in ASCII-8 will be

B3	B4	A1	B2
S	T	A	R

Since each character in ASCII-8 requires one bytes for its representation, and there are 4 characters in the word STAR, 4 bytes will be required for this representation.

SUMMARY

1. Binary coding schemes are used in computers to represent data internally. In binary coding, every symbol, which appears in the data, is represented by a group of bits. The group of its used to represent a symbol is called byte. Most modern computers use 8 bits to represent a symbol. Hence, the term byte is commonly used to mean a group of 8 bits.
2. The commonly used computer codes for internal representation of data are BCD, EBCDIC and ASCII.
3. BCD (Binary Coded Decimal) is a 6-bit code, which can represent 64 different characters.
4. EBCDIC (Extended Binary-Coded Decimal Interchange Code) is an 8-bit code, which can represent 256 different characters.
5. ASCII (American Standard Code for Information Interchange) is one of the most popular computer codes. It is of two types – ASCII-7 and ASCII-8. ASCII-7 is a 7-bit code, which can represent 128 different characters, and ASCII-8 in an 8-bit code, which can represent 256 different characters.

REVIEW EXERCISES

1. Define the term 'byte'. What is the different between a bit and a byte?
2. Write the 4-bit BCD code for the following numbers:
   (*a*) 25 10 (*b*) 64 10 (*c*) 128 10 (*d*) 1024 10
3. Using binary notation, show the BCD coding for the following words:
   (*a*) BIT (*b*) BYTE (*c*) CODE (*d*) ZERO
4. Using octal notation, show the BCD coding for the following words:
   (*a*) COMPUTER (*b*) INPUT (*c*) VIDEO (*d*) OUTPUT
5. Why was BCD code extended to EBCDIC?
6. How many different characters are possible for the following codes:
   (*a*) BCD (*b*) ASCII-7 (*c*) EBCDIC (*d*) ASCII-8
7. Why are octal and hexadecimal shortcut notations used? Identify the shortcut notations used for each of these computer codes:
   (*a*) BCD (*b*) EBCDIC (*c*) ASCII-7 (*d*) ASCII-8
8. Why do we have to packed decimal format? How does it differ from a zoned decimal format?
9. A new computer code is designed, which uses 9 hits. How many different characters are possible in this code?
10. Using binary notation, write the EBCDIC coding for the following words:
    (*a*) SUN (*b*) MOON (*c*) CAT (*d*) DOG
    How many bytes are required for each of these representations?

11. Using hexadecimal notation, write the EBCDIC coding for the following words:
    (*a*) PROGRAM (*b*) OUTPUT (*c*) BYTE (*d*) OCTAL
    How many bytes are required for each of these representations?
12. Using hexadecimal notation, write the zoned decimal coding for the following numbers:
    (*a*) 1256 (*b*) +439 (*c*) –63 (*d*) –786
    How many bytes are required for each of these representations?
13. Using hexadecimal notation, write the packed decimal coding for the following numbers:
    (*a*) 12915 (*b*) +9876 (*c*) 872 (*d*) –256
    How many bytes are required for each of these representations?
14. List out the similarities and differences between 7-bit and 8-bit ASCII.
15. Using binary notation, write the ASCII-7 and ASCII-8 codes for the following words:
    (*a*) DRY (*b*) WET (*c*) DAMP (*d*) TERM
    How many bytes are required for each of these representation?
16. Using hexadecimal notation, write the ASCII-7 and ASCII-8 codes for the following words:
    (*a*) PRINT (*b*) TYPE (*c*) RUB (*d*) GIVE
17. Explain the meaning of the term "collating sequence".
18. A computer uses EBCDIC as its internal representation of characters. In which order will this computer sort the following strings?
    (*a*) ABC (*b*) 123 (*c*) 245 (*d*) ADD
19. A computer uses ASCII. In which order will this computer sort the following strings?
    (*a*) BED (*b*) 512 (*c*) ADD (*d*) 128
    (*e*) BAD
20. Give the full form of the following abbreviations:
    (*a*) BCD (*b*) EBCDIC (*c*) ASCII.

7

COMPUTER LANGUAGE

CLASSIFICATION OF COMPUTER LANGUAGE

Machine Language

The lowest-level programming language (except for computers that utilize programmable microcode) Machine languages are the only languages understood by computers. While easily understood by computers, machine languages are almost impossible for humans to use because they consist entirely of numbers. Programmers, therefore, use either a high-level programming language or an assembly language. An assembly language contains the same instructions as a machine language, but the instructions and variables have names instead of being just numbers.

Programs written in high-level languages are translated into assembly language or machine language by a compiler. Assembly language programs are translated into machine language by a program called an assembler.

Every CPU has its own unique machine language. Programs must be rewritten or recompiled, therefore, to run on different types of computers.

Assembly Language

Assembly language commonly called assembly or asm, is a human-readable notation for the machine language that a specific computer architecture uses. Machine language, a pattern of bits encoding machine operations, is made readable by replacing the raw values with symbols is called mnemonics.

For example, a computer with the appropriate processor will understand this x86/IA-32 machine language :

```
10110000 01100001
```

For programmers, however, it is easier to remember the equivalent assembly language representation :

```
mov al, 061h
```

which means to move the hexadecimal value 61 (97′decimal) into the processor register with the name "al". The mnemonic "mov" is short for "move", and a comma-separated list of arguments or parameters follows it; this is a typical assembly language statement.

Transforming assembly into machine language is accomplished by an assembler, and the reverse by a disassembler. Unlike in high-level languages, there is usually a 1-to-1 correspondence between simple assembly statements and machine language instructions.

However, in some cases an assembler may provide pseudoinstructions which expand into several machine language instructions to provide commonly needed functionality. For example, for a machine that lacks a "branch if greater or equal" instruction, an assembler may provide a pseudo instruction that expands to the machine's "set if less than" and "branch if zero (on the result of the set instruction)".

Every computer architecture has its own machine language, and therefore its own assembly language. Computers differ by the number and type of operations that they support. They may also have different sizes and numbers of registers, and different representations of data types in storage. While all general-purpose computers are able to carry out essentially the same functionality, the way they do it differs, and the corresponding assembly language must reflect these differences.

In addition, multiple sets of mnemonics or assembly-language syntax may exist for a single instruction set. In these cases, the most popular one is usually that used by the manufacturer in their documentation.

Assembly language directives

In addition to codes for machine instructions, assembly languages have extra directives for assembling blocks of data, and assigning address locations for instructions or code.

They usually have a simple symbolic capability for defining values as symbolic expressions which are evaluated at assembly time, making it possible to write code that is easier to read and understand.

Like most computer languages, comments can be added to the source code; these often provide useful additional information to human readers of the code but are ignored by the assembler and so may be used freely.

They also usually have an embedded macro language to make it easier to generate complex pieces of code or data.

In practice, the absence of comments and the replacement of symbols with actual numbers makes the human interpretation of disassembled code considerably more difficult than the original (high level) source would be.

[edit]

Usage of assembly language

Historically, a large number of programs have been written entirely in assembly language. A classic example was the early IBM PC spreadsheet program Lotus 123. Even into the 1990s, the majority of console video games were written in assembly language, including most games written for the Sega Genesis and the Super Nintendo Entertainment System. The popular arcade game NBA Jam (1993) was also coded entirely using assembly language.

There is some debate over the continued usefulness of assembly language. It is often said that modern compilers can render higher-level languages into codes that run as fast as hand-written assembly, but counter-examples can be made, and there is no clear consensus on this topic. It is reasonably certain that, given the increase in complexity of modern processors, effective hand-optimization is increasingly difficult and requires a great deal of knowledge.

However, some discrete calculations can still be rendered into faster running code with assembly, and some low-level programming is actually easier to do with assembly. Some system-dependent tasks performed by operating systems simply cannot be expressed in high-level languages. In particular, assembly is often used in writing the low level interaction between the operating system and the hardware, for instance in device drivers. Many compilers also render high-level languages into assembly first before fully compiling, allowing the assembly code to be viewed for debugging and optimization purposes.

It's also common, especially in relatively low-level languages such as C, to be able to embed assembly language into the source code with special syntax. Programs using such facilities, such as the Linux kernel, often construct abstractions where different assembly language is used on each platform the program supports, but it is called by portable code through a uniform interface.

Many embedded systems are also programmed in assembly to obtain the absolute maximum functionality out of what is often very limited computational resources, though this is gradually changing in some areas as more powerful chips become available for the same minimum cost.

Another common area of assembly language use is in the system BIOS of a computer. This low-level code is used to initialize and test the system hardware prior to booting the OS and is stored in ROM. Once a certain level of hardware initialization has taken place, code written in higher level languages can be used, but almost always the code running immediately after power is applied is written in assembly language.

Assembly language is also valuable in reverse engineering, since many programs are distributed only in machine code form, and machine code is usually easy to translate into assembly language and carefully examine in this form, but very difficult to translate into a higher-level language. Tools such as the Interactive Disassembler make extensive use of disassembly for such a purpose.

MenuetOS, a floppy-based operating system with a fully functional GUI is written entirely in assembly. A 64 bit version is also available. The author claims that only through assembly language could he produce his system in less than 1.4 megabytes.

[edit]

Example listing of assembly language source code

* Addr	* Label	* Instruction *	* Object code *
		.begin	
		.org 2048	
	a_start	.equ 3000	
2048		ld [length],&r1	11000010 00000000 00101000 00101100

```
2052              ld [address],%r2   11000100 00000000 00101000 00110000
2056              addcc              10000110 10001000 11000000 00000000
                  %r3,%r0,%r3
2060  loop :      addcc              10000000 10001000 01000000 00000001
                  %r1,%r1,%r0
2064              be done            00000010 10000000 00000000 00000110
2068              addcc %r1,-4,%r1   10000010 10000000 01111111 11111100
2072              addcc              10001000 10000000 01000000 00000010
                  %r1,%r2,%r4
2076              ld %r4,%r5         11001010 00000001 00000000 00000000
2080              ba loop            00010000 10111111 11111111 11111011
2084              addcc              10000110 10000000 11000000 00000101
                  %r3,%r5,%r3
2088  done :      jmpl %r15+4,%r0    10000001 11000011 11100000 00000100
2092  length : 20                    00000000 00000000 00000000 00010100
2096  address: a_start               00000000 00000000 00001011 10111000
                  .org.a_start
3000  a:          25                 00000000 00000000 00000000 00011001
3004  -10                            11111111 11111111 11111111 11110110
3008  33                             00000000 00000000 00000000 00100001
3012  -5                             11111111 11111111 11111111 11111011
3016  7                              00000000 00000000 00000000 00000111
```

HIGH LEVEL LANGUAGE

A programming language such as C, FORTRAN, or Pascal that enables a programmer to wirte programs that are more or less independent of a particular type of computer. Such languages are considered high-level because they are closer to human languages and further from machine languages. In contrast, assembly languages are considered low-level because they are very close to machine languages.

The main advantage of high-level languages over low-level languages is that they are easier to read, write, and maintain. Ultimately, programs written in a high-level language must be translated into machine language by a compiler or interpreter.

The first high-level programming languages were designed in the 1950s. Now there are dozens of different languages, including Ada, Algol, BASIC, COBOL, C, C++, FORTRAN, LISP, Pascal, and Prolog.

BRIEF IDEA OF OPERATING SYSTEM

A batch system is one in which jobs are bundled together with the instructions necessary to allow them to be processed without intervention.

Often jobs of a similar nature can be bundled together to further increase economy.

The basic physical layout of the memory of a batch job computer is shown below :

```
Monitor (permanently resident)
          User Space
(compilers, programs, data, etc.)
```

The monitor is system software that is responsible for interpreting and carrying out the instructions in the batch jobs. When the monitor started a job, it handed over control of the entire computer to the job, which then controlled the computer until it finished.

A sample of several batch jobs might look like :

```
$JOB user spec; identify the user for accounting purposes
$FORTRAN; load the FORTRAN compiler
Source program cards
$LOAD; load the compiled program
$RUN; run the program
Data cards
$EOJ; end of job
$JOB user spec; identify a new user
$LOAD application
$RUN
Data
$EOJ
```

Often magnetic tapes and drums were used to store intermediate data and compiled programs.

1. *Advantages of batch systems*
   - Move much of the work of the operator to the computer
   - Increased performance since it was possible for job to start as soon as the previous job finished.
2. *Disadvantages*
   - Turn-around time can be large from user standpoint
   - More difficult to debug program
   - Due to lack of protection scheme, one batch job can affect pending jobs (read too many cards, etc.)
   - A job could corrupt the monitor, thus affecting pending jobs
   - A job could enter an infinite loop.

As mentioned above, one of the major shortcomings of early batch systems was that there was no protection scheme to prevent one job from adversely affecting other jobs.

The solution to this was a simple protection scheme, where certain memory (*e.g.*, where the monitor resides) were made off-limits to user programs. This prevented user programs from corrupting the monitor.

To keep user programs from reading too many (or not enough) cards, the hardware was changed to allow the computer to operate in one of two modes: one for the monitor and one for the user programs. IO could only be performed in monitor mode, so that IO requests from the user programs were passed to the monitor. In this way, the monitor could keep a job from reading past it's on $EOJ card.

OPERATING SYSTEM

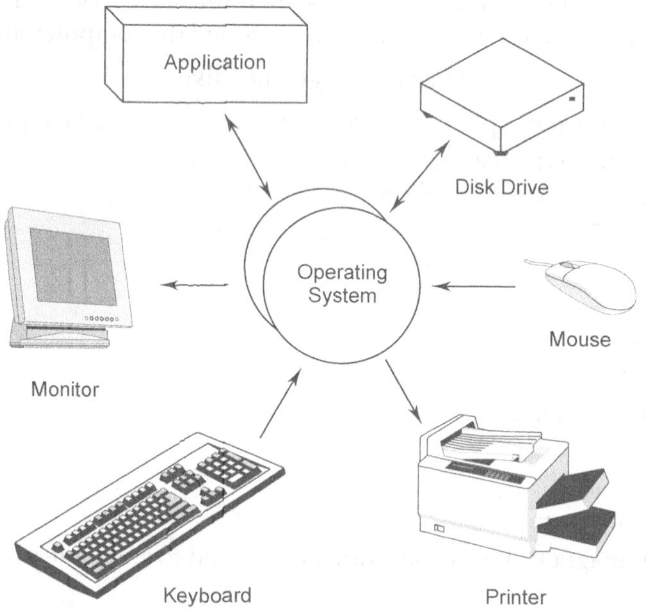

The most important program that runs on a computer. Every general-purpose computer must have an operating system to run other programs. Operating systems perform basic tasks, such as recognizing input from the keyboard, sending output to the display screen, keeping track of files and directories on the disk, and controlling peripheral devices such as disk drives and printers.

For large systems, the operating system has even greater responsibilities and powers. It is like a traffic cop — it makes sure that different programs and users running at the same time do not interfere with each other. The operating system is also responsible for security, ensuring that unauthorized users do not access the system.

Operating systems can be classified as follows :

- *multi-user:* Allows two or more users to run programs at the same time. Some operating systems permit hundreds or even thousands of concurrent users.
- *multiprocessing:* Supports running a program on more than one CPU.
- *multitasking:* Allows more than one program to run concurrently.
- *multithreading:* Allows different parts of a single program to run concurrently.
- *real time:* Responds to input instantly. General-purpose operating systems, such as DOS and UNIX, are not real-time.

Operating systems provide a software platform on top of which other programs, called application programs, can run. The application programs must be written to run on top of a particular operating system. Your choice of operating system, therefore, determines to a great extent the applications you can run. For PCs, the most popular operating systems are DOS, OS/2, and Windows, but others are available, such as Linux.

As a user, you normally interact with the operating system through a set of commands. For example, the DOS operating system contains commands such as COPY and RENAME for copying files and changing the names of files, respectively. The commands are accepted and executed by a part of the operating system called the command processor or command line interpreter. Graphical user interfaces allow you to enter commands by pointing and clicking at objects that appear on the screen.

SUMMARY

1. We can classify the computer languages according to Levels *e.g.*, machine level (Low level), Middle level and high level programming languages.
2. Machine level programming languages are understood by computers.
3. Assembly language commonly called assembly or asm, is an human readable notation. For the machine language that a specific computer architecture uses.
4. High level programming languages are closer to human language (English like statements) from machine language.
5. The main advantage of high-level languages over low-level languages is that they are easier to read, write and maintain.
6. The first high-level programming language were designed in the 1950s. Now, there are dozers of different language including Ada, Algol, BASIC, LOBOL, C, C++, JAVA, FORTRAN, LISP, Pascal etc.
7. Operating system provide the interface between the computer hardwares and softwares.
8. Operating system can be classified: Multiuser, multiprocessing multitasking, multithreading, Read time system.

REVIEW EXERCISES

1. Describe in brief of classification of computer languages.
2. Differentiate between machine level language & High level languages.
3. Discuss the advantages and disadvantages of batch system.
4. Which one is not high level programming language
   (*a*) ALGOL (*b*) Assembly (*c*) PASCAL (*d*) BASIC
5. Operating system provides the interface between
   (*a*) Hardware & Hard discs (*b*) Hardware & firmware
   (*c*) Hardware & Softwares (*d*) None

8

Compiler, Interpreter and Assembler

COMPILERS OVERVIEW

There are many aspects to be considered in the study of compilers. Usually the study encompasses more that just the strict definition of a compiler. According to **Webopedia**, a compiler is:

A program that translates source code into object code.

The textbook, Cooper & Torczon (CT) says that a compiler *"takes as input the specification for an executable program and produces as output the specification for another, equivalent executable program."*

Language Processors in General

We will concern ourselves with the study of the principles of compilation. However, the application of these principles and techniques are widely used in many other contexts. Examples of where you will find the such use are:

- static analysis tools
- testing tools
- XML tools for understanding and producing valid XML documents
- program rewriting and refactoring tools
- debuggers

For the purposes of this course, we will group all uses of the techniques into the category of language processors since we will be mostly concerned with understanding programming languages.

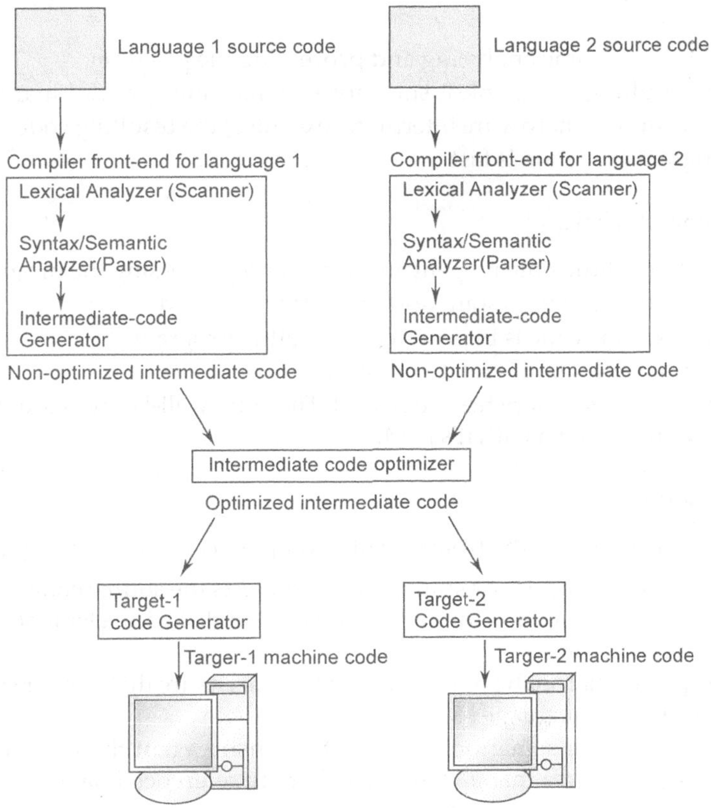

Fig. 8.1

Compiler vs. Interpreter

An interpreter translates some form of source code into a target representation that it can immediately execute and evaluate. The structure of the interpreter is similar to that of a compiler, but the amount of time it takes to produce the executable representation will vary as will the amount of optimization. The following diagram shows one representation of the differences.

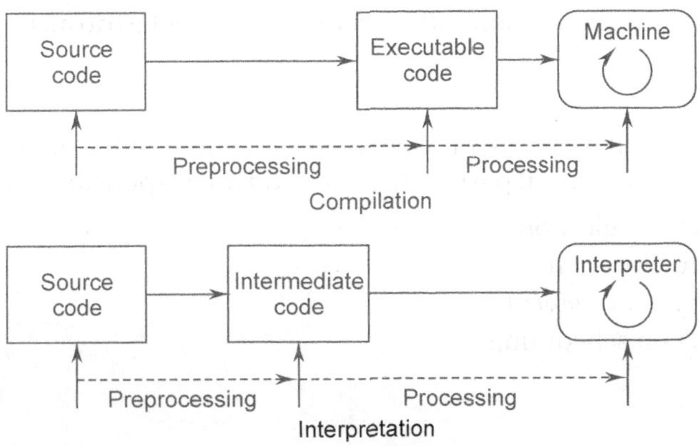

Fig. 8.2

Compiler Characteristics

- Spends a lot time analyzing and processing the program
- The resulting executable is some form of machine-specific binary code
- The computer hardware interprets (executes) the resulting code
- Program execution is fast

Interpreter Characteristics

- Relatively little time is spent analyzing and processing the program
- The resulting code is some sort of intermediate code
- The resulting code is interpreted by another program
- Program execution is relatively slow

The above characteristics are typical. There are well-known cases that are somewhere in between, such as Java with it's JVM.

Front End Structure

A typical structure for the front end of a compiler consists of three parts:

- The lexical analyzer, or scanner, that converts the source code into a stream of tokens. Each token represents the occurrence of a single lexical element, called a lexeme, in the source program.
- The parser that analyzes the token stream to ensure that it is a instance of a string that is in the source language.
- The context, or semantic, analyzer that ensures that the input is meaningful. For example, it ensures that all variables that are referenced have been declared (if that is a requirement of the language).

Middle Structure

- Most modern compilers have an optimization phase that sits between the front end and back end of the compiler. Usually, the optimizer consists of several cooperating modules that takes, as input, some intermediate form of the program under compilation and produces a transformation of it that is (hopefully) optimized.
- The optimization phases of most compilers today are composed of several modules because it is much easier to design and maintain the optimizer than if it were implemented as a single, monolithic, module that tried to do all optimizations.

Back End Structure

The back end of the compiler is responsible for emitting the final (executable) version of the source program. Typical parts of the back end are responsible for:

- instruction selection
- register allocation
- memory management
- instruction scheduling

A Simple Interpreter

- Writing a language processor is more than hacking together a few lines of code in a scripting language that transforms one form of a program to another. Even simple processors require some thought as to how the different parts will be distributed and collaborate.
- We will look at an example interpreter for a simple calculator and see how it is constructed, the tests, and how it evaluates expressions.

ASSEMBLY AND ASSEMBLERS

One of the early developments was a **symbolic assembler**. Instead of writing down a series of binary numbers, the programmer would write down a list of machine instructions, using human-readable symbols. A special program, the **assembler**, would convert these symbolic instructions into object or machine code. Assembly languages have the advantage that they are easier to understand than raw machine code, but still give access to all of the power of the computer (as each assembler symbol translates directly into a specific machine instruction). Assembly languages have the disadvantage that they are still very close to machine language. These can be difficult for a human to follow and understand and time-consuming for a human to write. Also, programs written in assembly are tied to a specific computer hardware and can't be reused on another kind of computer.

The human readable version of assembly code is known as **source code** (it is the source that the assembler converts into object code).

Fig. 8.3

HIGH LEVEL LANGUAGES

High level languages are designed to be easier to understand than assembly languages and allow a program to run on multiple different kinds of computers.

The source code written in high level languages need to be translated into object code. The two basic approaches are compilers and interpetters. Some programming languages are available in both interpreted and compiled versions.

High level languages have usually been designed to meet the needs of some particular kind of programming. For example, FORTRAN was originally intended for scientific programming. COBOL was originally intended for business programming and data processing. SQL was originally intended for data base queries. C was originally intended for systems programming. LISP was originally intended for list processing. PHP was originally intended for web scripting. Ada was originally intended for embedded systems. BASIC and Pascal were originally intended as teaching languages. Some high level languages were intended to be general purpose programming languages. Examples, include PL/I and Modula-2. Some languages that were originally intended for a specific purpose have turned into general purpose programming languages, such as C and Pascal.

INTERPRETERS

Interpreters convert each high level instruction into a series of machine instructions and then immediately run (or execute) those instructions. In some cases, the interpreter has a library of routines and looks up the correct routine from the library to handle each high level instruction.

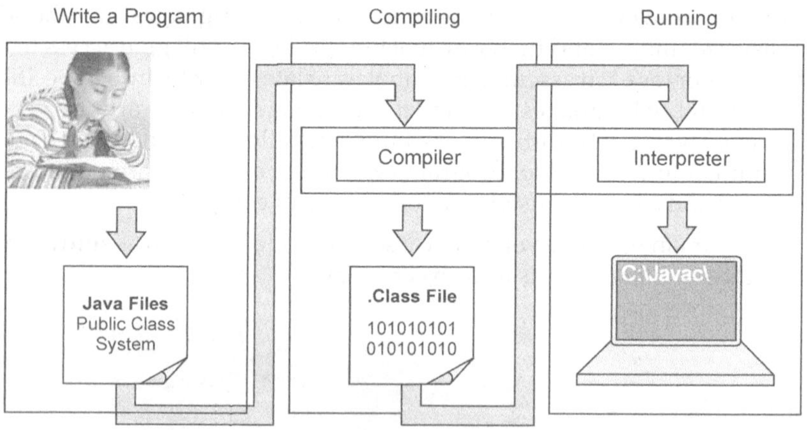

Fig. 8.4

COMPILERS

Compilers convert a finished program (or section of a program) into object code. This is often done in steps. Some compilers convert high level language instructions into assembly language instructions and then an assembler is used to create the finished object code.

Some compilers convert high level language instructions into an **intermediate language**. This intermediate language is platform-independent (it doesn't matter which actual computer hardware is eventually used). The intermediate language is then converted into object code for a specific kind of computer. This approach makes it easier to move (or **port**) a compiler from one kind of computer to another. Only the last step (or steps) need to be rewritten, while the main compiler is reused.

Compiled code almost always runs faster than interpreted code. An **optimizing compiler** examines a high level program and figures out ways to optimize the program so that it runs even faster.

LINKERS

As programs grow in size, requiring teams of programmers, there is a need to break them up into separate files so that different team members can work on their individual assignments without interfering with the work of others. Each file is compiled separately and then combined later.

Linkers are programs that combine the various parts of a large program into a single object program. Linkers also bring in support routines from **libraries**. These libraries contain utility and other support code that is reused over and over for lots of different programs. Historically, linkers also served additional purposes that are no longer necessary, such as resolving relocatable code on early hardware (so that more than one program could run at the same time).

LOADERS

A **loader** is a program that loads programs into main memory so that they can be run. In the past, a loader would have to be explicitely run as part of a job. In modern times the loader is hidden away in the operating system and called automatically when needed.

SUMMARY

1. **Compilers** convert a finished program (or section of a program) into object code. This is often done in steps. Some compilers convert high level language instructions into assembly language instructions and then an assembler is used to create the finished object code.
2. **Compiler characteristics:** There are mainly characteristics of a compiler that are as follows:
   - Spends a lot of time analyzing and processing the program
   - The resulting executable is some form of machine- specific binary code.
   - The computer hardware interprets (executes) the resulting code.
   - Program execution is fast.
3. A simple interpreter is a writing a language processor is more than hacking together a few lines of code in scripting languages that transforms one form of a program to another. Visual Interpreter(VI)editor in UNIX is the popular example of interpreter.
4. **Interpreter characteristics:** There are mainly **four** characteristics of a interpreter
   - Relatively little time is spent analyzing and processing the program.
   - The resulting code is some sort of intermediate code.
   - The resulting code is interpreted by another program.
   - Program execution is relatively slow.
5. **Linkers** are programs that combine the various parts of a large program into a single object program. Linkers also bring in support routines from **libraries.**
6. A **loader** is a program that loads programs into main memory so that they can be run. In the past, a loader would have to be explicitly run as part of a job.

REVIEW EXERCISES

1. Describe the language translators in brief.
2. What do you mean by a compiler and interpreter? Explain the characteristics of both.
3. Describe the difference between compiler and interpreter.
4. What is the main role of Linker and Loader in the programs?
5. Write a short notes on (*i*) Compiler (*ii*) Interpreter (*iii*) Linker (*iv*) Loader.

9

Need of Programming—Defining Problem

A **programming language** is an artificial language designed to express computations that can be performed by a machine, particularly a computer. Programming languages can be used to create programs that control the behavior of a machine, to express algorithms precisely, or as a mode of human communication.

Many programming languages have some form of written specification of their syntax (form) and semantics (meaning). Some languages are defined by a specification document. For example, the programming language is specified by an ISO Standard. Other languages, such as Perl, have a dominant implementation that is used as a reference.

Computer programming (often shortened to **programming** or **coding**) is the process of writing, testing, debugging/troubleshooting, and maintaining the source code of computer programs. This source code is written in a programming language. The code may be a modification of an existing source or something completely new. The purpose of programming is to create a program that exhibits a certain desired behaviour (customization). The process of writing source code often requires expertise in many different subjects, including knowledge of the application domain, specialized algorithms and formal logic.

Different programming languages support different styles of programming (called *programming paradigms*). The choice of language used is subject to many considerations, such as company policy, suitability to task, availability of third-party packages, or individual preference. Ideally, the programming language best suited for the task at hand will be selected. Trade-offs from this ideal involve finding enough programmers who know the language to build a team, the availability of compilers for that language, and the efficiency with which programs written in a given language execute.

The details look different in different languages, but a few basic instructions appear in just about every language:

- **input:** Get data from the keyboard, a file, or some other device.
- **output:** Display data on the screen or send data to a file or other device.
- **arithmetic:** Perform basic arithmetical operations like addition and multiplication.
- **conditional execution:** Check for certain conditions and execute the appropriate sequence of statements.
- **repetition:** Perform some action repeatedly, usually with some variation.

Many computer languages provide a mechanism to call functions provided by libraries. Provided the functions in a library follow the appropriate run time conventions (*e.g.*, method of passing arguments), then these functions may be written in any other language.

C (pronounced /si:/*see*) is a general-purpose computer programming language developed in 1972 by Dennis Ritchie at the Bell Telephone Laboratories for use with the Unix operating system.

Although C was designed for implementing system software, it is also widely used for developing portable application software.

C is one of the most popular programming languages and there are very few computer architectures for which a C compiler does not exist. C has greatly influenced many other popular programming languages, most notably C++, which originally began as an extension to C.

DESIGN

C is an imperative (procedural) systems implementation language. It was designed to be compiled using a relatively straightforward compiler, to provide low-level access to memory, to provide language constructs that map efficiently to machine instructions, and to require minimal run-time support. C was therefore useful for many applications that had formerly been coded in assembly language.

Despite its low-level capabilities, the language was designed to encourage machine-independent programming. A standards-compliant and portably written C program can be compiled for a very wide variety of computer platforms and operating systems with little or no change to its source code. The language has become available on a very wide range of platforms, from embedded microcontrollers to super computers.

C's design is tied to its intended use as a portable systems implementation language. It provides simple, direct access to any addressable object (for example, memory-mapped device control registers), and its source-code expressions can be translated in a straight forward manner to primitive machine operations in the executable code. Some early C compilers were comfortably implemented (as a few distinct passes communicating via intermediate files) on PDP-11 processors having only 16 address bits. C compilers for several common 8-bit platforms have been implemented as well.

CHARACTERISTICS

Like most imperative languages in the ALGOL tradition, C has facilities for structured programming and allows lexical variable scope and recursion, while a static type system prevents many unintended operations. In C, all executable code is contained within functions. Function parameters are always passed by value. Pass-by-reference is simulated in C by explicitly passing pointer values. Heterogeneous aggregate data types (struct) allow related data elements to be combined and manipulated as a unit. C program source text is free-format, using the semicolon as a statement terminator (not a delimiter).

C also exhibits the following more specific characteristics:

- variables may be hidden in nested blocks
- partially weak typing; for instance, characters can be used as integers
- low-level access to computer memory by converting machine addresses to typed pointers

- function and data pointers supporting *ad hoc* run-time polymorphism
- array indexing as a secondary notion, defined in terms of pointer arithmetic
- a preprocessor for macro definition, source code file inclusion, and conditional compilation
- complex functionality such as I/O, string manipulation, and mathematical functions consistently delegated to library routines
- A relatively small set of reserved keywords
- A lexical structure that resembles more than ALGOL, for example:
  - { ... } rather than either of ALGOL 60's begin ... end or ALGOL 68's (...)
  - = is used for assignment (copying), like Fortran, rather than ALGOL's :=
  - == is used to test for equality (rather than .EQ. in Fortran, or = in BASIC and ALGOL)
  - Logical "AND" and "OR" are represented with && and | | in place of ALGOL's ∧ and (∨ operators; note that the doubled-up operators will never evaluate the right operand if the result can be determined from the left alone (this is called short-circuit evaluation), and are semantically distinct from the bit-wise operators & and |
    - However Unix Version 6 & 7 versions of C used ALGOL's ∧ and ∨ operators (in ASCII), but for determining the infimum and supremum respectively.
  - a large number of compound operators, such as +=, -=, *= and ++ etc. (Equivalent to the ALGOL 68 operators +:=, –:=, *:= and +:=1)

ABSENT FEATURES

The relatively low-level nature of the language affords the programmer close control over what the computer does, while allowing special tailoring and aggressive optimization for a particular platform. This allows the code to run efficiently on very limited hardware, such as embedded systems.

C does not have some features that are available in some other programming languages:

- No nested function definitions
- No direct assignment of arrays or strings (copying can be done via standard functions; assignment of objects having struct or union type is supported)
- No automatic garbage collection
- No requirement for bounds checking of arrays
- No operations on whole arrays
- No syntax for ranges, such as the A..B notation used in several languages
- Prior to C99, no separate Boolean type (zero/nonzero is used instead)
- No formal closures or functions as parameters (only function and variable pointers)
- No generators or coroutines; intra-thread control flow consists of nested function calls, except for the use of the longjmp or setcontext library functions
- No exception handling; standard library functions signify error conditions with the global errno variable and/or special return values, and library functions provide non-local gotos
- Only rudimentary support for modular programming

- No compile-time polymorphism in the form of function or operator overloading
- Very limited support for object-oriented programming with regard to polymorphism and inheritance
- Limited support for encapsulation
- No native support for multithreading and networking
- No standard libraries for computer graphics and several other application programming needs.

A number of these features are available as extensions in some compilers, or are provided in some operating environments (e.g., POSIX), or are supplied by third-party libraries, or can be simulated by adopting certain coding disciplines.

UNDEFINED BEHAVIOR

Many operations in C that have undefined behavior are not required to be diagnosed at compile time. In the case of C, "undefined behavior" means that the exact behavior which arises is not specified by the standard, and exactly what will happen does not have to be documented by the C implementation. A famous, although misleading, expression in the newsgroups comp.std.c and comp.lang.c is that the program could cause "demons to fly out of your nose". Sometimes in practice what happens for an instance of undefined behavior is a bug that is hard to track down and which may corrupt the contents of memory. Sometimes a particular compiler generates reasonable and well-behaved actions that are completely different from those that would be obtained using a different C compiler. The reason some behavior has been left undefined is to allow compilers for a wide variety of instruction set architectures to generate more efficient executable code for well-defined behavior, which was deemed important for C's primary role as a systems implementation language; thus C makes it the programmer's responsibility to avoid undefined behavior, possibly using tools to find parts of a program whose behavior is undefined. Examples of undefined behavior are:

- accessing outside the bounds of an array
- overflowing a signed integer
- reaching the end of a non-void function without finding a return statement, when the return value is used
- reading the value of a variable before initializing it.

These operations are all programming errors that could occur using many programming languages; C draws criticism because its standard explicitly identifies numerous cases of undefined behavior, including some where the behavior could have been made well defined, and does not specify any run-time error handling mechanism.

Invoking fflush () on a stream opened for input is an example of a different kind of undefined behavior, not necessarily a programming error but a case for which some conforming implementations may provide well-defined, useful semantics (in this example, presumably discarding input through the next new-line) as an allowed *extension*. Use of such nonstandard extensions generally limits software portability.

C supports a rich set of operators, which are symbols used within an expression to specify the manipulations to be performed while evaluating that expression. C has operators for:

- arithmetic (+, -, *, / , %)
- equality testing (==, !=)
- order relations (<, <=, >, >=)

- boolean logic (!, &&, ||)
- bitwise logic (~, &, |, ^)
- bitwise shifts (<<, >>)
- assignment (=, +=, −=, *=, /=, %=, &=, |=, ^=, <<=, >>=)
- increment and decrement (++, −−)
- reference and dereference (&, *, [ ])
- conditional evaluation (? :)
- member selection (., ->)
- type conversion (( ))
- object size (sizeof)
- function argument collection (( ))
- sequencing (,)
- subexpression grouping (( ))

C has a formal grammar, specified by the C standard.

INTEGER-FLOAT CONVERSION AND ROUNDING

The type casting syntax can be used to convert values between an integer type and a floating-point type, or between two integer types or two float types with different sizes; *e.g.*, (long int) sqrt(1000.0), (double)(256*256), or (float)sqrt(1000.0). Conversions are implicit in several contexts, *e.g.*, when assigning a value to a variable or to a function parameter, when using a floating-point value as index to a vector, or in arithmetic operations on operand with different types.

Unlike some other cases of type casting (where the bit encoding of the operands are simply re-interpreted according to the target type), conversions between integers and floating-point values generally change the bit encoding so as to preserve the numerical value of the operand, to the extent possible. In particular, conversion from an integer to a floating-point type will preserve its numeric value exactly—unless the number of fraction bits in the target type is insufficient, in which case the least-significant bits are lost.

Conversion from a floating-point value to an integer type entails truncation of any fractional part (*i.e.*, the value is rounded "towards zero"). For other kinds of rounding, the C99 standard specifies (in <math.h>) the following functions:

- round(): round to nearest integer, halfway away from zero
- rint(), nearbyint(): round according to current floating-point rounding direction
- ceil(): smallest integral value not less than argument (round up)
- floor(): largest integral value (in double representation) not greater than argument (round down)
- trunc(): round towards zero (same as typecasting to an int).

All these functions take a double argument and return a double result, which may then be cast to an integer if necessary.

The conversion of a float value to the double type preserves the numerical value exactly, while the opposite conversion rounds the value to fit in the smaller number of fraction bits, usually towards zero. (Since float also has a smaller exponent range, the conversion may yield an infinite value.) Some compilers will silently convert float values to double in some contexts, *e.g.*, function parameters declared as float may be actually passed as double.

In machines that comply with the IEEE floating point standard, some rounding events are affected by the current rounding mode (which includes round-to-even, round-down, round-up, and round-to-zero), which may be retrieved and set using the fegetround()/ fesetround() functions defined in <fenv.h>.

SUMMARY

1. A "programming language" is an artificial language designed to express computations that can be performed by a machine, particularly a computer.
2. Programming or coding is the process of writing, testing, debugging/troubleshooting and maintaining the source code of computer.
3. Basic instructions in programming languages appess in – input, output, arithmetic, conditional execution, repetition.
4. 'C' is most popular programming language and developed by Dennis Ritchie in 1972 at the Bell Telephone Laboratories for use with the UNIX operating system.
5. 'C' is an imperative (procedural) system implementation language. C compiler for several common 8-bit platform have been implemented a well.

REVIEW EXERCISES

1. What do you mean by a good programming languages?
2. What are the features defined in the 'C' programming languages?
3. Describe the features of 'C' language those are not in other programming language.
4. Explain the undefined behavior of 'C' language.
5. Describe in brief 'C' language operators.

10

PLANNING THE COMPUTER PROGRAM

WHAT IS AN ALGORITHM ?

We saw above that planning a program involves defining its logic (the correct sequence of instructions needed to solve the problem at hand). The term algorithm is often used to refer to the logic of a program. It is a step-by-step description of how to arrive at the solution of the given problem. It may be formally defined as a sequence of instructions, designed in a manner that, if the instructions are executed in the specified sequence, the desired results will be obtained. In order to qualify as an algorithm, a sequence of instructions must possess the following characteristics :

1. Each and every instruction should be precise and unambiguous.
2. Each instruction should be such that it can be performed in a finite time.
3. One or more instructions should not be repeated infinitely. This ensures that the algorithm will ultimately terminate.
4. After performing the instructions, that is, after the algorithm terminates, the desired results must be obtained.

SAMPLE ALGORITHMS

To gain insight into algorithms, let us consider some simple examples.

Example: 50 students in a class appeared in their final examination. Their marksheet have been given to you the division column of the mark sheet contains the division (FIRST, SECOND, THIRD or FAIL) obtained by the student. Write an algorithm to calculate and print the total number of students who passed in FIRST division.

Algorithm :

Step 1 : Initialize Total_First_Division and Total_Marksheets_Checked to zero.

Step 2 : Take the mark sheet of the next student.

Step 3 : Check the division column of the marksheet to see if it is FIRST. If no, go to Step 5.

Step 4 : Add 1 to Total_First_Division.

Step 5 : Add 1 to Total_Marksheets_Checked.

Step 6 : Is Total_Marksheets_Checked = 50 ? If no, go to Step 2.

Step 7 : Print Total_First_Division.

Step 8 : Stop.

Example: There are 100 employees in an organization. The organization wants to distribute annual bonus to the employees based on their performance. The performance of the employees is recorded in their annual appraisal forms. Every employee's appraisal form contains his/her basic salary, and the grade for his/her performance during the year. The grade is of three categories – 'A' for outstanding, 'B' for good, and 'C' for average performance. It has been decided that the bonus of an employee will be 100% of the basic salary for outstanding performance, 70% of the basic salary for good performance, 40% of the basic salary for average performance, and zero for all other cases. Write an algorithm to calculate and print the total bonus amount to be distributed by the organization.

Algorithm :

Step 1 : Initialize Total_Bonus and Total_Employees_Checked to zero.

Step 2 : Initialize Bonus and Basic_Salary to zero.

Step 3 : Take the appraisal form of the next employee.

Step 4 : Read the employee's Basic_Salary and Grade.

Step 5 : If Grade = A, then Bonus = Basic_Salary. Go to Step 8.

Step 6 : If Grade = B, then Bonus = Basic_Salary × 0.7 Go to Step 8.

Step 7 : If Grade = C, then Bonus = Basic_Salary × 0.4.

Step 8 : Add Bonus to Total_Bonus.

Step 9 : Add 1 to Total_Employees_Checked.

Step 10 : If Total_Employees_Checked < 100, then go to Step 2.

Step 11 : Print Total_Bonus.

Step 12 : Stop.

Programmers design algorithms like these to solve complex programming problems. It must be clear to the readers from these examples that even for very simple problems, the development of algorithms is not so simple as it might initially appear, and requires some thinking. It may also be noted from the given examples that to solve a given problem, every instruction must be strictly carried out in a particular sequence. It is this fact, which a beginner to problem solving by computers finds difficult to appreciate.

REPRESENTATION OF ALGORITHMS

There are various ways in which an algorithm can be represented. Programmers normally use one or more of the following ways to represent their algorithms.

1. As programs
2. As flowcharts
3. As pseudocodes

When an algorithm is represented in the form of a programming language, it becomes a program. Hence, any program is an algorithm, although the reverse is not true.

Besides represented as programs, algorithms are often represented as flowcharts and pseudocodes. These are the commonly used tools used by programmers for program planning, which can often be of immense help in developing an effective and correct algorithm for a program, before is coded into a programming language. These program-planning tools are described below. Programmers generally select one of these tools depending on their choice to plan their programs.

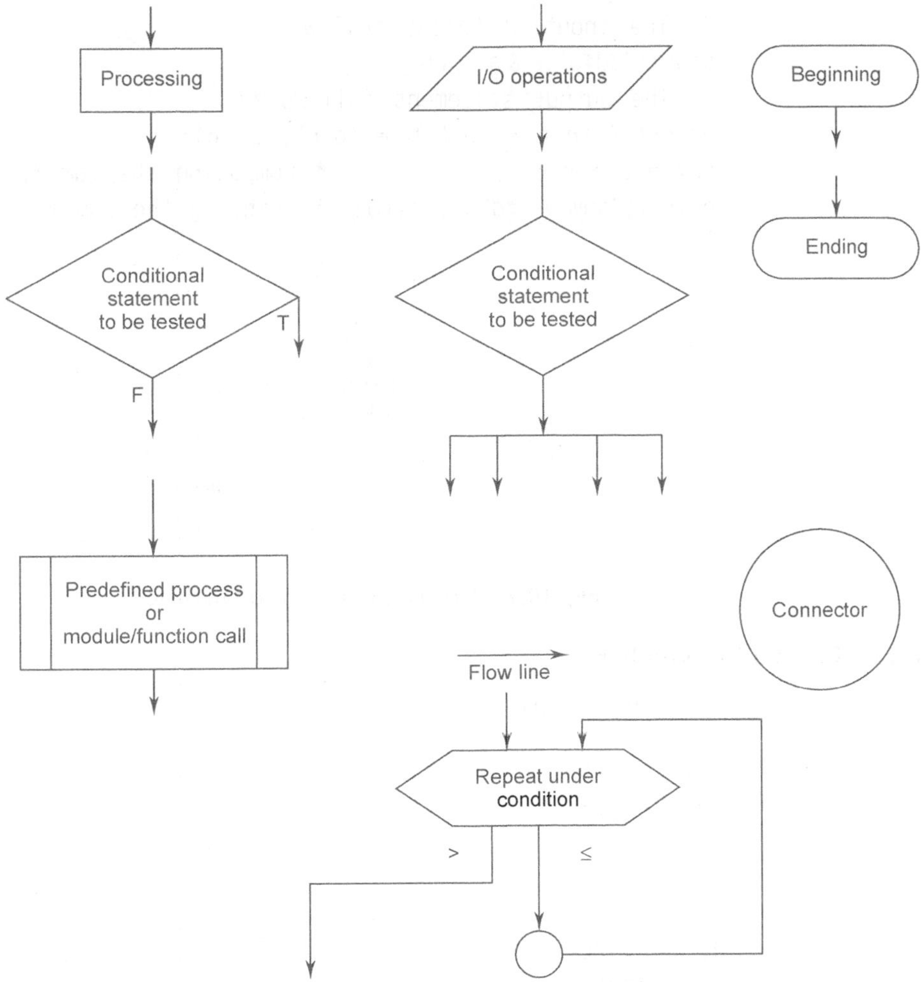

Fig. 10.1 *Flowchart symbols*

Sum of Two Given Numbers

```
/* Program to find the sum of two given numbers */
    # include<conio.h>         / * Including header file * /
    # include<stdio.h>
    Void main()
    {
        int a, b, sum;         /* Declaration of Variables */
        clrscr();
        /* A message is displayed on the monitor indicating the action
        to be taken by the user */
        printf ("\n\n Enter two numbers \n");
```

```
/* The input statement follows*/
scanf("%d%d", &a, &b);
/* The output statement follows */
printf ("\n a = %d\t b = %d\n", a, b);
Sum = a + b ;                 /* Computing the sum */
printf("sum = %d\n", sum); /* printing the sum */
}
```

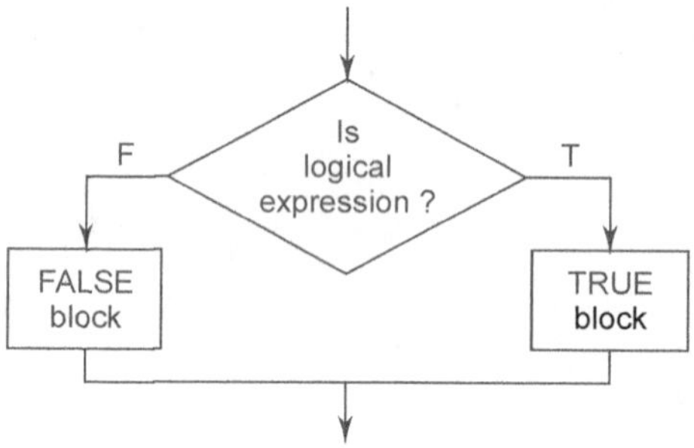

Fig. 10.2 *Flowchart for decision-making*

Largest of Two Given Numbers

```
if (logical expression)
{
        TRUE Block
        Statements
}
    else
    {
        FALSE Block
        Statements
    }
```

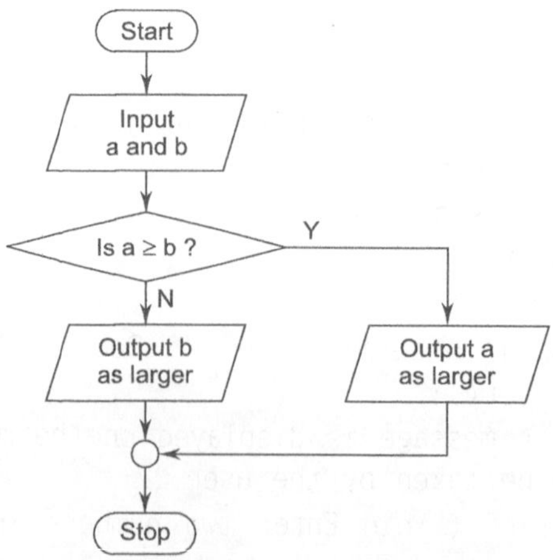

Fig. 10.3 *Flowchart for finding the larger*

Computing the Area of a Circle Given its Radius

```
# include<stdio.h>
# include<conio.h>
# define PI 3.1428    /* Using PI value is a symbolic constant */
Void main()
{
    float r, area;    /* Declaring variables */
    clrscru();
    printf ("\n\n Enter radius of the circle");
    scanf ("%f", &r); / * Entering radius of the circle */
    printf ("\n\n radius of the given circle: % f \n" , r);
    area = PI * r * r ; /* computing area of the circle */
    printf ("\n\n Area of the given circle : %f \n", area);
    }
```

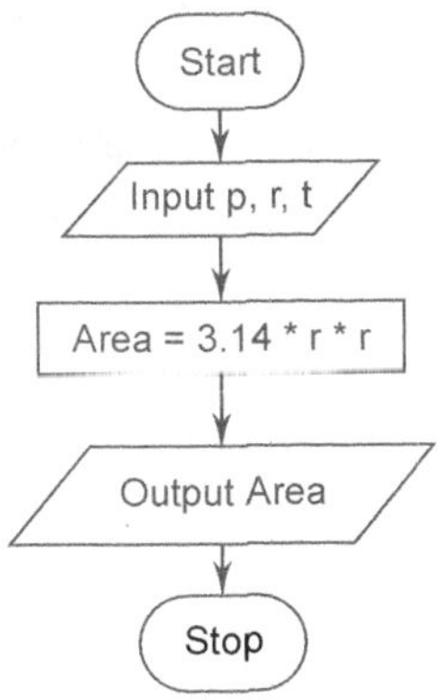

Fig. 10.4 *Flowchart for calculating the Area of a circle*

Computing the Area of a Triangle given all its sides

```
# include <conio.h>        /* Including header files */
# include <stdio.h>
# include <math.h>
    void main ()
    {
        float a, b, c, s, area ; /* Declaration of variables */
        clrscr();
        printf ("\n\n enter the three sides of the triangle\n");
        printf("such that sum of any two sides is greater than; the
        third_side. \n\n");
        scanf ("%f%f%f", &a, &b, &c);
        /* Entering three sides of the triangle such that sum of two sides
        should be greater than the third side */
```

```
printf("\n three sides of the triangle are:
a = %f\tb = %f\tc = %f\n", a, b, c);
S = (a+b+c)/2;
area = sqrt (s * (s - a) * (s - b) * (s - c));
/* computing area of the triangle */
printf ("\n\n Area of the triangle is %f\n", area);
}
```

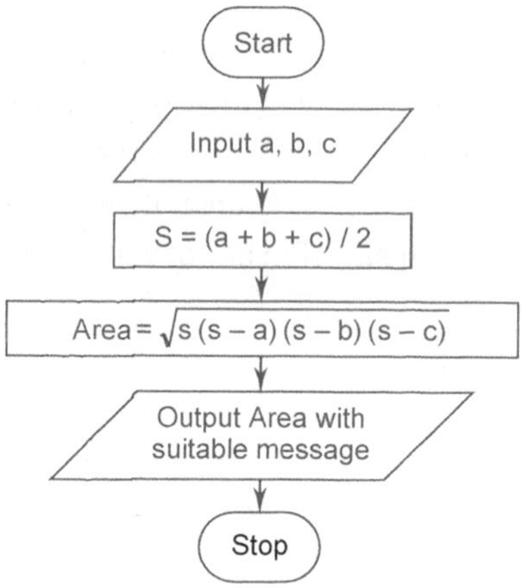

Fig. 10.5 *Flowchart for calculating the area of triangle*

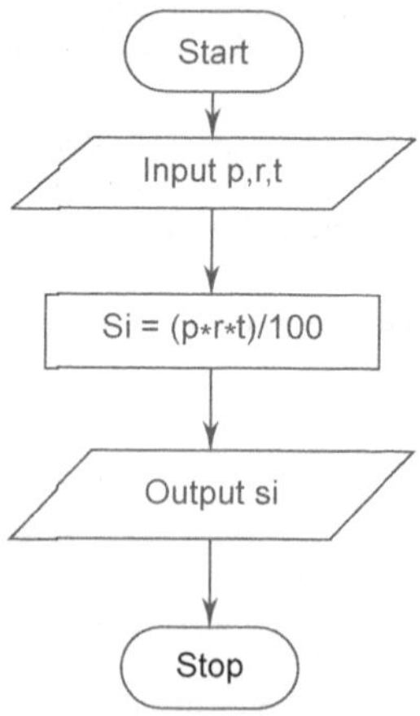

Fig. 10.6 *Flowchart for calculation simple interest*

Simple Interest Calculation

/* Program for single interest calculation */

```
# include <conio.h>       /* Including header file */
# include <stdio.h>
    Void main()
```

```
{
    float p, r, t, si ; /*Declaring variables */
    clrscr();
    printf ("\n\n Enter principle, rate of interest, time \n\n\n");
    Scanf ("%f%f%f", &p, &r, &t);
    /* Entering principle = % f\t Rate of interest and time */
    printf ("\n principle = %f\t Rate of interest = %.2f\t
    Time = %. 2f\n", p, r, t);
    Si = (p * r * t )/100 ; /* Computing simple interest */
    printf ("\n\n Simple Interest = %. 2f\n", Si);
    }
```

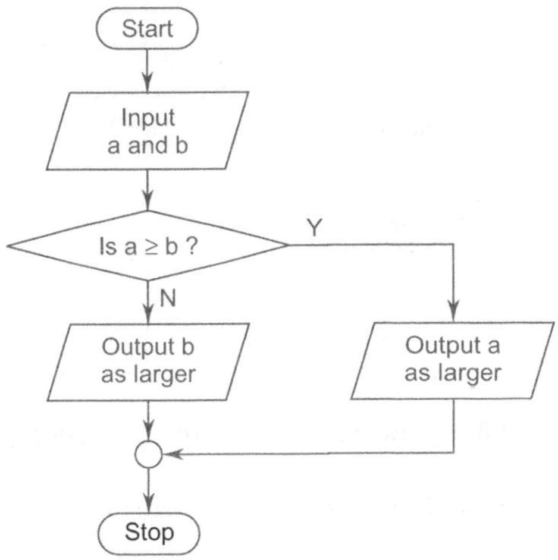

Fig.10.7 *Flowchart for finding the largest of two numbers*

Finding the Largest of the Given two Numbers

```
# include <stdio.h>
# include <conio.h>
Void main()
{
    int a, b ;
    clrscr();
    printf ("Enter any two numbers \n");
    scanf ("%d%d", &a, &b);
    printf ("\n the given two numbers are : a = %d, b = %d\n", a, b);
    if ( a >= b)
    printf ("\n a = %d is the largest number", a) :
    else
    printf ("\n b = %d is the largest number", b);
    }
```

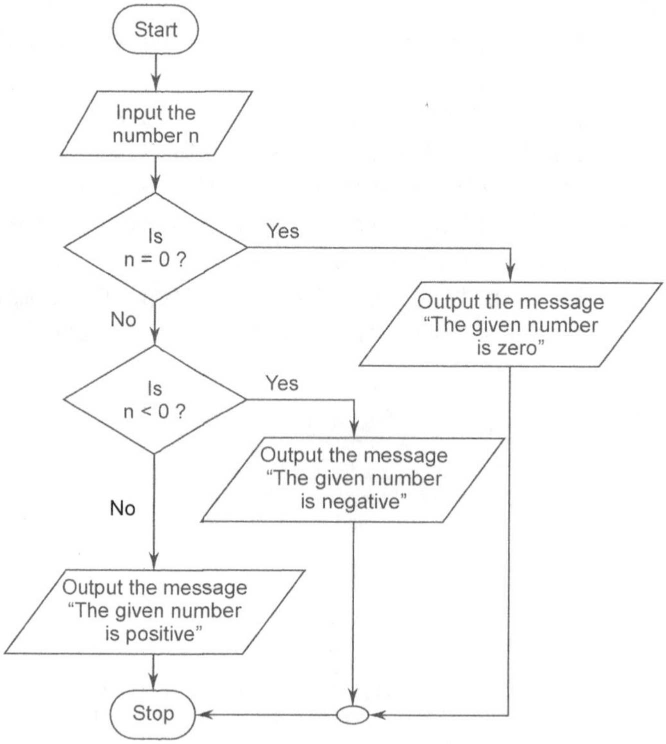

Fig. 10.8 *Flowchart for find out number is positive or negative*

To Find out whether a given Integer is zero, the or – ve

```
# include <conio.h>   /* Including header file */
# include <stdio.h>
void main()
{
    int number ;
    clrscr();
    printf ("\n\n Enter an integer number \n\n");
    scanf ("%d", & number); /* Read a number */
    printf ("\n Number, %d \n\n", number);
    if (number == 0)
    printf ("The number is zero. \n");
    else
    if (number < 0)
    printf ("%d is negative, \n", number);
    else
    printf ("%d is positive, \n", number);
    }
```

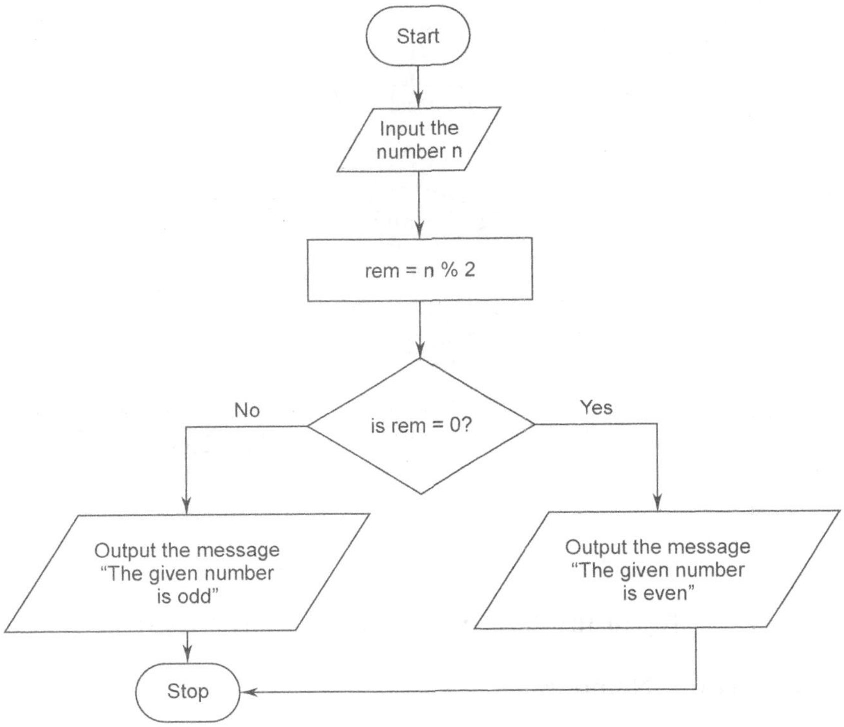

Fig. 10.9 *Flowchart for find out number is odd or even*

Determining whether a Given integer Number is Odd or Even

```
# include <stdio.h>
# include <conio.h>
Void main()
{
    int number, rem ;
    clrscr();
    print f ("Enter an integer number :");
    scanf ("%d", &number); /* Read an integer */
    printf ("\n Number is %d \n", number);
    / * Dividing number by 2, if the reminder is zero it is even otherwise,
    it is odd */
    rem = number%2;
    if (rem == 0)
    printf ("The number %d is even. \n", number);
    else
    printf ("The number %d is odd. \n", number);
    }
```

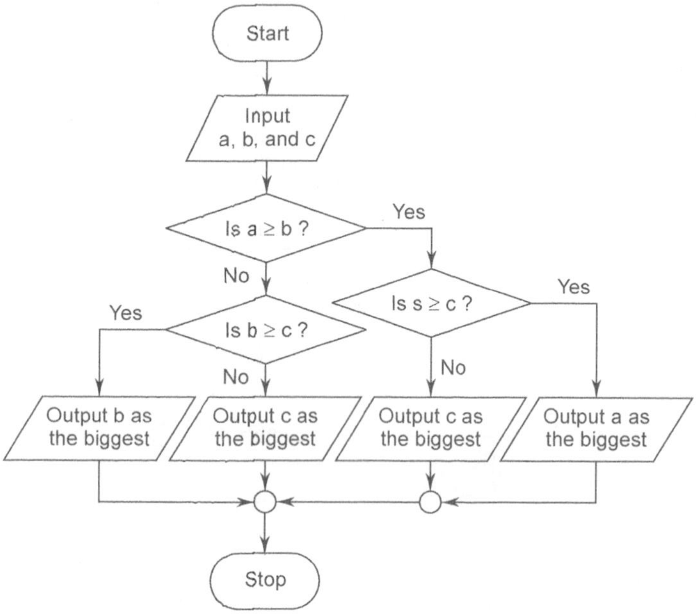

Fig. 10.10 *Flowchart for finding largest of given three numbers*

Largest of Given three Numbers

```
/* Program to find biggest of three numbers */
/* Here num1, num2 and num3 are used instead of a, b and c */
# include <stdio.h>
# include <conio.h>
    Void main()
    {
        int num1, num2, num3 ;
        clrscr();
        printf ("Enter three numbers : \n");
        scanf ("%d%d%d", &num1, &num2, &num3); /*Reading three numbers*/
        printf ("\n the three numbers are \t % d\t % d\t % d\n\n", num1,
        num2, num3);
        if (num1 >= num2) /* Comparing first with second */
        {
        if (num1 >= num3) /* Comparing first with third */
        printf ("\n%d is biggest \n", num 1);
        else
        printf ("\n%d is biggest \n", num3);
        {
    }
```

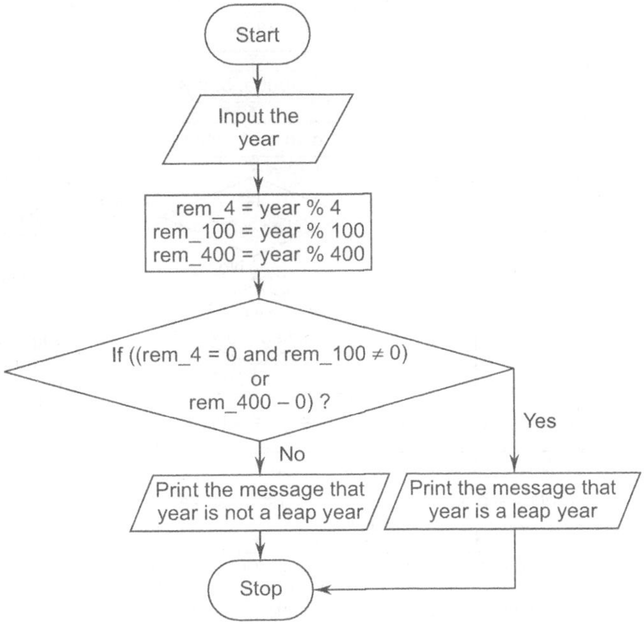

Fig.10.11

To Find out whether a Given year is a Leap year or not

```
# include<stdio.h>
# include <conio.h>
    Void main()
    {
        int year, rem_4,rem_100,rem_400;
        clrscr();
        printf ("Enter the year to be tested\n");
        scanf ("%d", &year);
        rem_4 = year % 4 ;
        rem_100 = year % 100 ;
        rem_400 = year % 400 ;
        if ((rem_4 = 0 ** rem_100 ! = 0) "rem_400 == 0)
        printf ("the given year %d is a leap year", year);
        else
        printf ("The given year %d is not a leap year", year);
        }
```

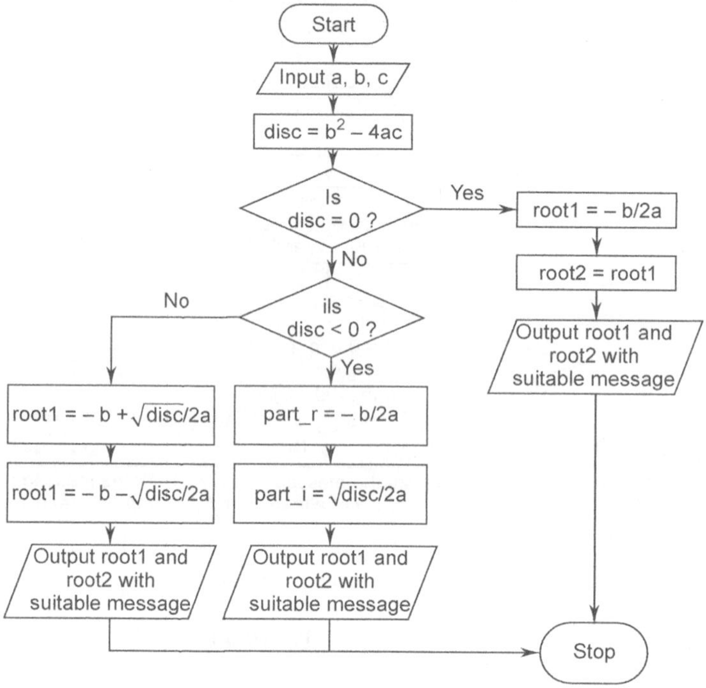

Fig.10.12 *Flowchart for solving quadratic equation*

Solving a given Quadratic Equation

```
/* To find the roots of a given quadratic equation */
# include <conio.h>
# include <stdio.h>    /* Including header files */
# include <math.h>
    Void main()
    {
        float a, b, c, disc, root2, root2, part = r, part-i ; /*
        Declaring variables */
        clrscr();    /* Clearing the screen */
        printf ("\n\n Enter co-efficients of the quadratic equation
        \n\n");
        scanf ("%f%f%f", &a, &b, &c);
        printf ("\n co-efficients are a = %f\t is = %f\t c = %f\n\n", a,
        b, c);
        disc = b * b - 4 * a * c ; /* Calculating discriminant*/
        if (disc == 0)
        /* If discriminant is zero roots are real and equal */
        {
            printf ("Roots are real and equal \n");
            root1 = - b/(2.0 * a);
```

```
root2 = root1;
printf ("/n Root1 = %f\t Root2 = %f\n", root1, root2);
}
    else
        if (disc < 0)
        /* If discriminant is less than zero roots are
        complex */
        {
        printf ("Roots are complex /n");
        part_r = - b/(2.0 * a);
        part_i = sqrt (- disc)/2.*a);
        printf ("\ Root1 = %f t i %f\t Root 2 = %f - i
        %f\n", part_r,part_i,part_r,part_i);
        }
        else
        /* As disc is greater than zero roots are real and
        distinct */
        {
            printf ("Roots are real and distinct \n");
            root1 = (- b + sqrt (disc))/(2.0 * a);
            root2 = (- b - sqrt (disc))/(2.0 * a);
            printf ("\n Root1 = %f\t Root2 = %f\n" root1,
            root2);
        }
{
```

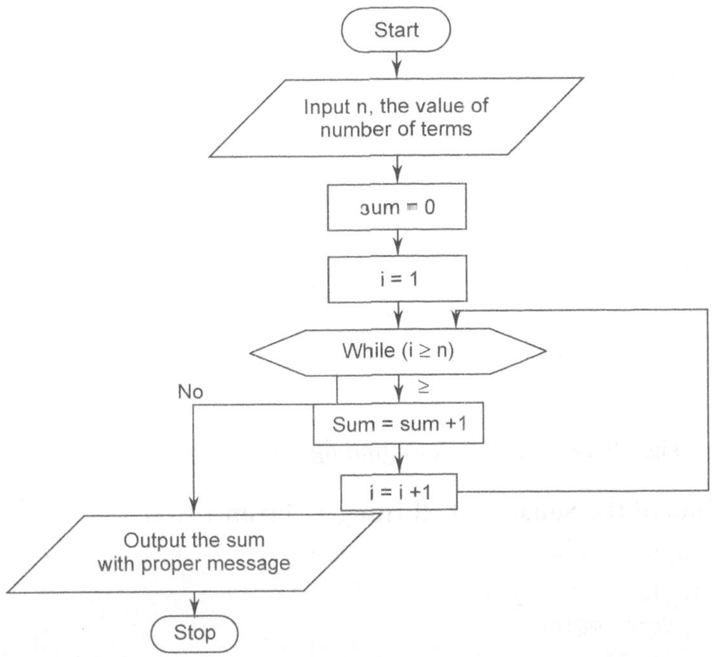

Fig. 10.13 *Flowchart for finding the sum of n natural numbers*

Finding the Sum of first n Natural Numbers

```
# include <conio.h>    /* Including header file */
# include <stdio.h>
   void main()
   {
        int n, i = 1, sum = 0;  /* Initializing i to one and sum to zero */
        clrscr();
        printf ("\n\n Enter value of n \n");
        Scanf ("%d", &n);
        printf ("n = %d\n", n);
        /* Repeat while i is less than or equation */
        while (i <= n)
        {
             sum = sum + i ;    /* Adding is to sum */
             i = i + 1;         /* Incrementing i by 1 */
        }
        printf ("\n Sum of first %d natural numbers is %d\n", n, sum);
        }
```

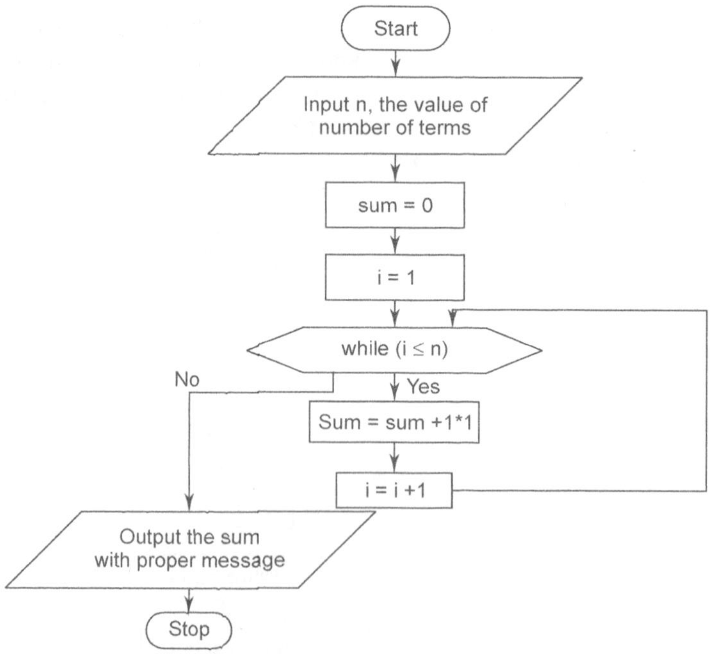

Fig. 10.14 *Flowchart for finding sum of squares of all integers from 1 to n*

To Find the Sum of the Squares of all Integers From 1 to n

```
# include <conio.h>         /* Including header & files */
# include <stdio.h>
   Void main()
   {
```

```
int n, i = 1, sum = 0 ;     /* Initializing i to 1 and sum to 0 */
clrscr();
printf ("\n\n Enter value of n \n");
scanf ("%d", &n);
printf ("n = %d\n", n);
while (i <= n) /* Repeat while i is less than or eual to n */
{
    sum+ = i * i ;    /* Adding i to sum */
    i++;              /* Incrementing i by 1 */
}
printf ("\n sum of squares of numbers from 1 to %d is %d\n, n,
sum);
}
```

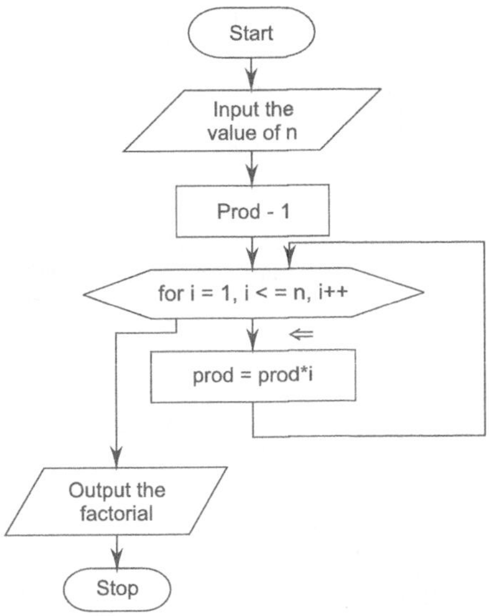

Fig. 10.15 *Flowchart for find the factorial of a given integer*

To Find the Factorial of a Given Integer

```
# include < stdio.h >
# include < conio.h >
Void main()
    {
        long n, i, prod = 1 ;
        clrscr();
        printf ("Input the value of n \n");
        scanf ("%id", &n);
    for (i = 1 ; i < = n ; i++)
    {
        prod = prod * i ;
    }
        printf ("\n the value of %id factorial is : %id\n", n, prod);
    }
```

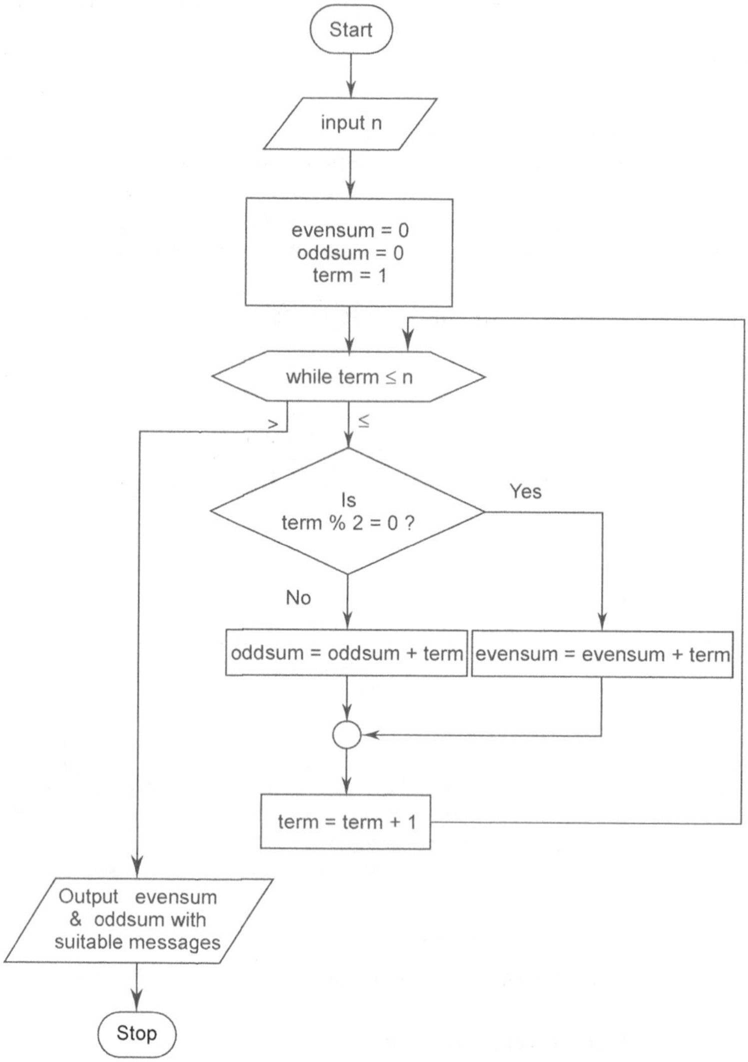

Fig. 10.16 *Flowchart for finding the sum of odd numbers and sum of even numbers from 1 to n*

Finding the Sum of Odd numbers and Sum of Even numbers from 1 to n

```
# include <stdio.h>
# include <conio.h>
    Void main()
    {
        int n, even_sum = 0, odd_sum = 0, i = 1 ;
        /* Initializing even sum and odd sum to zero and i to 1 */
        clrscr();
```

```
        printf ("Enter value of n \n");
        scanf ("%d", &n);
        printf ("\nn = %d\n", n);
        while (i <= n)     /* Repeat while i is less than or equal to n*/
    {
        /* If the remainder after dividing number by 2 is zero then it
        is even, add to even sum */
        if (i % 2 == 0)
        even_sum + = i ;
        else
        /* If the remainder after dividing number by 2 is non zero then
        it is odd, add to odd sum */
        odd_sum + = i ;
        i++;                /* Increment i by 1 */
        }
        printf ("\n sum of odd numbers from 1 to %d\n", n, odd_sum);
        printf ("\n sum of even numbers from 1 to %d is %d\n", n, even_sum
        }
```

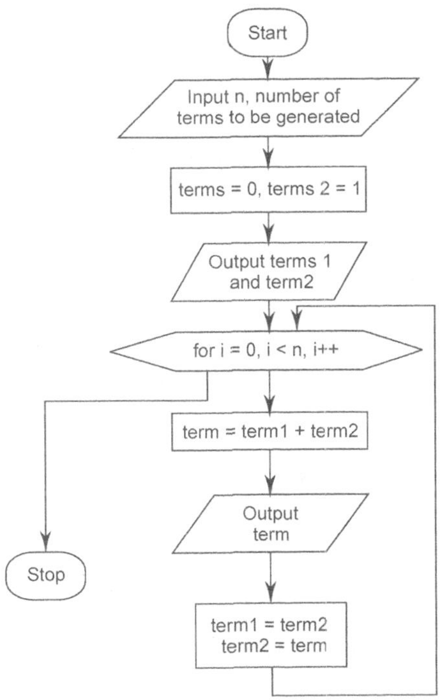

Fig. 10.17 *Flowchart for find & generation of fibonacci sequence*

Generation of required Number of terms of the Fibonacci sequence

```
# include <stdio.h>
# include <conio.h>
    Void main()
{
```

```
        int n, term1 = 0, term2 = 1, term, i ;
        /* Initializing first and second numbers to 0 and 1 respectively */
        clrscr();
        printf ("Enter the value of n, the number of terms to be generated
        \n");
        scanf ("%d", &n);
        printf ("\nn = %d\n", n);
        printf ("\n first %d fibonicci numbers are : \n", n + 2);
        /* Printing first and second number */
        printf ("\n%d\n%d", term1, term2);
        /* Repeating for n times since already two numbers are printed */
        for (i = 0, i < n ; i++)
    {
        term = term1 + term2 ;
        printf = ("\n%d", term);
        term1 = term2 ;
        term2 = term ;
    }
}
```

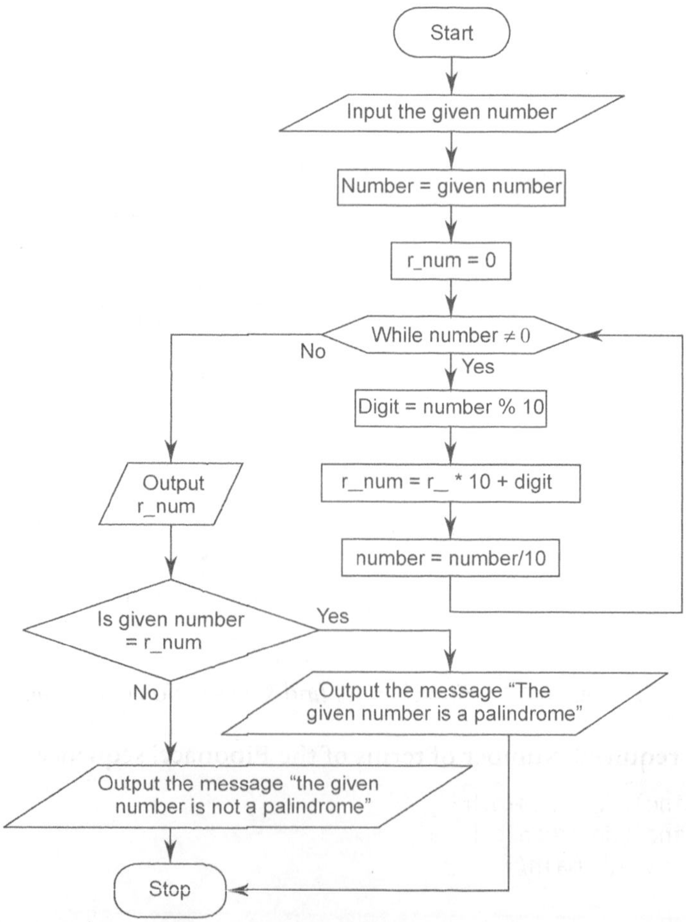

Fig. 10.18 *Flowchart for finding the number is palindrome or not*

Reversing a Number and to Check whether it is Palindrome or not

```
# include <conio.h>   /* Including header file */
# include <stdio.h>
    Void main()
    {
    int num, r_num, digit, n ;
    clrscr();
    printf ("\n\n Enter an integer number \n");
    scanf ("%d", &num);
    n = num ;    /* Keep the value of num in n for later use */
    r_num = 0 ;
    printf ("\n number = %d\t", num);
    while (num ! = 0) /* Repeat while num is not zero */
    {
    digit = num %10 ;
        /* obtain the remainder by dividing num by 10, so that last
        digit is obtained */
    r_num = r_num * 10 + digit ;
        /* r_num is multiplied by 10 and added to digit*/
    num = num/10 ; /* Dividing number by 10 to get quotient */
    }
    printf ("\n the reverse of the given number is %d is %d \n\n", n,
    r_num);
    if (n = r_num)
        /* If number and reverse are same then it is palindrome
        otherwise not */
    printf ("reverse = %d, given number is %d is a palindrome \n",
    r_num, n);
    else
        printf ("reverse = %d, given number %d is not a palindrome \n",
        r_num, n);
    }
```

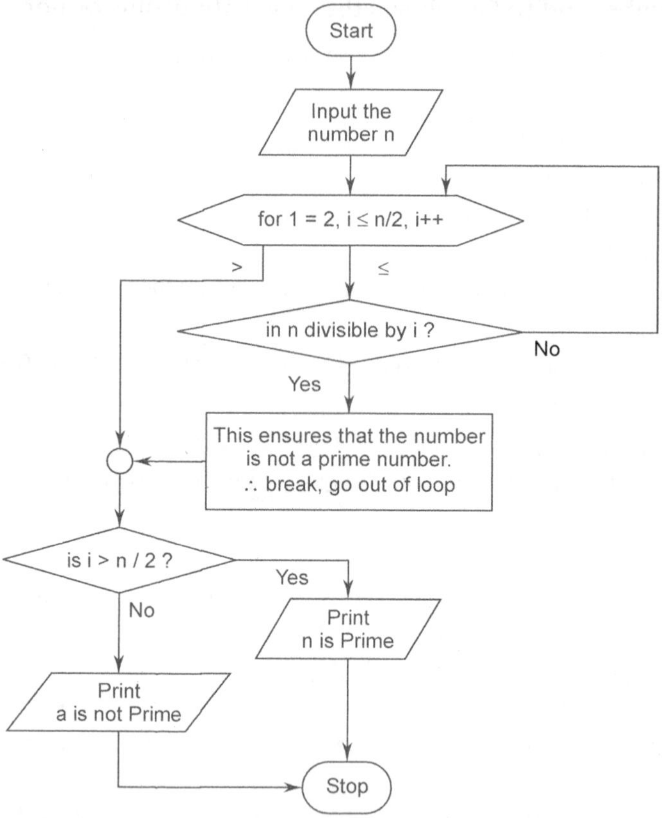

Fig. 10.19 *Flowchart for finding a number is prime or not.*

To Find out whether a Given integer Number is Prime or not

```
# include <stdio.h>
# include <conio.h>
    void main()
    {
        int n, i ;
        clrscr();
        printf ("\n Enter an integer number \n");
        scanf ("%d", & n)
        printf ("Given number = %d\n",n);
        for (i = 2 ; i <= i++)
        {
        /* Dividing number n by i, if remainder is zero it is not a
        prime */
            if(n%i==0)
            break;
        }
```

```
                if (i > n/2)
            printf ("%d is prime \n", n);
        else
            printf ("%d is not a prime \n", n);
        }
}
```

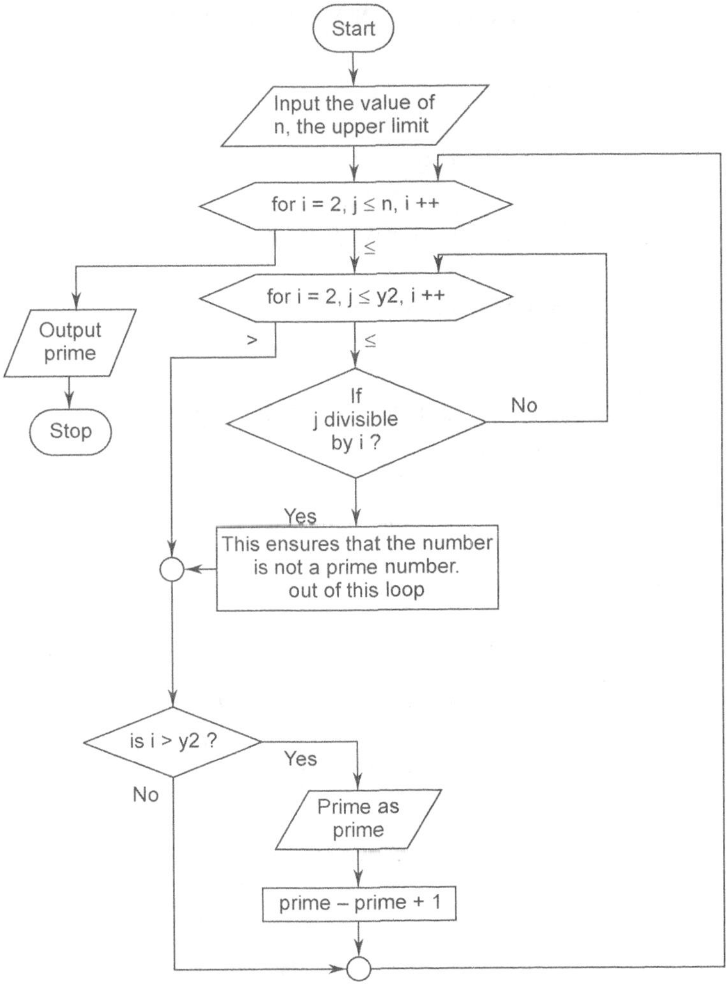

Fig. 10.20 *Flowchart for finding prime number between 1 & N*

Prime Numbers Between 1 and N

```
#include <stdio.h>
#include <math.h>
void main()
{
    int i = 2, n, s = 1, x, pwr = 1, dr;
```

```
float nr = 1, x1, sum;
clrscr();
printf("\n\n\t ENTER THE ANGLE....:");
scanf("%d", &x);
x1 = 3.142 * (x/180.0);
sum = x1;
printf("\n\t ENTER THE NUMBER OF TERMS....:");
scanf("%d", &n);
while(i <=n)
{
       pwr = pwr + 2;
       dr = dr * pwr * (pwr - 1);
       sum = sum + (nr \ dr)* s;
       s = s * (-1);
       nr = nr * x1 * x1;
       i+ = 2;
}
printf("\n\t THE SUM OF THE SINE SERIES IS...%0.3f", sum);
getch();
}
```

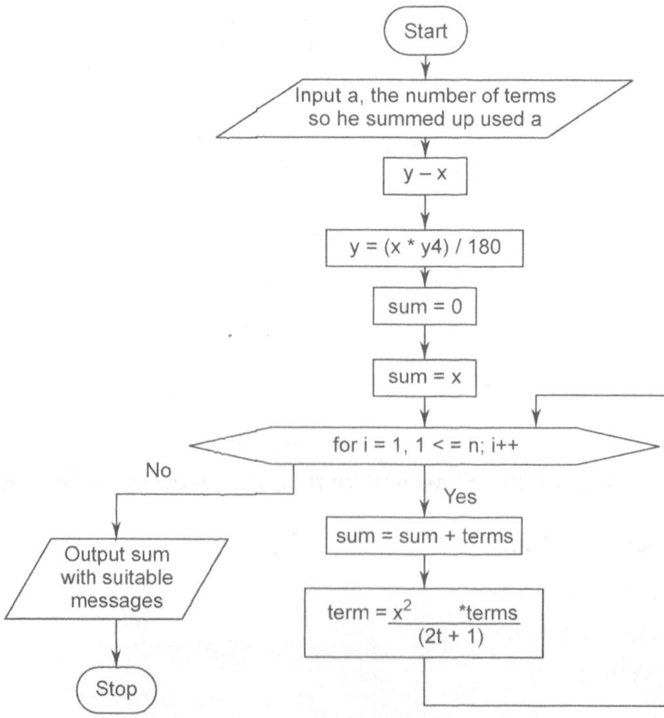

Fig. 10.21 *Flowchart for finding first N terms in the expansion of sine series*

Sum of first N terms in the Expansion of Sine series

```
# include <stdio.h>
# include <conio.h>
# include <math.h>
    void main()
    {
        int n, i ;
        float sum = 0, term, x, y ;
        clrscr();
        printf ("Enter the value of x and n \n"});
        scanf ("%f%d", &x, &n);
        printf ("X = %f\tn = %d\n", x, n);
        y = x ;
        x = x * 3 .14 /180 ;
        term = x ;
        for (i = 1; i <= n ; ++i)
    {
        sum + = term ;
        term * = - x * i / (2 * i * (2 * i + 1)) / i
    }
        printf ("Value of sin (% . F) up to %f terms is %f\n", y, n,
        sum);
        printf ("Value of sin (% . F) using library function < %f\n",
        y, sin (y));
    }
```

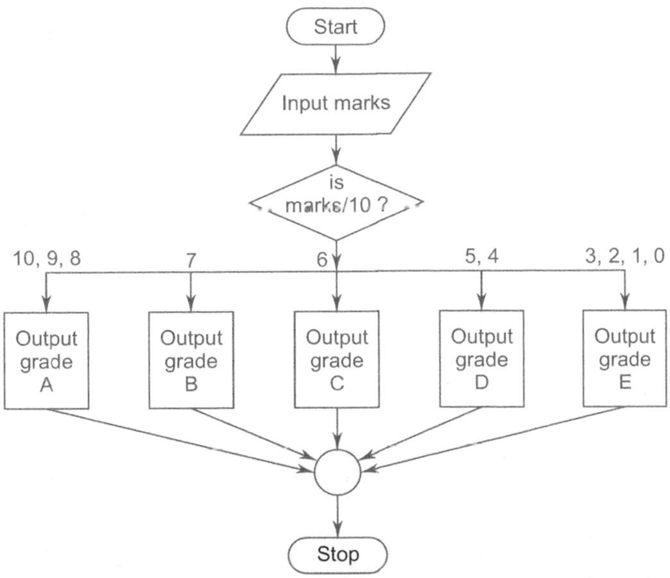

Fig. 10.22 *Flowchart for finding grade based marks i+ + in examination*

Awarding Grades Based on marks Scored in an Examination

```
# include <stdio.h>
# include <conio.h>
    Void main()
    {
        int marks;
        clrscr();
        printf ("Enter the marks\n");
        scanf ("%d", &marks);
        if (marks > 100) exit (1);
        switch (marks/10)
        {
            case 10:
            case 9 :
            case 8 : printf ("Grade is A\n");
                     break ;
            case 7 : printf ("Grade is B\n");
                     break ;
            case 6 : printf ("Grade is C\n");
            case 5 : break ;
            case 4 : printf ("Grade is D\n");
                     break ;
            default: printf ("Grade is E\n");
                     break ;
        }
    }
```

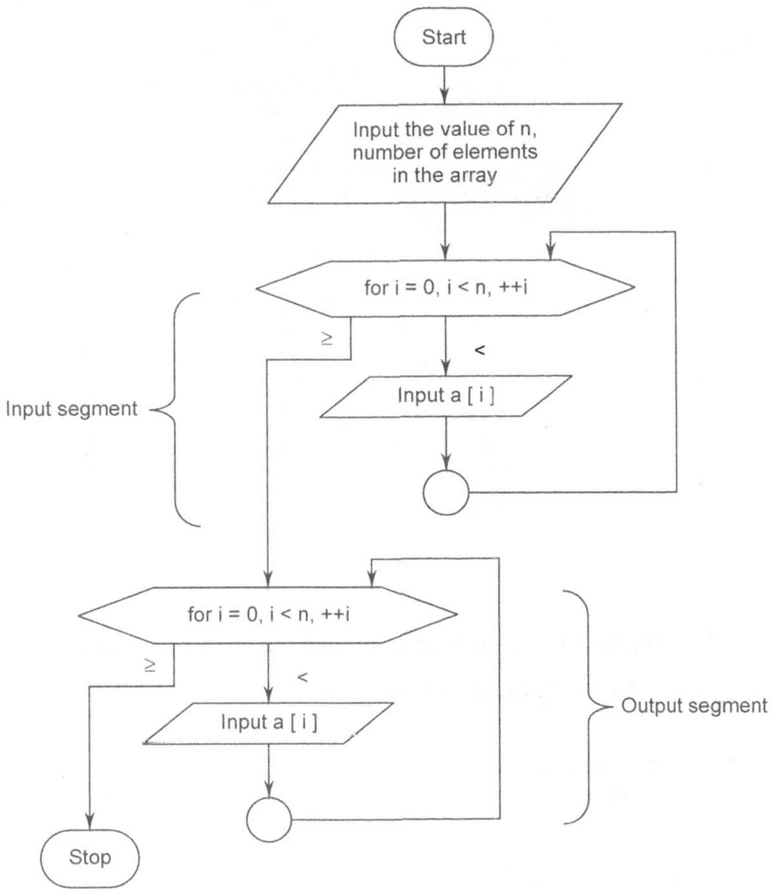

Fig. 10.23 *Flowchart for read and print the 1-Dimensional array*

Reading in an Array and to Print the same (1-Dimensional)

```
# include <stdio.h>
# include <conio.h>
    Void main()
    {
        int a [25], i, n ;
        clrscr();
        printf ("Enter the value of n\n");
        scanf ("%d", &n);
        printf ("\n Size of the array is %d\n\n", n);
        printf ("Enter the elements of the array \n\n");
        for (i = 0 ; i < n ; i++)
        scanf ("%d", * a [i]);
        printf ("\n\t the elements of the array are \n\n");
        For (i = 0, i < n ; i++)
            printf ("\t %d", a [i]);
        }
```

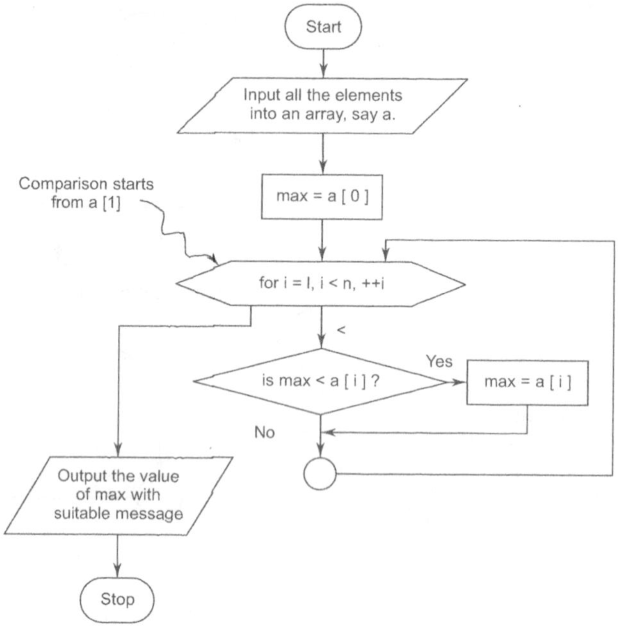

Fig. 10.24 *Flowchart for finding biggest among given 'n' numbers*

Biggest Among given 'n' Integer Numbers

```
# include <stdio.h>
# include <conio.h>
    Void main()
    {
        int a [25], i, n, max ;
        clrscr();
        printf ("Input the value of n \n");
        scanf ("%d", &n);
        printf("Size of the array is %d", n);
        printf ("\n Input the array elements \n");
        for (i = 0; i < n; i ++)
        scanf ("%d", & a [n]);
        printf ("The elements of the array are \n");
        for (i = 0; i < n; i++)
        printf ("%d\t", a\ej);
        Max = a [0]
        for(i=1;i<n;i++)
    {
        if (max < a [i])
    {
        max = a [i] ;
    }
}
    printf ("\n the biggest is %d among the given elements of the
    array", max);
}
```

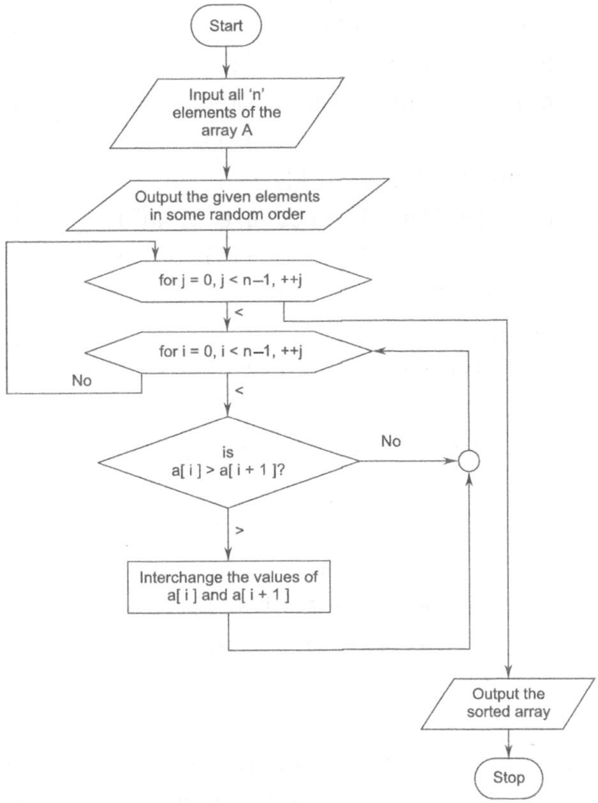

Fig. 10.25 *Flowchart for. sorting 'n' numbers in ascending order using bubble sort*

Sorting 'n' numbers in ascending order using bubble sort

```
# include <conio.h>
# include <stdio.h>
    void main()
    {
        int i, j, n, a [20], temp ;
        clrscr();
        printf ("\n Enter n, number of elements \n");
```

```
scanf ("%d", &n);
printf ("n = %d\n", n);
printf ("Enter the elements \n");
For (i = 0 ; i < n ; ++i)
scanf ("%d", &a [i]);
printf ("\n Elements are : \n");
for (i = 0 ; i < n ; ++i)
printf ("%d\t", a [i] ;
printf ("\n");
for (j = 0 ; j < n - 1 ; ++j)
{
     for (i = 0 ; i < n - 1 ; ++i)
     if (a [i] > a [i + 1]
     {
          temp = a [i] ;
          a [i] = a [i + 1] ;
          a [i + 1] = temp ;
     }
}
          printf ("\n sorted elements are : \n");
          For (i = 0 ; i < n ; ++i)
          printf ("%d\t", a [i]);
          printf ("\n");
}
```

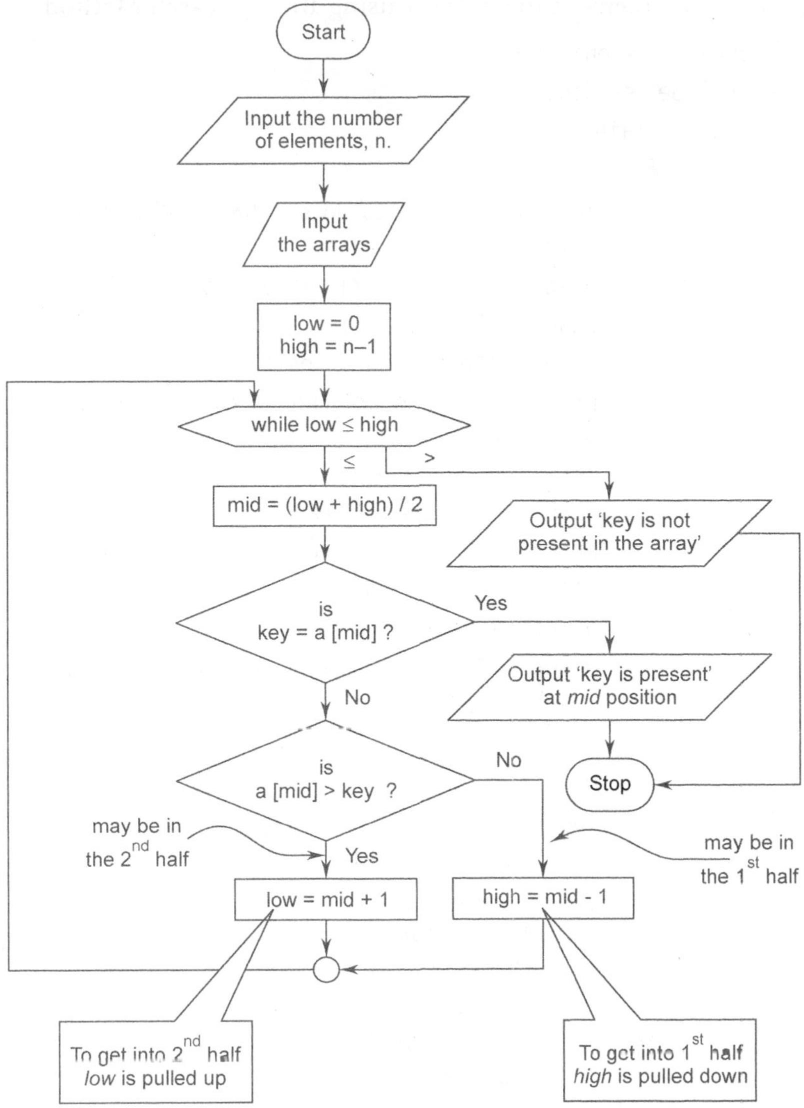

Fig. 10.26 *Flowchart for binary search method*

Searching for a given Element in an Array using Binary search Method

```
# include <conio.h>
# include <stdio.h>
    Void main()
        {
            int i, n, a [20], key, low, high, mid ;
            clrscr();
            printf ("\n\n Enter value for n\n");
            scanf ("%d", &n );
            printf ("n = %d\n", n);
            printf ("\n Enter the elements of array a in ascending
            order \n") ;
            for (i = 0 ; i < n ; i++)
            scanf ("%d", &a [i]);
            printf ("Elements are \n");
            for (i = 0; i < n; ++i)
            printf ("%d\n", a [i]);
            printf ("\n Enter key element to be searched \n");
            scanf ("%d", & key) ;
            printf ("key = %d\n", key) ;
            high = n - 1;
            low = 0;
            while (low <= high)
            {
                mid = (low + high)/2 ;
                if (key == a [mid])
                break;
        else if (key > a[mid])
                low = mid + 1;
                else
                high = mid - 1;
        }
                if (a [mid] == key)
        {
            printf ("Search is successful \n");
            printf ("%d is found in position number %d\n", key mid + 1];
        }
            else
            printf ("Search is unsuccessful, %d is not found \n", key) ;
        }
```

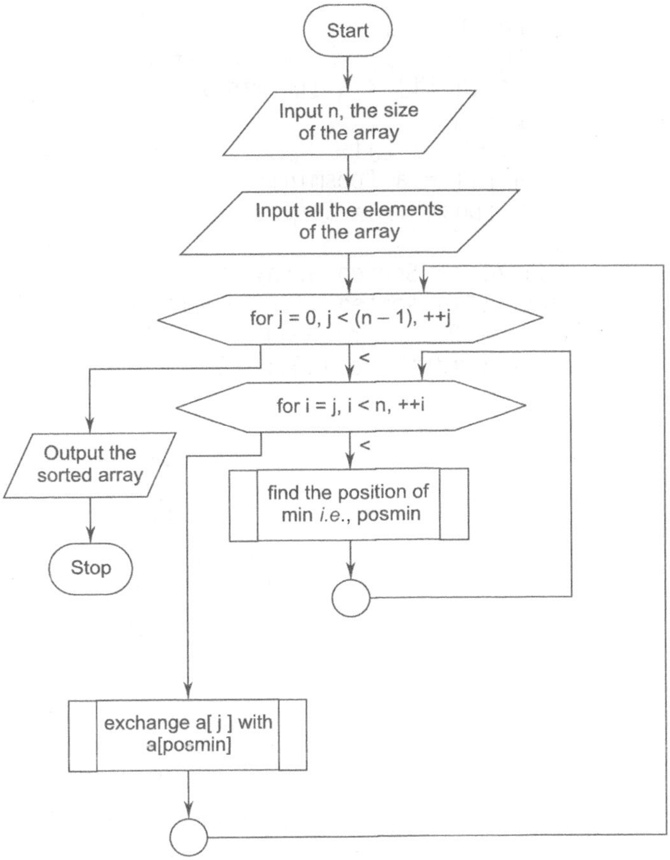

Fig. 10.27 *Flowchart for selection sort*

Sorting the Given set of Elements in Ascending order using Selection Sort

```
# include <stdio.h>
# include <conio.h>
    void main()
    {
          int a [20], n, i, j, posmin, temp ;
          clrscr();
          printf ("Enter the number of elements \n") ;
          scanf ("%d", &n) ;
          printf ("Number of elements = %d\n", n);
          printf ("Enter the elements \n") ;
          for (i = 0; i < n; ++i)
          scanf ("%d", &a [i]);
          printf ("\n Given list of elements \n") ;
          for (i = 0; i < n; ++i)
          printf ("%d\t", a [i]) ;
          for (j = 0; j < n - 1; ++j)
          {
```

```
        posmin = j;
        for (i = j + 1; i < n; ++i)
        if (a [i] < a [posmin])
        posmin = i;
        temp = a [j];
        a [j] = a [posmin];
        a [posmin] = temp;
    }
    /* Printing Sorted array */
    printf ("\n sorted list of elements \n\n") ;
    for (i = 0; i < n; ++i)
    printf ("%d\t", a [i]);
    }
```

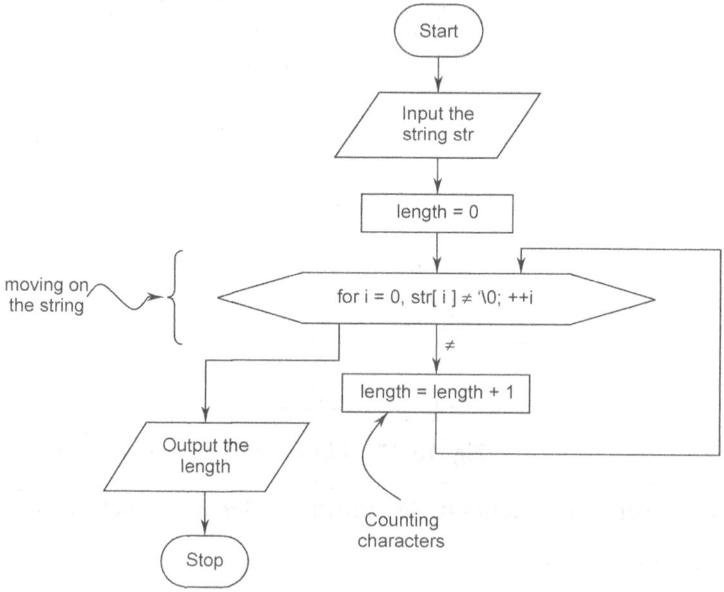

Fig. 10.28 *Flowchart for find the length of given string*

Program to Find the Length of a given String

```
# include < stdio.h>
    void main()
        {
            chrstr [' '];
            int length, i;
            clrscr();
            printf ("Enter a string : \n");
            gets (str);
            length = 0;
            for (i = 0; str [i] ! = '\0'; ++i)
            length ++;
            printf ("The length of the given string is : %d\n" length);
        }
```

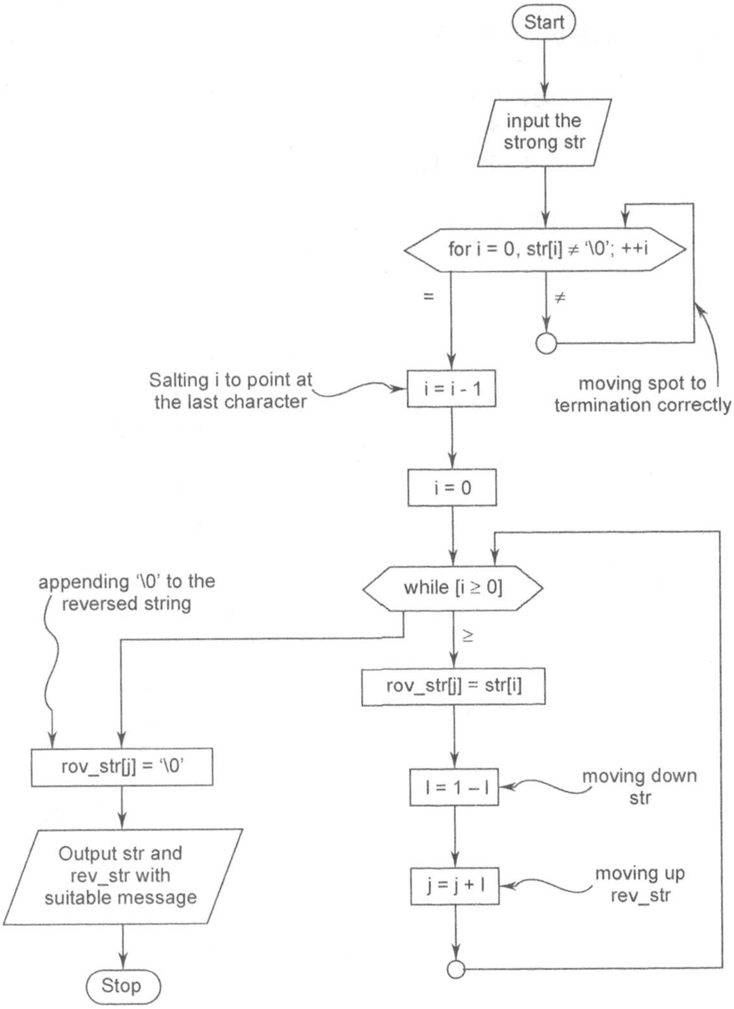

Fig. 10.29 *Flowchart for reserves a given string*

Reversing a Given String

```
# include < stdio.h>
    Void main()
    {
        int i, j;
        char str [' ']. rev_str ['' ];
        clrscr();
        printf ("Input a string : \n");
        gets (str);
        printf ("\n\n the input string is : \n");
        puts (str);
        for (i = 0; str[i] ! '\0', i++) ;
        i = i - 1;
```

```
j = 0;
while (i >= 0)
{
    rev-str [i] = str [i];
    i = i - 1;
    j = j + 1;
}
    [j] = '10;
    printf ("the reverse of the given string is %s", rev-str);
}
```

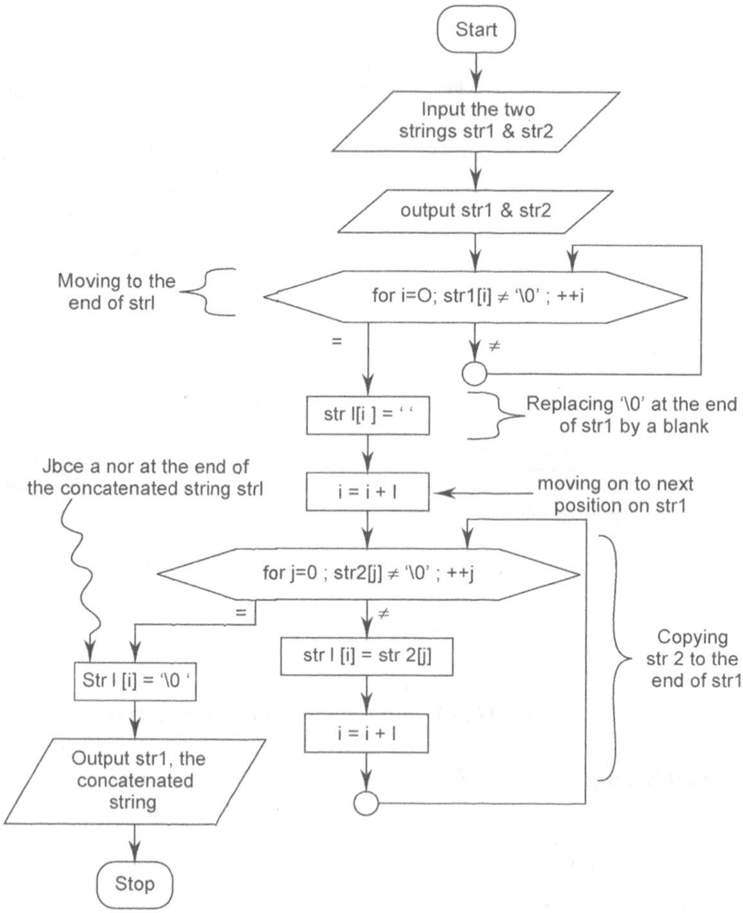

Fig. 10.30 *Flowchart for concatenation of two strings*

Concatenating two Given Strings

```
# include <stdio.h>
    Void main()
    {
        int i,j;
        chrstrl [' '], str2 [' '];
```

```
clrscr();
printf ("Input the first string : \n");
gets (str1);
printf ("first string is : %s\n", str1);
printf ("Input the second string : \n");
gets (str2);
printf ("Second string is : %s\n", str2);
for (i = 0; str1 [i]! = '\0' = i++);
str1 [i] = ' ';
i = i + 1;
for (j = 0; str2 [j]! = '\0'; j++)
    {
        str1 [i] = str2 [j];
        i = i +1;
}
    str1 [i] = '\0';
    printf ("The concatenated string is : %s", str1);
}
```

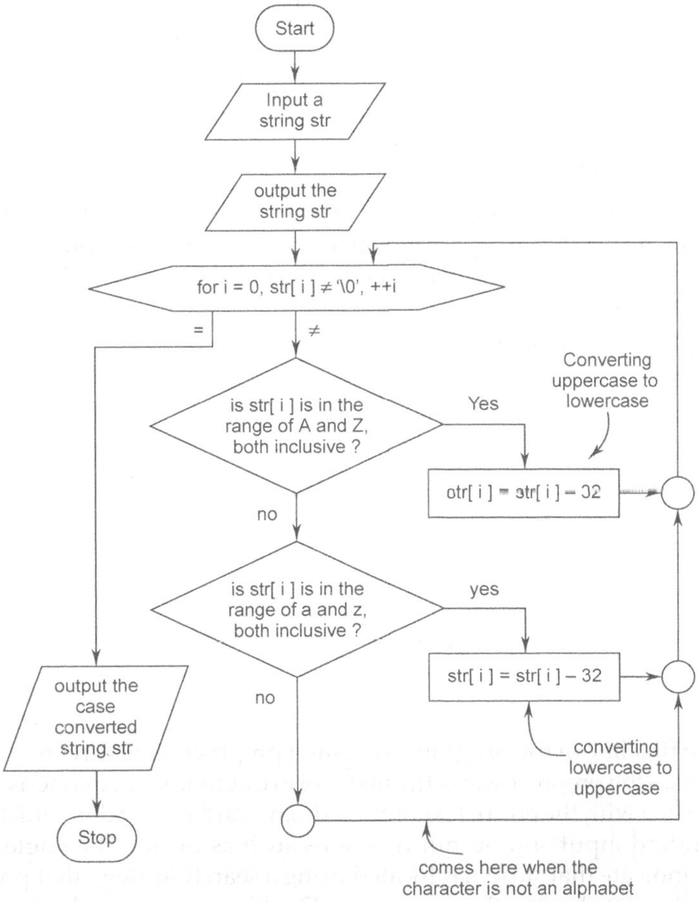

Fig. 10.31 *Flowchart for converting the uppercase alphabets into lower case alphabets*

Converting the Uppercase Alphabets into Lower case Alphabets in a given String

```
# include <stdio.h>
# inlcude <conio.h>
     Void main()
          {
               char str[‘’];
               int i;
               clrscr();
               printf (“\n\n Enter a string \n”);
               gets(str);
               printf (“\n Given string is : %s\n”, str);
               for (i = 0; str [i]! = ‘\0’; i++)
               {
               if (str [i] >= ‘A’ && str [i] <= ‘Z’)
               str [i] = str [i] + 32;
               else if (str[i] >= ‘a’ & & str[i] < = ‘z’)
                    str[i]=str[i]-32;
               }
               printf (“\n case converted string is : %s\n”, str];
          }
```

“Hello, world” example

The “hello, world” example which appeared in the first edition of K&R has become the model for an introductory program in most programming textbooks, regardless of programming language. The program prints “hello, world” to the standard output, which is usually a terminal or screen display.

The original version was:

```
main()
{
    printf(“hello, world\n”);
}
A standard-conforming “hello, world” program is:
#include <stdio.h>
int main(void)
{
    printf(“hello, world\n”);
    return 0;
}
```

The first line of the program contains a preprocessing directive, indicated by #include. This causes the preprocessor—the first tool to examine source code as it is compiled-to substitute the line with the entire text of the stdio.h standard header, which contains declarations for standard input and output functions such as printf. The angle brackets surrounding stdio.h indicate that stdio.h is located using a search strategy that prefers standard headers to other headers having the same name. Double quotes may also be used to include local or project-specific header files.

The next line indicates that a function named main is being defined. The main function serves a special purpose in C programs: The run-time environment calls the main function to begin program execution. The type specifier int indicates that the *return value,* the value that is returned to the invoker (in this case the run-time environment) as a result of evaluating the main function, is an integer. The keyword void as a parameter list indicates that the main function takes no arguments.

The opening curly brace indicates the beginning of the definition of the main function.

The next line *calls* (diverts execution to) a function named printf, which was declared in stdio.h and is supplied from a system library. In this call, the printf function is *passed* (provided with) a single argument, the address of the first character in the string literal "hello, world*n*". The string literal is an unnamed array with elements of type char, set up automatically by the compiler with a final 0-valued character to mark the end of the array (printf needs to know this). The \n is an *escape sequence* that C translates to a *newline* character, which on output signifies the end of the current line. The return value of the printf function is of type int, but it is silently discarded since it is not used. (A more careful program might test the return value to determine whether or not the printf function succeeded.) The semicolon ; terminates the statement.

The *return* statement terminates the execution of the main function and causes it to return the integer value 0, which is interpreted by the run-time system as an exit code indicating successful execution.

The closing curly brace indicates the end of the code for the main function.

DATA STRUCTURES

Chas a static weak typing type system that shares some similarities with that of other ALGOL descendants such as Pascal . There are built-in types for integers of various sizes, both signed and unsigned, floating-point numbers, characters, and enumerated types (enum). C99 added a boolean datatype. There are also derived types including arrays, pointers, records (struct), and untagged unions (union).

C is often used in low-level systems programming where escapes from the type system may be necessary. The compiler attempts to ensure type correctness of most expressions, but the programmer can override the checks in various ways, either by using a *type cast* to explicitly convert a value from one type to another, or by using pointers or unions to reinterpret the underlying bits of a value in some other way.

Pointers

C supports the use of pointers, a very simple type of reference that records, in effect, the address or location of an object or function in memory. Pointers can be *dereferenced* to access data stored at the address pointed to, or to invoke a pointed-to function. Pointers can be manipulated using assignment and also pointer arithmetic. The run-time representation of a pointer value is typically a raw memory address (perhaps augmented by an offset-within-word field), but since a pointer's type includes the type of the thing pointed to, expressions including pointers can be type-checked at compile time. Pointer arithmetic is automatically scaled by the size of the pointed-to data type. (See Array-pointer interchangeability below.) Pointers are used for many different purposes in C. Text strings are commonly manipulated using pointers into arrays of characters. Dynamic memory allocation, which is described below, is performed using pointers. Many data types, such as trees, are commonly implemented as dynamically allocated struct objects linked together using pointers. Pointers to functions are useful for callbacks from event handlers.

A *null pointer* is a pointer value that points to no valid location (it is often represented by address zero). Dereferencing a null pointer is therefore meaningless, typically resulting in a run-time error. Null pointers are useful for indicating special cases such as no *next* pointer in the final node of a linked list, or as an error indication from functions returning pointers.

Void pointers (void *) point to objects of unknown type, and can therefore be used as "generic" data pointers. Since the size and type of the pointed-to object is not known, void pointers cannot be dereferenced, nor is pointer arithmetic on them allowed, although they can easily be (and in many contexts implicitly are) converted to and from any other object pointer type.

Careless use of pointers is potentially dangerous. Because they are typically unchecked, a pointer variable can be made to point to any arbitrary location, which can cause undesirable effects. Although properly-used pointers point to safe places, they can be made to point to unsafe places by using invalid pointer arithmetic; the objects they point to may be deallocated and reused (dangling pointers); they may be used without having been initialized (wild pointers); or they may be directly assigned an unsafe value using a cast, union, or through another corrupt pointer. In general, C is permissive in allowing manipulation of and conversion between pointer types, although compilers typically provide options for various levels of checking. Some other programming languages address these problems by using more restrictive reference types.

Arrays

Array types in C are traditionally of a fixed, static size specified at compile time. (The more recent C99 standard also allows a form of variable-length arrays.) However, it is also possible to allocate a block of memory (of arbitrary size) at run-time, using the standard library's malloc function, and treat it as an array. C's unification of arrays and pointers (see below) means that true arrays and these dynamically-allocated, simulated arrays are virtually interchangeable. Since arrays are always accessed (in effect) via pointers, array accesses are typically *not* checked against the underlying array size, although the compiler may provide bounds checking as an option. Array bounds violations are therefore possible and rather common in carelessly written code, and can lead to various repercussions, including illegal memory accesses, corruption of data, buffer overruns, and run-time exceptions.

C does not have a special provision for declaring multidimensional arrays, but rather relies on recursion within the type system to declare arrays of arrays, which effectively accomplishes the same thing. The index values of the resulting "multidimensional array" can be thought of as increasing in row-major order.

Although C supports static arrays, it is not required that array indices be validated (bounds checking). For example, one can try to write to the sixth element of an array with five elements, generally yielding undesirable results. This type of bug, called a *buffer overflow* or *buffer overrun*, is notorious for causing a number of security problems. Since bounds checking elimination technology was largely nonexistent when C was defined, bounds checking came with a severe performance penalty, particularly in numerical computation. A few years earlier, some Fortran compilers had a switch to toggle bounds checking on or off; however, this would have been much less useful for C, where array arguments are passed as simple pointers.

Multidimensional arrays are commonly used in numerical algorithms (mainly from applied linear algebra) to store matrices. The structure of the C array is well suited to this particular task. However, since arrays are passed merely as pointers, the bounds of the array must be known fixed values or else explicitly passed to any subroutine that requires them, and dynamically sized arrays of arrays cannot be accessed using double indexing. (A workaround for this is to allocate the array with an additional "row vector" of pointers to the columns.)

C99 introduced "variable-length arrays" which address some, but not all, of the issues with ordinary C arrays.

C Programming Language - Data Types

In this tutorial you will learn about C language data types, Primary data type, Integer Type, Floating Point Types, Void Type, Character Type, Size and Range of Data Types on 16 bit machine, derived data type, Declaration of Variables, User defined type declaration, Declaration of Storage Class, auto, static, extern, register, Defining Symbolic Constants, Declaring Variable as Constant and Volatile Variable.

A C language programmer has to tell the system before-hand, the type of numbers or characters he is using in his program. These are data types. There are many data types in C language. A C programmer has to use appropriate data type as per his requirement.

C language data types can be broadly classified as:

Primary data type

Derived data type

User-defined data type

Primary data type

All C Compilers accept the following fundamental data types:

1.	Integer	int
2.	Character	char
3.	Floating Point	float
4.	Double precision floating point	double
5.	Void	void

The size and range of each data type is given in the table below:

Data Type	*Range of Values*
char	–128 to 127
int	–32768 to +32767
float	3.4 e–38 to 3.4 e+38
double	1.7 e–308 to 1.7 e+308

Integer Type

Integers are whole numbers with a machine dependent range of values. A good programming language as to support the programmer by giving a control on a range of numbers and storage space. C has 3 classes of integer storage namely short int, int and long int. All of these data types have signed and unsigned forms. A short int requires half the space than normal integer values. Unsigned numbers are always positive and consume all the bits for the magnitude of the number. The long and unsigned integers are used to declare a longer range of values.

Floating Point Types

Floating point number represents a real number with 6 digits precision. Floating point numbers are denoted by the keyword float. When the accuracy of the floating point number is insufficient, we can use the double to define the number. The double is same as float but with longer precision. To extend the precision further we can use long double which consumes 80 bits of memory space.

Void Type

Using void data type, we can specify the type of a function. It is a good practice to avoid functions that does not return any values to the calling function.

Character Type

A single character can be defined as a character type of data. Characters are usually stored in 8 bits of internal storage. The qualifier signed or unsigned can be explicitly applied to char. While unsigned characters have values between 0 and 255, signed characters have values from –128 to 127.

Size and range of data types on 16 bit machine

Type	*Size (Bits)*	*Range*
Char or Signed Char	8	–128 to 127
Unsigned Char	8	0 to 255
Int or Signed int	16	–32768 to 32767
Unsigned int	16	0 to 65535
Short int or Signed short int	8	–128 to 127
Unsigned short int	8	0 to 255
Long int or signed long int	32	–2147483648 to 2147483647
Unsigned long int	32	0 to 4294967295
Float	32	3.4 e–38 to 3.4 e+38
Double	64	1.7e–308 to 1.7e+308
Long Double	80	3.4 e–4932 to 3.4 e+4932

Declaration of Variables

Every variable used in the program should be declared to the compiler. The declaration does two things.

1. Tells the compiler the variables name.
2. Specifies what type of data the variable will hold.

The general format of any declaration

datatype $v_1, v_2, v_3, \ldots\ldots v_n;$

where v_1, v_2, v_3 are variable names. Variables are separated by commas. A declaration statement must end with a semicolon.

Example:

```
int sum;
int number, salary;
```

Double average, mean;

Datatype	*Keyword Equivalent*
Character	char
Unsigned Character	unsigned char
Signed Character	signed char
Signed Integer	signed int (or) int
Signed Short Integer	signed short int (or) short int (or) short
Signed Long Integer	signed long int (or) long int (or) long
UnSigned Integer	unsigned int (or) unsigned
UnSigned Short Integer	unsigned short int (or) unsigned short
UnSigned Long Integer	unsigned long int (or) unsigned long
Floating Point	float
Double Precision Floating Point	double
Extended Double Precision Floating Point	long double

User defined type declaration

In C language a user can define an identifier that represents an existing data type. The user defined datatype identifier can later be used to declare variables. The general syntax is

```
typedef type identifier;
```

here type represents existing data type and 'identifier' refers to the 'row' name given to the data type.

Example:

```
typedef int salary;
typedef float Average;
```

Here salary symbolizes int and average symbolizes float. They can be later used to declare variables as follows:

```
Units dept1, dept2;
Average section1, section2;
```

Therefore, dept1 and dept2 are indirectly declared as integer datatype and section1 and section2 are indirectly float data type

The second type of user defined datatype is enumerated data type which is defined as follows.

```
Enum identifier {value1, value2 …. value n};
```

The identifier is a user defined enumerated datatype which can be used to declare variables that have one of the values enclosed within the braces. After the definition we can declare variables to be of this 'new' type as below.

```
enum identifier v1,v2,v3,………vn
```

The enumerated variables V1, V2, ….. Vn can have only one of the values value1, value2 ….. value n

Example:

```
enum day {Monday, Tuesday, …. Sunday};
enum day week_st, week_end;
```

```
week_st = Monday;
week_end = Friday;
if(wk_st == Tuesday)
week_en = Saturday;
```

Declaration of Storage Class

Variables in C have not only the data type but also storage class that provides information about their location and visibility. The storage class divides the portion of the program within which the variables are recognized.

auto : It is a local variable known only to the function in which it is declared. Auto is the default storage class.

static : Local variable which exists and retains its value even after the control is transferred to the calling function.

extern : Global variable known to all functions in the file

register : Social variables which are stored in the register.

Defining Symbolic Constants

A symbolic constant value can be defined as a preprocessor statement and used in the program as any other constant value. The general form of a symbolic constant is

```
# define symbolic_name value of constant
```

Valid examples of constant definitions are :

```
# define marks 100
# define total 50
# define PI 3.14159
```

These values may appear anywhere in the program, but must come before it is referenced in the program.

It is a standard practice to place them at the beginning of the program.

Declaring Variable as Constant

The values of some variable may be required to remain constant through-out the program. We can do this by using the qualifier constant at the time of initialization.

Example:

```
constant int class_size = 40;
```

The constant data type qualifier tells the compiler that the value of the int variable class_size may not be modified in the program.

Volatile Variable

A volatile variable is the one whose values may be changed at any time by some external sources.

Example:

```
volatile int num;
```

The value of data may be altered by some external factor, even if it does not appear on the left hand side of the assignment statement. When we declare a variable as volatile the compiler will examine the value of the variable each time it is encountered to see if an external factor has changed the value.

OPERATORS INTRODUCTION

An operator is a symbol which helps the user to command the computer to do a certain mathematical or logical manipulations. Operators are used in C language program to operate on data and variables. C has a rich set of operators which can be classified as

1. Arithmetic Operators
2. Relational Operators
3. Logical Operators
4. Assignment Operators
5. Increments and Decrement Operators
6. Conditional Operators
7. Bitwise Operators
8. Special Operators

1. Arithmetic Operators

All the basic arithmetic operations can be carried out in C. All the operators have almost the same meaning as in other languages. Both unary and binary operations are available in C language. Unary operations operate on a singe operand, therefore the number 5 when operated by unary — will have the value -5.

Arithmetic Operators

Operator	*Meaning*
+	Addition or Unary Plus
–	Subtraction or Unary Minus
*	Multiplication
/	Division
%	Modulus Operator

Examples of arithmetic operators are

```
x + y
x – y
(–x) + y
a * b + c
(–a) * b
```

here a, b, c, x, y are known as operands. The modulus operator is a special operator in C language which evaluates the remainder of the operands after division.

Example:

```
#include<stdian> //include header file stdio.h
void main() //tell the compiler the start of the program
{
int numbl, num2, sum, sub, mul, div, mod; //declaration of variables
```

```
scanf ("%d %d", &num1, &num2); //inputs the operands
sum = num1+num2; //addition of numbers and storing in sum.
printf("\n The sum is = %d", sum); //display the output
sub = num1-num2; //subtraction of numbers and storing in sub.
printf("\n Thu difference is = %d", sub); //display the output
mul = num1*num2; //multiplication of numbers and storing in mul.
printf("\n Thu product is = %d", mul); //display the output
div = num1/num2; //division of numbers and storing in div.
printf("\n Thu division is = %d", div); //display the output
mod = num1%num2; //modulus of numbers and storing in mod.
printf("\n The  modulus is = %d", mod); //display the output
}
```

Integer Arithmetic

When an arithmetic operation is performed on two whole numbers or integers than such an operation is called as integer arithmetic. It always gives an integer as the result. Let $x = 27$ and $y = 5$ be 2 integer numbers. Then the integer operation leads to the following results.

$x + y = 32$
$x - y = 22$
$x * y = 115$
$x \% y = 2$
$x / y = 5$

In integer division the fractional part is truncated.

Floating point arithmetic

When an arithmetic operation is preformed on two real numbers or fraction numbers such an operation is called floating point arithmetic. The floating point results can be truncated according to the properties requirement. The remainder operator is not applicable for floating point arithmetic operands.

Let x = 14.0 and y = 4.0 then

x + y = 18.0
x − y = 10.0
x * y = 56.0
x / y = 3.50

Mixed mode arithmetic

When one of the operand is real and other is an integer and if the arithmetic operation is carried out on these 2 operands then it is called as mixed mode arithmetic. If any one operand is of real type then the result will always be real thus 15/10.0 = 1.5

2. Relational Operators

Often it is required to compare the relationship between operands and bring out a decision and program accordingly. This is when the relational operator come into picture. C supports the following relational operators.

Operator	*Meaning*
<	is less than
<=	is less than or equal to
>	is greater than
>=	is greater than or equal to
==	is equal to
!=	is not equal to

It is required to compare the marks of 2 students, salary of 2 persons, we can compare them using relational operators.

A simple relational expression contains only one relational operator and takes the following form.

```
exp1 relational operator exp2
```

where exp1 and exp2 are expressions, which may be simple constants, variables or combination of them. Given below is a list of examples of relational expressions and evaluated values.

```
6.5 <= 25 TRUE
-65 > 0 FALSE
10 < 7 + 5 TRUE
```

Relational expressions are used in decision-making statements of C language such as if, while and for statements to decide the course of action of a running program.

3. Logical Operators

C has the following logical operators, they compare or evaluate logical and relational expressions.

Operator	*Meaning*
&&	Logical AND
||	Logical OR
!	Logical NOT

Logical AND (&&)

This operator is used to evaluate 2 conditions or expressions with relational operators simultaneously. If both the expressions to the left and to the right of the logical operator is true then the whole compound expression is true.

Example:

```
a>b && x==10
```

The expression to the left is a > b and that on the right is x == 10 the whole expression is true only if both expressions are true *i.e.*, if a is greater than b and x is equal to 10.

Logical OR (||)

The logical OR is used to combine 2 expressions or the condition evaluates to true if any one of the 2 expressions is true.

Example:

```
a < m || a < n
```

The expression evaluates to true if any one of them is true or if both of them are true. It evaluates to true if a is less than either m or n and when a is less than both m and n.

Logical NOT (!)

The logical not operator takes single expression and evaluates to true if the expression is false and evaluates to false if the expression is true. In other words it just reverses the value of the expression.

For example:

! (x >= y) the NOT expression evaluates to true only if the value of x is neither greater than or equal to y.

4. Assignment Operators

The Assignment Operator evaluates an expression on the right of the expression and substitutes it to the value or variable on the left of the expression.

Example:

```
x = a + b
```

Here the value of a + b is evaluated and substituted to the variable x.

In addition, C has a set of shorthand assignment operators of the form.

```
var oper = exp;
```

Here var is a variable, exp is an expression and oper is a C binary arithmetic operator. The operator oper = is known as shorthand assignment operator.

Example:

```
x + = 1 is same as x = x + 1
```

The commonly used shorthand assignment operators are as follows

Shorthand assignment operators

Statement with simple assignment operator	*Statement with shorthand operator*
a = a + 1	a += 1
a = a – 1	a –= 1
a = a * (n+1)	a *= (n+1)
a = a / (n+1)	a /= (n+1)
a = a % b	a %= b

Example for using shorthand assignment operator

```
#define N 100 //creates a variable N with constant value 100
#define A 2 //creates a variable A with constant value 2

void main() //start of the program
{
int a; //variable a declaration
a = A; //assigns value 2 to a

while (a < N) //while value of a is less than N
{ //evaluate or do the following
printf("%d \n",a); //print the current value of a
a *= a; //shorthand form of a = a * a
} //end of the loop
} //end of the program
```

Output

```
2
4
16
```

Arithmetic Expressions

An expression is a combination of variables constants and operators written according to the syntax of C language. In C every expression evaluates to a value *i.e.*, every expression results in some value of a certain type that can be assigned to a variable. Some examples of C expressions are shown in the table given below.

Algebraic Expression	*C Expression*
a x b – c	a * b – c
(m + n) (x + y)	(m + n) * (x + y)
(ab / c)	a * b / c
$3x^2$ +2x + 1	3*x*x+2*x+1
(x / y) + c	x / y + c

Evaluation of Expressions

Expressions are evaluated using an assignment statement of the form

```
Variable = expression;
```

Variable is any valid C variable name. When the statement is encountered, the expression is evaluated first and then replaces the previous value of the variable on the left hand side. All variables used in the expression must be assigned values before evaluation is attempted.

Example of evaluation statements are

```
x = a * b - c
y = b / c * a
z = a - b / c + d;
```

The following program illustrates the effect of presence of parenthesis in expressions.

```
main ()
{
float a, b, c x, y, z;
a = 9;
b = 12;
c = 3;
x = a - b / 3 + c * 2 - 1;
y = a - b / (3 + c) * (2 - 1);
z = a - ( b / (3 + c) * 2) - 1;
printf ("x = %fn",x);
printf ("y = %fn",y);
printf ("z = %fn",z);
}
```

Output

```
x = 10.00
y = 7.00
z = 4.00
```

Precedence in Arithmetic Operators

An arithmetic expression without parenthesis will be evaluated from left to right using the rules of precedence of operators. There are two distinct priority levels of arithmetic operators in C.

High priority * / %

Low priority +, -

Rules for evaluation of expression

- First parenthesized sub expression left to right are evaluated.
- If parenthesis are nested, the evaluation begins with the innermost sub expression.
- The precedence rule is applied in determining the order of application of operators in evaluating sub expressions.
- The associability rule is applied when two or more operators of the same precedence level appear in the sub expression.
- Arithmetic expressions are evaluated from left to right using the rules of precedence.
- When Parenthesis are used, the expressions within parenthesis assume highest priority.

Type conversions in expressions

Implicit type conversion

C permits mixing of constants and variables of different types in an expression. C automatically converts any intermediate values to the proper type so that the expression can be evaluated without loosing any significance. This automatic type conversion is know as implicit type conversion

During evaluation it adheres to very strict rules and type conversion. If the operands are of different types the lower type is automatically converted to the higher type before the operation proceeds. The result is of higher type.

The following rules apply during evaluating expressions

All short and char are automatically converted to int then

1. If one operand is long double, the other will be converted to long double and result will be long double.
2. If one operand is double, the other will be converted to double and result will be double.
3. If one operand is float, the other will be converted to float and result will be float.
4. If one of the operand is unsigned long int, the other will be converted into unsigned long int and result will be unsigned long int.
5. If one operand is long int and other is unsigned int then
   (*a*) If unsigned int can be converted to long int, then unsigned int operand will be converted as such and the result will be long int.
   (*b*) Else both operands will be converted to unsigned long int and the result will be unsigned long int.
6. If one of the operand is long int, the other will be converted to long int and the result will be long int.

7. If one operand is unsigned int the other will be converted to unsigned int and the result will be unsigned int.

Explicit Conversion

Many times there may arise a situation where we want to force a type conversion in a way that is different from automatic conversion.

Consider for example the calculation of number of female and male students in a class

$$\text{Ratio} = \frac{\text{female\_students}}{\text{male\_students}}$$

Since if female_students and male_students are declared as integers, the decimal part will be rounded off and its ratio will represent a wrong figure. This problem can be solved by converting locally one of the variables to the floating point as shown below.

Ratio = (float) female_students / male_students

The operator float converts the female_students to floating point for the purpose of evaluation of the expression. Then using the rule of automatic conversion, the division is performed by floating point mode, thus retaining the fractional part of the result. The process of such a local conversion is known as explicit conversion or casting a value. The general form is

```
(type_name) expression
```

Operator Precedence and Associativity

Each operator in C has a precedence associated with it. The precedence is used to determine how an expression involving more than one operator is evaluated. There are distinct levels of precedence and an operator may belong to one of these levels. The operators of higher precedence are evaluated first.

The operators of same precedence are evaluated from right to left or from left to right depending on the level. This is known as associativity property of an operator.

Arrays are used to store large set of data and manipulate them but the disadvantage is that all the elements stored in an array are to be of the same data type. If we need to use a collection of different data type items it is not possible using an array. When we require using a collection of different data items of different data types we can use a structure. Structure is a method of packing data of different types. A structure is a convenient method of handling a group of related data items of different data types.

```
structure definition:
general format:
struct tag_name
{
data type member1;
data type member2;
...
...
}
```

Example:

```
struct lib_books
{
```

```
char title[20];
char author[15];
int pages;
float price;
};
```

the keyword struct declares a structure to holds the details of four fields namely title, author pages and price. These are members of the structures. Each member may belong to different or same data type. The tag name can be used to define objects that have the tag names structure. The structure we just declared is not a variable by itself but a template for the structure.

We can declare structure variables using the tag name any where in the program. For example the statement,

```
struct lib_books book1,book2,book3;
```

declares book1,book2,book3 as variables of type struct lib_books each declaration has four elements of the structure lib_books. The complete structure declaration might look like this

```
struct lib_books
{
char title[20];
char author[15];
int pages;
float price;
};
struct lib_books, book1, book2, book3;
```

structures do not occupy any memory until it is associated with the structure variable such as book1. the template is terminated with a semicolon. While the entire declaration is considered as a statement, each member is declared independently for its name and type in a separate statement inside the template. The tag name such as lib_books can be used to declare structure variables of its data type later in the program.

We can also combine both template declaration and variables declaration in one statement, the declaration

```
struct lib_books
{
char title[20];
char author[15];
int pages;
float price;
} book1,book2,book3;
is valid. The use of tag name is optional for example
struct
{
...
...
...
}
```

book1, book2, book3 declares book1,book2,book3 as structure variables representing 3 books but does not include a tag name for use in the declaration.

A structure is usually defines before main along with macro definitions. In such cases the structure assumes global status and all the functions can access the structure.

Giving values to members

As mentioned earlier the members themselves are not variables they should be linked to structure variables in order to make them meaningful members. The link between a member and a variable is established using the member operator '.' Which is known as dot operator or period operator.

For example:

```
book1.price
```

Is the variable representing the price of book1 and can be treated like any other ordinary variable. We can use scanf statement to assign values like

```
scanf("%s",book1.file);
scanf("%d",& book1.pages);
```

Or we can assign variables to the members of book1

```
strcpy(book1.title,"basic");
strcpy(book1.author,"E.balagurusamy");
book1.pages=250;
book1.price=28.50;
```

```
/* Example program for using a structure*/
#include< stdio.h>
void main()
{
int id_no;
char name[20];
char address[20];
char combination[3];
int age;
}newstudent;
printf("Enter the student information"),
printf("Now Enter the student id_no");
scanf("%d",&newstudent.id_no);
printf("Enter the name of the student");
scanf("%s",&new student.name);
printf("Enter the address of the student");
scanf("%s",&new student.address);

printf("Enter the combination of the student");
scanf("%d",&new student.combination);

printf("Enter the age of the student");
scanf("%d",&new student.age);
printf("Student information\n");
printf("student id_number=%d\n",newstudent.id_no);
```

```
printf("student name=%s\n",newstudent.name);
printf("student Address=%s\n",newstudent.address);
printf("students combination=%s\n",newstudent.combination);
printf("Age of student=%d\n",newstudent.age);
}
```

Initializing structure

Like other data type we can initialize structure when we declare them. As for initalization goes structure obeys the same set of rules as arrays we initalize the fields of a structure by the following structure declaration with a list containing values for weach fileds as with arrays these values must be evaluate at compile time.

Example:

Struct student newstudent

```
{
12345,
"kapildev"
"Pes college";
"Cse";
19;
};
```

this initializes the id_no field to 12345, the name field to "kapildev", the address field to "pes college" the field combination to "cse" and the age field to 19.

Functions and structures

We can pass structures as arguments to functions. Unlike array names however, which always point to the start of the array, structure names are not pointers. As a result, when we change structure parameter inside a function, we don't effect its corresponding argument.

Passing structure to elements to functions:

A structure may be passed into a function as individual member or a separate variable.

A program example to display the contents of a structure passing the individual elements to a function is shown below.

```
# include < stdio.h >
void main()
{
int emp_id;
char name[25];
char department[10];
float salary;
};

static struct emp1={125,"sampath","operator",7500.00};
/* pass only emp_id and name to display function*/
display(emp1.emp_id,emp1.name);
}
/* function to display structure variables*/
display(e_no,e_name)
```

```
int e_no,e_name;
{
printf("%d%s",e_no,e_name);}
```

in the declaration of structure type, emp_id and name have been declared as integer and character array. When we call the function display() using display(emp1.emp_id,emp1.name); we are sending the emp_id and name to function display(0);

it can be immediately realized that to pass individual elements would become more tedious as the number of structure elements go on increasing a better way would be to pass the entire structure variable at a time.

Passing entire Function to Functions

In case of structures having to having numerous structure elements passing these individual elements would be a tedious task. In such cases we may pass whole structure to a function as shown below:

```
# include stdio.h>
{
int emp_id;
char name[25];
char department[10];
float salary;
};
void main()
{
static struct employee emp1=
{
12,
"sadanand",
"computer",
7500.00
};
/*sending entire employee structure*/
display(emp1);
}
/*function to pass entire structure variable*/
display(empf)
struct employee empf
{
printf("%d%s,%s,%f", empf.empid,empf.name,empf.department,empf.salary);
}
```

Arrays of Structure

It is possible to define a array of structures for example, if we are maintaining information of all the students in the college and if 100 students are studying in the college. We need to use an array than single variables. We can define an array of structures as shown in the following example:

```
structure information
{
int id_no;
char name[20];
char address[20];
char combination[3];
int age;
}
student[100];
```

An array of structures can be assigned initial values just as any other array can. Remember that each element is a structure that must be assigned corresponding initial values as illustrated below.

```
#include< stdio.h >
{
struct info
{
int id_no;
char name[20];
char address[20];
char combination[3];
int age;
}
struct info std[100];
int I,n;
printf("Enter the number of students");
scanf("%d",&n);
printf("Enter Id_no,name address combination age\m");
for(I=0;I < n;I++)
scanf(%d%s%s%s%d",&std[I].id_no,std[I].name,std[I].address,std[I].
combination,&std[I].age);
printf("\n Student information");
for (I=0;I< n;I++)
printf("%d%s%s%s%d\n",
",std[I].id_no,std[I].name,std[I].address,std[I].combination,std[I].age);
}
```

Structure within a Structure

A structure may be defined as a member of another structure. In such structures the declaration of the embedded structure must appear before the declarations of other structures.

```
struct date
{
int day;
int month;
int year;
```

```
};
struct student
{
int id_no;
char name[20];
char address[20];
char combination[3];
int age;
structure date def;
structure date doa;
}oldstudent, newstudent;
```

the structure student contains another structure date as its one of its members.

UNION

Unions like structure contain members whose individual data types may differ from one another. However the members that compose a union all share the same storage area within the computers memory where as each member within a structure is assigned its own unique storage area. Thus unions are used to observe memory. They are useful for application involving multiple members. Where values need not be assigned to all the members at any one time. Like structures union can be declared using the keyword union as follows:

```
union item
{
int m;
float p;
char c;
}
code;
```

this declares a variable code of type union item. The union contains three members each with a different data type. However, we can use only one of them at a time. This is because if only one location is allocated for union variable irrespective of size. The compiler allocates a piece of storage that is large enough to access a union member we can use the same syntax that we use to access structure members. That is

```
code.m
code.p
code.c
```

are all valid member variables. During accessing we should make sure that we are accessing the member whose value is currently stored.

For example a statement such as

```
code.m=456;
code.p=456.78;
printf("%d",code.m);
```

Would produce erroneous result.

In effect a union creates a storage location that can be used by one of its members at a time. When a different number is assigned a new value the new value supercedes the previous members value. Unions may be used in all places where a structure is allowed. The notation for accessing a union member that is nested inside a structure remains the same as for the nested structure.

C BASICS

A Very Simple Program

This program which will print out the message. This is a C program

```
#include <stdio.h>
main()
{
                printf ("This is a C program\n");
}
```

Every C program contains a function called main. This is the start point of the program. #include <stdio.h> allows the program to interact with the screen, keyboard and filesystem of your computer. You will find it at the beginning of almost every C program.
main() declares the start of the function, while the two curly brackets show the start and finish of the function. Curly brackets in C are used to group statements together as in a function, or in the body of a loop. Such a grouping is known as a compound statement or a block.

```
printf ("This is a C program\n");
```

prints the words on the screen. The text to be printed is enclosed in double quotes. The \n at the end of the text cells the program to print a new line as part of the output.

Most C programs are in lower case letters. You will usually find upper case letters used in preprocessor definitions (which will be discussed later) or inside quotes as parts of character strings. C is case sensitive, that is, it recognises a lower case letter and its's upper case equivalent as being different.

Fibonacci Series Using an Array

We have now used a variety the features of C. This final example will introduce the array. The program prints out a table of Fibonacci numbers. These are defined by a series in which any element is the sum of the previous two elements. This program stores the series in an array, and after calculating it, prints the numbers out as a table.

```
#include <stdio.h>
main()
{
                int fib[24];
                int i;
                fib[0] = 0;
                fib[1] = 1;
```

```
for(i = 2; i < 24; i++)
            fib[1] = fib[i-1] + fib[i-2];
            for (i = 0; i < 24; i++)
            printf("%3d %6d\n", i, fib[i]);
}
```

One new construct has been introduced here.

int fib[24];

This defines an array called fib of 24 integers. In C, the array index is bounded by square brackets (this avoids confusion with a function call). Also, the first element of the array has index zero, and for this 24 element array, the last element is index 23.

The C Compiler (cc)

The simplest method is to type

```
cc testprog.c
```

This will try to compile testprog.c, and, if successful, will produce a runnable file called a.out. If you want to give the runnable file a better name you can type

```
cc testprog.c -o testprog
```

This will compile testprog.c, creating runnable file testprog.

VARIABLES

In C, a variable must be declared before it can be used. Variables can be declared at the start of any block of code, but most are found at the start of each function. Most local variables are created when the function is called, and are destroyed on return from that function.

A declaration begins with the type, followed by the name of one or more variables. For example,

```
int high, low, results[20];
```

Declarations can be spread out, allowing space for an explanatory comment. Variables can also be initialised when they are declared, this is done by adding an equals sign and the required value after the declaration.

```
int high = 250;     /* Maximum Temperature */
int low = -40;          /* Minimum Temperature */
int results[20];    /* Series of Temperature readings */
```

C provides a wide range of types. The most common are

```
int An  Integer
float  A floating point (real) number
char   A single byte of memory, enough to hold a character
```

There are also several variants on these types.

```
short           An integer, possibly of reduced range
```

long	An integer, possibly of increased range
unsigned	An integer with no negative range, the spare capacity being used to increase the positive range
unsigned long	Like unsigned, possibly of increased range
double	A double precision floating point number.

All of the integer types plus the char are called the integral types. Float and double are called the real types.

Variable Names

Every variable has a name and a value. The name identifies the variable, the value stores data. There is a limitation on what these names can be. Every variable name in C must start with a letter, the rest of the name can consist of letters, numbers and underscore characters. C recognises upper and lower case characters as being different. Finally, you cannot use any of C's keywords like main, while, switch etc., as variable names.

Examples of legal variable names include :

```
x          result     outfile     bestyet
x1         x2         out_file    best_yet
power      impetus    gamma       hi_score
```

It is conventional to avoid the use of capital letters in variable names. These are used for names of constants.

Global Variables

Local variables are declared within the body of a function, and can only be used within that function. This is usually no problem, since when another function is called, all required data is passed to it as arguments. Alternatively, a variable can be declared globally so it is available to all functions. Modern programming practice recommends against the excessive use of global variables. They can lead to poor program structure, and tend to clog up the available name space.

A global variable declaration looks normal, but is located outside any of the program's functions. This is usually done at the beginning of the program file, but after preprocessor directives. The variable External Variables.

Where a global variable is declared in one file, but used by functions from another, then the variable is called an external variable in these functions, and must be declared as such. The declaration must be preceeded by the word extern. The declaration is required so the compiler can find the type of the variable without having to search through several source files for the declaration.

Global and external variables can be of any legal type. They can be initialised, but the initialisation takes place when the program starts up, before entry to the main function is not declared again in the body of the functions which access it.

Static Variables

Another class of local variable is the static type. A static can only be accessed from the function in which it was declared, like a local variable. The static variable is not destroyed on exit from the function, instead its value is preserved, and becomes available again when the function is next called. Static variables are declared as local variables, but the declaration is preceeded by the word static.

```
static int counter;
```

Static variables can be initialised as normal, the initialisation is performed once only, when the program starts up.

CONSTANTS

A C constant is usually just the written version of a number. For example 1, 0, 5.73, 125e9. We can specify our constants in octal or hexadecimal, or force them to be treated as long integers.

- Octal constants are written with a leading zero - 015.
- Hexadecimal constants are written with a leading 0x - 0x1ae.
- Long constants are written with a trialing L - 890L.

Character constants are usually just the character enclosed in single quotes; 'a', 'b', 'c'. Some characters can't be represented in this way, so we use a 2 character sequence.

```
'\n'     new line
 '\t'    tab
'\\'     backslash
'\'      single quote
'\0'     null (used automatically to terminate character strings).
```

In addition, a required bit pattern can be specified using its octal equivalent.

```
'\044' produces bit pattern 00100100.
```

Character constants are rarely used, since string constants are more convenient. A string constant is surrounded by double quotes *e.g.*, "Brian and Dennis". The string is actually stored as an array of characters. The null character '\0' is automatically placed at the end of such a string to act as a string terminator.

A character is a different type to a single character string. This is important.

We will meet strings and characters again when we deal with the input/output functions in more detail Arrays

An array is a collection of variables of the same type. Individual array elements are identified by an integer index. In C the index begins at zero and is always written inside square brackets.

We have already met single dimensioned arrays which are declared like this

```
int results[20];
```

Arrays can have more dimensions, in which case they might be declared as

```
int  results_2d[20][5];
int  results_3d[20][5][3];
```

Each index has its own set of square brackets.

Where an array is declared in the main function it will usually have details of dimensions included. It is possible to use another type called a pointer in place of an array. This means that dimensions are not fixed immediately, but space can be allocated as required. This is an advanced technique which is only required in certain specialised programs.

When passed as an argument to a function, the receiving function need not know the size of the array. So for example if we have a function which sorts a list (represented by an array) then the function will be able to sort lists of different sizes. The drawback is that the function is unable to determine what size the list is, so this information will have to be passed as an additional argument.

As an example, here is a simple function to add up all of the integers in a single dimensioned array.

```
int add_array(int array[], int size)
{        int i;
         int total = 0;
         for(i = 0; i < size; i++)
                  total += array[i];
         return(total);
}
```

EXPRESSIONS AND OPERATORS

One reason or the power of C is its wide range of useful operators. An operator is a function which is applied to values to give a result. You should be familiar with operators such as +, –,/.

Arithmetic operators are the most common. Other operators are used for comparison of values, combination of logical states, and manipulation of individual binary digits. The binary operators are rather low level for so are not covered here.

Operators and values are combined to form expressions. The values produced by these expressions can be stored in variables, or used as a part of even larger expressions.

Assignment Statement

The easiest example of an expression is in the assignment statement. An expression is evaluated, and the result is saved in a variable. A simple example might look like

```
y = (m * x) + c
```

This assignment will save the value of the expression in variable *y*.

Arithmetic operators

Here are the most common arithmetic operators

```
+ Addition
- Subtraction
* Multiplication
/ Division
% Modulo Reduction (Remainder from integer division)
```

*, / and % will be performed before + or – in any expression. Brackets can be used to force a different order of evaluation to this. Where division is performed between two integers, the result will be an integer, with remainer discarded. Modulo reduction is only meaningful between integers. If a program is ever required to divide a number by zero, this will cause an error, usually causing the program to crash.

Here are some arithmetic expressions used within assignment statements.

```
velocity = distance / time;
force = mass * acceleration;
count = count + 1;
```

C has some operators which allow abbreviation of certain type of arithmetic assignment statements.

Shorthand	Equivalent
`i++; or ++i;`	`i = i + 1;`
`i--; or --i;`	`i = i - 1;`

These operators are usually very efficient. They can be combined with another expression.

```
x = a * b++; is equivalent to    x = a * b;
                                 b = b + 1;
```

Versions where the operator occurs before the variable name change the value of the variable before evaluating the expression, so

```
x = --i * (a + b); is equivalent to i = i - 1;
                                    x = i * (a + b);
```

These can cause confusion if you try to do too many things on one command line. You are recommended to restrict your use of ++ and – to ensure that your programs stay readable.

Another shorthand notation is listed below:

Shorthand	Equivalent
`i += 10;`	`i = i + 10;`
`i -= 10;`	`i = i - 10;`
`i *= 10;`	`i = i * 10;`
`i /= 10;`	`i = i / 10;`

These are simple to read and use.

Type conversion

You can mix the types of values in your arithmetic expressions. char types will be treated as int. Otherwise where types of different size are involved, the result will usually be of the larger size, so a float and a double would produce a double result. Where integer and real types meet, the result will be a double.

There is usually no trouble in assigning a value to a variable of different type. The value will be preserved as expected except where;

- The variable is too small to hold the value. In this case it will be corrupted (this is bad).
- The variable is an integer type and is being assigned a real value. The value is rounded down. This is often done deliberately by the programmer.

Values passed as function arguments must be of the correct type. The function has no way of determining the type passed to it, so automatic conversion cannot take place. This can lead to corrupt results. The solution is to use a method called casting which temporarily disguises a value as a different type.

For example, the function sqrt finds the square root of a double.

```
int i = 256;
int root
root = sqrt( (double) i);
```

The cast is made by putting the bracketed name of the required type just before the value. (double) in this example. This result of sqrt((double) i); is also a double, but this is automatically converted to an int on assignment to root.

Comparison

C has no special type to represent logical or boolean values. It improvises by using any of the integral types char, int, short, long, unsigned, with a value of 0 representing false and any other value representing true. It is rare for logical values to be stored in variables. They are usually generated as required by comparing two numeric values. This is where the comparison operators are used, they compare two numeric values and produce a logical result.

C notation	Meaning
==	Equal to
>	Greater than
<	Less than
>=	Greater than or equal to
<=	Less than or equal to
!=	Not equal to

Note that == is used in comparisons and = is used in assignments. Comparison operators are used in expressions like the ones below.

```
x == y
i > 10
a + b != c
```

In the last example, all arithmetic is done before any comparison is made.

These comparisons are most frequently used to control an if statement or a for or a while loop. These will be introduced in a later chapter.

Logical Connectors

These are the usual And, Or and Not operators.

Symbol	Meaning
&&	And
||	Or
!	Not

They are frequently used to combine relational operators, for example

```
x < 20 && x >= 10
```

In C these logical connectives employ a technique known as lazy evaluation. They evaluate their left hand operand, and then only evaluate the right hand one if this is required. Clearly false && anything is always false, true || anything is always true. In such cases the second test is not evaluated.

Not operates on a single logical value, its effect is to reverse its state. Here is an example of its use.

```
if ( ! acceptable )
        printf("Not Acceptable !!\n");
```

CONTROL STATEMENTS

A program consists of a number of statements which are usually executed in sequence. Programs can be much more powerful if we can control the order in which statements are run.

Statements fall into three general types;

- Assignment, where values, usually the results of calculations, are stored in variables.
- Input / Output, data is read in or printed out.
- Control, the program makes a decision about what to do next.

This section will discuss the use of control statements in C. We will show how they can be used to write powerful programs by;

- Repeating important sections of the program.
- Selecting between optional sections of a program.

The if else Statement

This is used to decide whether to do something at a special point, or to decide between two courses of action.

The following test decides whether a student has passed an exam with a pass mark of 45

```
if (result >= 45)
        printf("Pass\n");
else
        printf("Fail\n");
```

It is possible to use the if part without the else.

```
if (temperature < 0)
        print("Frozen\n");
```

Each version consists of a test, (this is the bracketed statement following the if). If the test is true then the next statement is obeyed. If it is false then the statement following the else is obeyed if present. After this, the rest of the program continues as normal.

If we wish to have more than one statement following the if or the else, they should be grouped together between curly brackets. Such a grouping is called a compound statement or a block.

```
if (result >= 45)
{               printf("Passed\n");
                printf("Congratulations\n")
}
else
                printf("Failed\n");
                printf("Good luck in the resits\n");
}
```

Sometimes we wish to make a multi-way decision based on several conditions. The most general way of doing this is by using the else if variant on the if statement. This works by cascading several comparisons. As soon as one of these gives a true result, the following statement or block is executed, and no further comparisons are performed. In the following example we are awarding grades depending on the exam result.

```
if (result >= 75)
                    printf("Passed: Grade A\n");
else if (result >= 60)
                    printf("Passed: Grade B\n");
else if (result >= 45)
                    printf("Passed: Grade C\n");
else
                    printf("Failed\n");
```

In this example, all comparisons test a single variable called result. In other cases, each test may involve a different variable or some combination of tests. The same pattern can be used with more or fewer else if's, and the final lone else may be left out. It is up to the programmer to devise the correct structure for each programming problem.

The Switch Statement

This is another form of the multi-way decision. It is well-structured, but can only be used in certain cases where;

- Only one variable is tested, all branches must depend on the value of that variable. The variable must be an integral type. (int, long, short or char).
- Each possible value of the variable can control a single branch. A final, catch all, default branch may optionally be used to trap all unspecified cases.

Hopefully an example will clarify things. This is a function which converts an integer into a vague description. It is useful where we are only concerned in measuring a quantity when it is quite small.

```
estimate(number)
int number;
/* Estimate a number as none, one, two, several, many */
{                      switch(number) {
                       case 0 :
                                     printf("None\n");
                                     break;
                       case 1 :
                                     printf("One\n");
                                     break;
                       case 2 :
                                     printf("Two\n");
                                     break;
                       case 3 :
                       case 4 :
                       case 5 :
                                     printf("Several\n");
                                     break;
                       default  :
                                     printf("Many\n");
                                     break;
                       }
}
```

Each interesting case is listed with a corresponding action. The break statement prevents any further statements from being executed by leaving the switch. Since case 3 and case 4 have no following break, they continue on allowing the same action for several values of number.

Both if and switch constructs allow the programmer to make a selection from a number of possible actions.

The other main type of control statement is the loop. Loops allow a statement, or block of statements, to be repeated. Computers are very good at repeating simple tasks many times, the loop is C's way of achieving this.

LOOPS

C gives you a choice of three types of loop, while, do while and for.

- The while loop keeps repeating an action until an associated test returns false. This is useful where the programmer does not know in advance how many times the loop will be traversed.
- The do while loops is similar, but the test occurs after the loop body is executed. This ensures that the loop body is run at least once.
- The for loop is frequently used, usually where the loop will be traversed a fixed number of times. It is very flexible, and novice programmers should take care not to abuse the power it offers.

The while Loop

The while loop repeats a statement until the test at the top proves false.

As an example, here is a function to return the length of a string. *Remember that the string is represented as an array of characters terminated by a null character '\0'.

```
int string_length(char string[])
{                          int i = 0;
                           while (string[i] != '\0')
                                                       i++;
                           return(i);
}
```

The string is passed to the function as an argument. The size of the array is not specified, the function will work for a string of any size.

The while loop is used to look at the characters in the string one at a time until the null character is found. Then the loop is exited and the index of the null is returned. While the character isn't null, the index is incremented and the test is repeated.

The do while Loop

This is very similar to the while loop except that the test occurs at the end of the loop body. This guarantees that the loop is executed at least once before continuing. Such a setup is frequently used where data is to be read. The test then verifies the data, and loops back to read again if it was unacceptable.

```
do
{                         printf("Enter 1 for yes, 0 for no :");
                          scanf("%d", &input_value);
} while (input_value != 1 && input_value != 0)
```

The for Loop

The for loop works well where the number of iterations of the loop is known before the loop is entered. The head of the loop consists of three parts separated by semicolons.

- The first is run before the loop is entered. This is usually the initialisation of the loop variable.
- The second is a test, the loop is exited when this returns false.
- The third is a statement to be run every time the loop body is completed. This is usually an increment of the loop counter.

The example is a function which calculates the average of the numbers stored in an array. The function takes the array and the number of elements as arguments.

```
float average(float array[], int count)
     {                          float total = 0.0;
                                int i;
                                for(i = 0; i < count; i++)
                                                  total += array[i];
                        return(total / count);
}
```

The for loop ensures that the correct number of array elements are added up before calculating the average.

The three statements at the head of a for loop usually do just one thing each, however any of them can be left blank. A blank first or last statement will mean no initialisation or running increment. A blank comparison statement will always be treated as true. This will cause the loop to run indefinitely unless interrupted by some other means. This might be a return or a break statement.

It is also possible to squeeze several statements into the first or third position, separating them with commas. This allows a loop with more than one controlling variable. The example below illustrates the definition of such a loop, with variables hi and lo starting at 100 and 0 respectively and converging.

```
for (hi = 100, lo = 0; hi >= lo; hi--, lo++)
```

The for loop is extremely flexible and allows many types of program behaviour to be specified simply and quickly.

The Break Statement

We have already met break in the discussion of the switch statement. It is used to exit from a loop or a switch, control passing to the first statement beyond the loop or a switch.

With loops, break can be used to force an early exit from the loop, or to implement a loop with a test to exit in the middle of the loop body. A break within a loop should always be protected within an if statement which provides the test to control the exit condition.

The Continue Statement

This is similar to break but is encountered less frequently. It only works within loops where its effect is to force an immediate jump to the loop control statement.

- In a while loop, jump to the test statement.
- In a do while loop, jump to the test statement.
- In a for loop, jump to the test, and perform the iteration.

Like a break, continue should be protected by an if statement. You are unlikely to use it very often.

The goto Statement

C has a goto statement which permits unstructured jumps to be made. Its use is not recommended, so we'll not teach it here. Consult your textbook for details of its use.

FUNCTIONS IN C

Almost all programming languages have some equivalent of the function. You may have met them under the altenrative names subroutine or procedure.

Some languages distinguish between functions which return variables and those which don't. C assumes that every function will return a value. If the programmer wants a return value, this is achieved using the return statement. If no return value is required, none should be used when calling the function.

Here is a function which raises a double to the power of an unsigned, and returns the result.

```
double power (double val, unsigned pow)
{
                        double ret_val = 1.0;
                        unsigned i;
                        for(i = 0; i < pow; i++0
                                    ret_val *= val;
                        return(ret_val);
}
```

The function follows a simple algorithm, multiplying the value by itself pow times. A for loop is used to control the number of multiplications, and variable ret_val stores the value to be returned. Careful programming has ensured that the boundary condition is correct too. *i.e.,*

Let us examine the details of this function.

```
double power(double val, unsigned pow)
```

This line begins the function definition. It tells us the type of the return value, the name of the function, and a list of arguments used by the function. The arguments and their types are enclosed in brackets, each pair separated by commas.

The body of the function is bounded by a set of curly brackets. Any variables declared here will be treated as local unless specifically declared as static or extern types.

```
return(ret_val);
```

On reaching a return statement, control of the program returns to the calling function. The bracketed value is the value which is returned from the function. If the final closing curly bracket is reached before any return value, then the function will return automatically, any return value will then be meaningless.

The example function can be called by a line in another function which looks like this

```
result = power(val, pow);
```

This calls the function power assigning the return value to variable result.

Here is an example of a function which does not return a value.

```
void error_line(int line)
{                  fprintf (stderr, "Error in input data: line %d\n",
                   line);
}
```

The definition uses type void which is optional. It shows that no return value is used. Otherwise the function is much the same as the previous example, except that there is no return statement. Some void type functions might use return, but only to force an early exit from the function, and not to return any value. This is rather like using break to jump out of a loop.

This function also demonstrates a new feature.

```
fprintf(stderr, "Error in input data: line %d\n", line);
```

This is a variant on the printf statement, fprintf sends its output into a file. In this case, the file is stderr, is a special UNIX file which serves as the channel for error messages. It is usually connected to the console of the computer system, so this is a good way to display error messages from your programs. Messages sent to stderr will appear on screen even if the normal output of the program has been redirected to a file or a printer.

The function would be called as below

```
error_line(line_number);
```

Scope of Function Variables

Only a limited amount of information is available within each function. Variables declared within the calling function can't be accessed unless they are passed to the called function as arguments. The only other contact a function might have with the outside world is through global variables.

Local variables are declared within a function. They are created a new each time the function is called, and destroyed on return from the function. Values passed to the function as arguments can also be treated like local variables.

Static variables are slightly different, they don't die on return from the function. Instead their last value is retained, and it becomes available when the function is called again.

Global variables don't die on return from a function. Their value is retained, and is available to any other function which accesses them.

POINTERS IN C

Pointers are not exclusive to functions, but this seems a good place to introduce the pointer type.

Imagine that we have an int called i. Its address could be represented by the symbol &i. If the pointer is to be stored as a variable, it should be stored like this.

```
int *pi = &i;
```

int * is the notation for a pointer to an int. & is the operator which returns the address of its argument. When it is used, as in &i we say it is referencing i.

The opposite operator, which gives the value at the end of the pointer is *. An example of use, known as de-referencing pi, would be

```
i = *pi;
```

Take care not to confuse the many uses of the * sign; Multiplication, pointer declaration and pointer de-referencing.

This is a very confusing subject, so let us illustrate it with an example. The following function fiddle takes two arguments, x is an int while y is a pointer to int. It changes both values.

```
fiddle(int x, int *y)
{           printf(" Starting fiddle: x = %d, y = %d\n", x, *y);
            x ++;
            (*y)++;
            printf("Finishing fiddle: x = %d, y = %d\n", x, *y);
}
```

since *y* is a pointer, we must de-reference it before incrementing its value.

A very simple program to call this function might be as follows.

```
main()
{           int i = 0;
            int j = 0;
            printf(" Starting main : i =, %d, j = %d\n", i, j);
            printf("Calling fiddle now\n");.
            fiddle(i, &j);
            printf("Returned from fiddle\n");
            printf("Finishing main : i = %d, j = %d\n", i, j);
  }
```

Note here how a pointer to int is created using the & operator within the call fiddle (i, & j);.

The result of running the program will look like this.

```
Starting main : i = 0, j = 0
Calling fiddle now
Starting fiddle: x = 0, y = 0
Finishing fiddle: x = 1, y = 1
Returned from fiddle
Finishing main : i = 0, j = 1
```

After the return from fiddle the value of i is unchanged while j, which was passed as a pointer, has changed.

To summarise, if you wish to use arguments to modify the value of variables from a function, these arguments must be passed as pointers, and de-referenced within the function.

Where the value of an argument isn't modified, the value can be passed without any worries about pointers.

ARRAYS AND POINTERS

An array is actually a pointer to the 0th element of the array. Dereferencing the array name will give the 0th element. This gives us a range of equivalent notations for array access. In the following examples, arr is an array.

Array Access	*Pointer Equivalent*
arr[0]	*arr
arr[2]	*(arr + 2)
arr[n]	*(arr + n)

There are some differences between arrays and pointers. The array is treated as a constant in the function where it is declared. This means that we can modify the values in the array, but not the array itself, so statements like arr ++ are illegal, but arr[n] ++ is legal.

Since an array is like a pointer, we can pass an array to a function, and modify elements of that array without having to worry about referencing and de-referencing. Since the array is implemented as a hidden pointer, all the difficult stuff gets done automatically.

A function which expects to be passed an array can declare that parameter in one of two ways.

```
int arr[]; or int *arr;
```

Either of these definitions is independent of the size of the array being passed. This is met most frequently in the case of character strings, which are implemented as an array of type char. This could be declared as char string[]; but is most frequently written as char *string; In the same way, the argument vector argv is an array of strings which can be supplied to function main. It can be declared as one of the following.

```
char **argv; or char *argv[];
```

Don't panic if you find pointers confusing. While you will inevitably meet pointers in the form of strings, or as variable arguments for functions, they need not be used in most other simple types of programs.

Recursive Functions

A recursive function is one which calls itself. This is another complicated idea which you are unlikely to meet frequently. Recursive functions are useful in evaluating certain types of mathematical function. You may also encounter certain dynamic data structures such as linked lists or binary trees. Recursion is a very useful way of creating and accessing these structures.

Here is a recursive version of the Fibonacci function. We saw a non recursive version of this earlier.

```
int fib(int num)
/* Fibonacci value of a number */
{       switch(num)  {
        case 0 :
                        return(0);
                        break;
                case 1:
                        return(1);
                        break;
                default: /* Including recursive calls */
```

```
                        return (fib(num - 1) + fib(num - 2));
                        break;
                }
    }
```

We met another function earlier called power. Here is an alternative recursive version.

```
double power(double val, unsigned pow)
    {
                if(pow == 0) /* pow(x, 0) returns 1 */
                        return(1.0);
                else
                        return(power(val, pow - 1) * val);
    }
```

The definition of fib is interesting, because it calls itself twice when recursion is used. Consider the effect on program performance of such a function calculating the fibonacci function of a moderate size number.

Input Value	*Number of times fib is called*
0	1
1	1
2	3
3	5
4	9
5	15
6	25
7	41
8	67
9	109
10	177

INPUT AND OUTPUT

The same mechanisms can be used to read or write data from and to files. It is also possible to threat character strings in a similar way, constructing or analysing them and storing results in variables. These variants of the basic input and output commands are discussed in the next section. The Standard Input Output File

```
#include <stdio.h>
```

near the start of the program file.

If you do not do this, the compiler may complain about undefined functions or datatypes.

Character Input / Output

This is the lowest level of input and output. It provides very precise control, but is usually too fiddly to be useful. Most computers perform buffering of input and output. This means that they'll not start reading any input until the return key is pressed, and they'll not print characters on the terminal until there is a whole line to be printed.

- getchar
- putchar

getchar

getchar returns the next character of keyboard input as an int. If there is an error then EOF (end of file) is returned instead. It is therefore usual to compare this value against EOF before using it. If the return value is stored in a char, it will never be equal to EOF, so error conditions will not be handled correctly.

As an example, here is a program to count the number of characters read until an EOF is encountered. EOF can be generated by typing Control - d.

```
#include < stdio.h>
main()
{          int ch, i = 0;
           while((ch = getchar ()) != EOF)
                     i ++;
           printf("%d\n", i);
}
```

putchar

putchar puts its character argument on the standard output (usually the screen).

The following example program converts any typed input into capital letters. To do this it applies the function to upper from the character conversion library ctype.h to each character in turn.

```
#include <ctype.h>        /* For definition of toupper */
#include <stdio.h>  /* For definition of getchar, putchar, EOF */
main()
{          int ch;
           while ((ch = getchar()) != EOF)
           putchar(toupper(ch));
}
```

Formatted Input / Output

- printf
- scanf

printf

This offers more structured output than putchar. Its arguments are, in order; a control string, which controls what gets printed, followed by a list of values to be substituted for entries in the control string.

Control String Entry	What Gets Printed
%d	A Decimal Integer
%f	A Floating Point Value
%c	A Character
%S	A Character String

scanf

scanf allows formatted reading of data from the keyboard. Like printf it has a control string, followed by the list of items to be read. However scanf wants to know the address of the items to be read, since it is a function which will change that value. Therefore, the names of variables are preceeded by the & sign. Character strings are an exception to this. Since a string is already a character pointer, we give the names of string variables unmodified by a leading &.

Whole Lines of Input and Output

Where we are not too interested in the format of our data, or perhaps we cannot predict its format in advance, we can read and write whole lines as character strings. This approach allows us to read in a line of input, and then use various string handling functions to analyse it at our leisure.

- gets

gets

gets reads a whole line of input into a string until a newline or EOF is encountered. It is critical to ensure that the string is large enough to hold any expected input lines.

When all input is finished, NULL as defined in stdio.h is returned.

puts

puts writes a string to the output, and follows it with a newline character.

Example: Program which uses gets and puts to double space typed input.

```
#include <stdio.h>
main()
{
        char line[256]; /* Define string sufficiently large to
        store a line of input */
        while(gets(line) != NULL)     /* Read line        */
        {   puts(line);               /* Print line       */
            printf("\n");             /* Print blank line */
        }
```

Note that putchar, printf and puts can be freely used together. So can getchar, scanf and gets.

C File Handling - File Pointers

C communicates with files using a new datatype called a file pointer. This type is defined within stdio.h, and written as FILE*. A file pointer called output_file is declared in a statement like

```
FILE *output_file;
```

Opening a file pointer using fopen

Your program must open a file before it can access it. This is done using the fopen function, which returns the required file pointer. If the file cannot be opened for any reason then the value NULL will be returned. You will usually use fopen as follows

```
if ((output_file = fopen("output_file", "w")) == NULL)
        fprintf(stderr, "Cannot open %s\n", "output_file");
```

fopen takes two arguments, both are strings, the first is the name of the file to be opened, the second is an access character, which is usually one of:

```
"r" Open file for reading
"w" Create file for writing
"a" Open file for appending
```

As usual, use the man command for further details by typing man fopen.

Closing a file using fclose

The fclose command can be used to disconnect a file pointer from a file. This is usually done so that the pointer can be used to access a different file. Systems have a limit on the number of files which can be open simultaneously, so it is a good idea to close a file when you have finished using it.

This would be done using a statement like

```
fclose(output_file);
```

If files are still open when a program exits, the system will close them for you. However, it is usually better to close the files properly.

Input and Output using file pointers

Having opened a file pointer, you will wish to use it for either input or output. C supplies a set of functions to allow you to do this. All are very similar to input and output functions that you have already met.

Character Input and Output with Files

This is done using equivalents of getchar and putchar which are called getc and putc. Each takes an extra argument, which identifies the file pointer to be used for input or output.

```
putchar(c) is equivalent to putc(c, stdout)
getchar() is equivalent to getc(stdin)
```

Formatted Input Output

```
with File Pointers
```

Similarly there are equivalents to the functions printf and scanf which read or write data to files. These are called fprintf and fscanf. You have already seen fprintf being used to write data to stderr.

The functions are used in the same way, except that the fprintf and fscanf take the file pointer as an additional first argument.

Formatted Input Output with Strings

These are the third set of the printf and scanf families. They are called sprintf and sscanf.

sprintf puts formatted data into a string which must have sufficient space allocated to hold it. This can be done by declaring it as an array of char. The data is formatted according to a control string of the same form as that for printf.

sscanf takes data from a string and stores it in other variables as specified by the control string. This is done in the same way that scanf reads input data into variables.

sscanf is very useful for converting strings into numeric v values.

Whole Line Input and Output using File Pointers

Predictably, equivalents to gets and puts exist called fgets and fputs. The programmer should be careful in using them, since they are incompatible with gets and puts, gets requires the programmer to specify the maximum number of characters to be read. fgets and fputs retain the trailing newline character on the line they read or write, whereas gets and puts discard the newline.

When transferring data from files to standard input/output channels, the simplest way to avoid incompatibility with the newline is to use fgets and fputs for files and standard channels too.

For example, read a line from the keyboard using

```
fgets(data_string, 80, stdin);
```

and write a line to the screen using

```
fputs(data_string, stdout);
```

EOF, The End of File Marker

EOF is a character which indicates the end of a file. It is returned by read commands of the getc and scanf families when they try to read beyond the end of a file.

Other String Handling Functions

As well as sprintf and sscanf, the UNIX system has a number of other string handling functions within its libraries. A number of the most useful ones are contained in the <strings.h> file, and are made available by putting the line

```
#include <strings.h>
```

near to the head of your program file.

A couple of the functions are described below.

```
strcpy(str1, str2)  copies str2 into str1.
strcmp(str1, str2)  compares the contents of str1 and str2. Returns
                    0 (false) if both are equal.
```

A full list of these functions can be seen using the man command by typing.

```
man 3 strings
```

STRUCTURES IN C

A structure is a collection of variables under a single name. These variables can be of different types, and each has a name which is used to select it from the structure. A structure is a convenient way of grouping several pieces of related information together.

A structure can be defined as a new named type, thus extending the number of available types. It can use other structures, arrays or pointers as some of its members, though this can get complicated unless you are careful.

Defining a Structure

A structure type is usually defined near to the start of a file using a typedef statement.

typedef defines and names a new type, allowing its use throughout the program. typedefs usually occur just after the #define and #include statements in a file.

Here is an example structure definition.

```
typedef   struct {
                      char  name[64];
                      char  course[128];
                      int  age;
                      int  year;
} student;
```

This defines a new type student variables of type student can be declared as follows.

```
student  st_rec;
```

Notice how similar this is to declaring an int or float.

The variable name is st_rec, it has members called name, course, age and year.

Accessing Members of a Structure

Each member of a structure can be used just like a normal variable, but its name will be a bit longer. To return to the examples above, member name of structure st_rec will behave just like a normal array of char, however we refer to it by the name.

```
st_rec.name
```

Here the dot is an operator which selects a member from a structure.

Where we have a pointer to a structure we could dereference the pointer and then use dot as a member selector. This mehod is a little clumsy to type. Since selecting a member from a structure pointer happens frequently, it has its own operator -> which acts as follows.

Assume that st_ptr is a pointer to a structure of type student. We would refer to the name member as

```
st_ptr -> name
```

Structures as Function Arguments

A structure can be passed as a function argument just like any other variable. This raises a few practical issues.

Where we wish to modify the value of members of the structure, we must pass a pointer to that structure. This is just like passing a pointer to an int type argument whose value we wish to change.

If we are only interested in one member of a structure, it is probably simpler to just pass that member. This will make for a simpler function, which is easier to re-use. Of course if we wish to change the value of that member, we should pass a pointer to it.

When a structure is passed as an argument, each member of the structure is copied. This can prove expensive where structures are large or functions are called frequently. Passing and working with pointers to large structures may be more efficient in such cases.

Further Uses of Structures

As we have seen, a structure is a good way of storing related data together. It is also a good way of representing certain types of information. Complex numbers in mathematics inhabit a two dimensional plane (stretching in real and imaginary directions). These could easily be represented here by

```
typedef   struct {
                      double real;
                      double imag;
} complex;
```

THE C PREPROCESSOR

The C preprocessor is a tool which filters your source code before it is compiled. The preprocessor allows constants to be named using the #define notation. The preprocessor provides several other facilities which will be described here. It is particularly useful for selecting machine dependent pieces of code for different computer types, allowing a single program to be compiled and run on several different computers.

Using #define to Implement Constants

We have already met this facility, in its simplest form it allows us to define textual substitutions as follows.

```
#define MAXSIZE 256
```

This will lead to the value 256 being substituted for each occurrence of the word MAXSIZE in the file.

Using #define to Create Functional Macros

define can also be given arguments which are used in its replacement. The definitions are then called macros. Macros work rather like functions, but with the following minor differences.

- Since macros are implemented as a textual substitution, there is no effect on program performance (as with functions).
- Recursive macros are generally not a good idea.
- Macros don't care about the type of their arguments. Hence, macros are a good choice where we might want to operate on reals, integers or a mixture of the two. Programmers sometimes call such type flexibility polymorphism.
- Macros are generally fairly small.

Macros are full of traps for the unwary programmer. In particular the textual substitution means that arithmetic expressions are liable to be corrupted by the order of evaluation rules.

Here is an example of a macro which won't work.

```
#define DOUBLE(x) x+x
```

Now if we have a statement

```
a = DOUBLE(b) * c;
```

This will be expanded to

```
a = b+b * c;
```

And since * has a higher priority than +, the compiler will treat it as.

```
a = b + (b * c);
```

The problem can be solved using a more robust definition of DOUBLE

```
#define DOUBLE(x) (x + x)
```

Here the brackets around the definition force the expression to be evaluated before any surrounding operators are applied. This should make the macro more reliable.

In general it is better to write a C function than risk using a macro.

Reading in Other Files using #include

The preprocessor directive #include is an instruction to read in the entire contents of another file at that point. This is generally used to read in header files for library functions. Header files contain details of functions and types used within the library. They must be included before the program can make use of the library functions.

Library header file names are enclosed in angle brackets, <>. These tell the preprocessor to look for the header file in the standard location for library definitions. This is /usr/include for most UNIX systems.

For example:

```
#include <stdio.h>
```

PRECEDENCE OF C OPERATORS

The following table shows the precedence of operators in C. Where a statement involves the use of several operators, those with the lowest number in the table will be applied first.

<table>
<tr><th></th><th>Description</th><th>Represented By</th></tr>
<tr><td>1</td><td>Parenthesis</td><td>()</td></tr>
<tr><td>1</td><td>Structure Access</td><td>- -></td></tr>
<tr><td>2</td><td>Unary</td><td>! - ++ -- - * &</td></tr>
<tr><td>3</td><td>Multiply, Divide, Modulus</td><td>* / %</td></tr>
<tr><td>4</td><td>Add, Subtract</td><td>+ -</td></tr>
<tr><td>5</td><td>Shift Right, Left</td><td>>> <<</td></tr>
<tr><td>6</td><td>Greater, Less Than, etc</td><td>> < =</td></tr>
<tr><td>7</td><td>Equal, Not Equal</td><td>== !=</td></tr>
<tr><td>8</td><td>Bitwise AND</td><td>&</td></tr>
<tr><td>9</td><td>Bitwise Exclusive OR</td><td>^</td></tr>
<tr><td>10</td><td>Bitwise OR</td><td>|</td></tr>
<tr><td>11</td><td>Logical AND</td><td>&&</td></tr>
<tr><td>12</td><td>Logical OR</td><td>||</td></tr>
<tr><td>13</td><td>Conditional Expression</td><td>?:</td></tr>
<tr><td>14</td><td>Assignment</td><td>= += -= etc</td></tr>
<tr><td>15</td><td>Comma</td><td>,</td></tr>
</table>

Some of these operators have not been described in this course, consult a textbook if you want details about them.

Special Characters

The following special patterns are used to represent a single character in C programs. The leading backslash in the single quotes indicates that more information is to follow.

C code	Meaning
'\014'	Bit pattern for Form Feed
'\n'	Newline
'\t'	Tab
'\\'	Backslash
'\' '	Single Quote
'\" '	Double Quote
'\b'	Backspace
'\r'	Carriage Return
'\f'	Form Fed
'\0'	NULL (String Terminator)

C Language Keywords

The following names are reserved by the C language. Their meaning is already defined, and they cannot be re-defined to mean anything else.

auto	break	case	char	continue	default
do	double	else	enum	exterm	float
for	goto	if	int	long	register
return	short	sizeof	static	struct	switch
typedef	union	unsigned	void	while	

Other than these names, you can choose any names of reasonable length for variables, functions etc. The names must begin with a letter or underscore (letters are better) and then can contain letters, numbers and underscores.

ENCLOSURE

List of Laboratory Exercises

1. **Algorithms:**
   1. Determine average of given three numbers.
   2. Determine area and perimeter of a rectangle, while length a and width b are given.
   3. Find area of triangle, while its side a, b and c are given.
   4. Determine largest number among given three nos.
   5. Determine roots of a quadratic equation.
2. **C Programming Basics:**
   1. Average of two numbers.
   2. Calculate perimeter and area of triangle.
   3. Convert the temperature from Fahrenheit to the corresponding Centigrade.
3. **Control Structures:**
   1. Determine roots of a quadratic equation.
   2. Determine largest of given three numbers.
4. **Loops:**
   1. Prints out the numbers from 1 to 10 each on separate line.
   2. Sum and average of indefinite number of the number indicate end of data with 0.
   3. The sum of first n numbers 1 + 2 + 3 ... + n using do while.
   4. Sum up the series $1 + 2^2 + 3^2 + 4^2 + ... + n^2$ while n is input.
   5. Sum up the series $1 + X + X^2 + X^3 + ... + X^n$ while n and X are input.
   6. Print numbers in given shape.
   7. Create a given shape using for loop.
   8. Create a given shape using while loop.
   9. Reverse digits of number.
   10. Generate N terms of a Fibonacci Series
5. **Functions:**
   1. Function to calculate average of two nos.
   2. Write function is leap year and use it to determine if a given year is a leap year.
   3. Write a function which determine if a number is prime number, use this function to print first 10 prime number.
   4. Calculate factorial of a given number N using recursion.

6. **Arrays:**
    1. Write a program which reads in n (at most 10) positive values into an array and output maximum among them.
    2. Write a program which reads in n (at most 10) values into an array and outputs sum and average of these values.
    3. Write a program which reads in Roll no. and marks of n students of a class (at most 10) and output roll no and marks of students having marks less than their average.
    4. Write function to read, print bubble sort and uses them to sort an array.
    5. Write function to add two matrices.
    6. Write a function to compute product c of two matrices a, b.
7. **Pointers:**
    1. Swap function using pointers.
    2. Write a program which reads in arrays using pointers and calculate its sum by accessing through pointers.
8. **Strings:**
    1. Read a name and output it in uppercase.
    2. Function to copy a string into another string.
    3. Function to reverse a string.
    4. Function which takes two string as parameter and concatenate (appends) second string to first string.
    5. Program to find the Palindrome of a given string.
    6. Function to c compares the two strings.
    7. Function to find the length of a string.
    8. Read a name and output it in lowercase.
9. **Structures and Union:**
    1. Using structures input name and marks in three subjects of students, calculate percentage marks and output the same.
10. **File handling:**
    1. Read a line from a file.
    2. Converts a file into uppercase.

(*Ashish Kumar Sharma*)

Lecturer,

Deptt. of CSE & I.T ., PCE, Kota

Programming Exercises

Q.1. *Program to calculate the area of a triangle using both the methods.*

```
#include<stdio.h>
#include<conio.h>
#include<math.h>
#include<process.h>
void main()
{
float a,b,c,h,s,area;
```

```
char  ch1,ch2;
clrscr();
printf("Do you know the measure of height of triangle? (y/n)");
ch1 = getche();
if(ch1 == 'y' || ch1 == 'Y')
   {
   printf("\n Do you know base length? (y/n)");
   ch2 = getche();
   if(ch2 == 'y' || ch2 == 'Y')
      {
      printf("\n\n Enter the height: ");
      scanf("%f", &h);
      printf("\n Enter the base length: ");
      scanf("%f", &a);
      area = (a * h)/2;
      printf("\n\n Area of triangle = %f sq. units", area);
      }
   else
      printf("\n\n Data insufficient to calculate the area of
      triangle");
   }
else
   {
   printf("\n Do you know the measure of all three sides? (y/n)");
   ch1 = getche();
   if(ch1 == 'y' || ch1 == 'Y')
         {
         printf("\n\n Enter 1st side: ");
         scanf("%f", &a);
         printf("\n Enter 2nd side: ");
         scanf("%f", &b);
         printf("\n Enter 3rd side: ");
         scanf("%f", &c);
         s = (a + b + c)/2;
         area = sqrt(s * (s - a) * (s - b) * (s - c));
         if(area <= 0)
                  {
                  printf("\n\n Triangle not feasible");
                  getch();
                  exit(0);
                  }
         printf("\n\n Area of triangle = %f sq. units", area);
         }
      else
```

```
            printf("\n\n Data insufficient to calculate the area of
            triangle");
        }
getche();
}
```

OUTPUT:

Do you know the measure of height of triangle? (y/n)Y

Do you know base length? (y/n)Y

Enter the height: 12

Enter the base length: 24

Area of triangle = 144.000000 sq. units

Q.2. *Program to calculate Gross Salary.*
Given:

Gross Salary = 20% HRA + 60% DA + Basic Salary

```
#include<stdio.h>
#include<conio.h>
void main()
{
float gross, basic, hra, da;
clrscr();
printf("Enter your Basic salary: ");
scanf("%f", &basic);
printf("\n Enter your HRA: ");
scanf("%f", &hra);
printf("\n Enter your DA: ");
scanf("%f", &da);
gross = basic + (hra * 0.20) + (da * 0.60);
printf("\n\n Your Gross Salary is: %f", gross);
getch();
}
```

OUTPUT:

Enter your Basic salary: 1000

Enter your HRA: 200

Enter your DA: 100

Your Gross Salary is: 1100.000000

Q.3. *Program to calculate area and circumference of a circle.*

```
#include<stdio.h>
#include<conio.h>
void main()
{
float r, area, circum;
```

```
clrscr();
printf("Enter the radius of the circle: ");
scanf("%f", &r);
printf("\n\n Area of the circle is: %f", 3.14 * r * r);
printf("\n\n Circumference of the circle is: %f", 2 * 3.14 * r);
getch();
}
```

OUTPUT:

Enter the radius of the circle: 5

Area of the circle is: 78.500000

Circumference of the circle is: 31.400000

Q.4. *Program to calculate Simple Interest.*

```
#include<stdio.h>
#include<conio.h>
void main()
{
float p, r, t, si;
clrscr();
printf("Enter the principle amount: ");
scanf("%f", &p);
printf("\n Enter rate per annum: ");
scanf("%f", &r);
printf("\n Enter time in years: ");
scanf("%f", &t);
printf("\n\n The Simple Interest on %f amount for %f years\n", p, t);
printf("at a rate of %f percent per annum is: %f", r, (p * r * t)/100);
getch();
}
```

OUTPUT:

Enter the principle amount: 2000

Enter rate per annum: 2

Enter time in years: 3

The Simplest Interest on 2000.000000 amount for 3.000000 years at a rate of 2.000000 percent per annum is: 120.000000

Q.5. *Convert Centrigrade to Fahrenheit*

```
#include<stdio.h>
#include<conio.h>
void main()
{
float c, f;
clrscr();
printf("Enter the temperature in Centigrade: ");
```

```
scanf("%f", &c);
f = (9/5) * c + 32;
printf("\n\n Temperature in Fahrenheit is: %f", f);
getch();
}
```

OUTPUT:

Enter the temperature in Centigrade: 30

Temperature in Fahrenheit is: 62.000000

Q.6. *Program to find the roots of a quadratic equation.*

```
#include<stdio.h>
#include<conio.h>
#include<math.h>
#include<process.h>
void main()
{
int a, b, c;
float x1, x2, temp, discr;
clrscr();
printf("Enter the coefficient of x * x: ");
scanf("%d", &a);
printf("\n Enter the coefficient of x: ");
scanf("%d", &b);
printf("\n Enter the constant term: ");
scanf("%d", &c);
discr = b * b - 4 * a * c;
if(discr<0)
   {
   printf("\n\n Roots are Imaginary and thus can't be displayed.");
   getch();
   exit(0);
   }
else
   {
   x1 = (– b + sqrt(discr))/2;
   x2 = (– b – sqrt(discr))/2;
   printf("\n\n Roots are: %f & %f", x1, x2);
   }
getch();
}
```

OUTPUT:

Enter the coefficient of x * x: 1

Enter the coefficient of x: –2

Enter the constant term: 1

Roots are: 1.000000 & 1.000000

Q.7. *To find the factorial of a given number*

```
#include<stdio.h>
#include<conio.h>
void main()
{
int n, i, fact = 1;
clrscr();
printf("Enter the number whose factorial is to be known/n");
scanf("%d", &n);
for(i = n; i > 0; i--)
fact = fact * i;
printf("Factorial = %d", fact);
getch();
}
```

OUTPUT:

Enter the number whose factorial is to be known 5

Factorial = 20

Q.8. *To find the sum of the digits of a number*

```
#include<stdio.h>
#include<conio.h>
void main()
{
int n, x, sum = 0;
clrscr();
printf("Enter the number sum of whose digits is to be found\n");
scanf("%d", &n);
while(n > 0)
    {
    x = n%10;
    n = n/10;
    sum = sum + x;
    }
printf("Sum = %d", sum);
getch();
}
```

OUTPUT:

Enter the number sum of whose digits is to be found 1632

Sum = 12

Q.9. *WAP to reverse a number.*

```
#include<stdio.h>
#include<conio.h>
void main()
{
```

```
int num, rev, q, r;
clrscr();
printf("Enter the number :");
scanf("%d", &num);
fflush(stdin);
rev = 0;
for(q = num; q; q = q/10)
{
r = q%10;
rev = rev * 10 + r;
}
printf("\n The reverse of %d is %d", num, rev);
getch();
}
```

OUTPUT:

Enter the number : 1234

The reverse of 1234 is 4321

Q.10. *WAP to print Fibonacci Series.*

```
#include<stdio.h>
#include<conio.h>
void main()
{
int a = 1, b = 1, c, n, i;
clrscr();
printf("Enter number of steps:");
scanf("%d", &n);
printf("%d %d ", a, b);    //We print first two numbers manually
for(i = 0; i < n - 2; i++) //Other numbers are printed through this
                             loop
        {
        c = a + b;
        a = b;
        b = c;
        printf("%d ", c);
        }
getch();
}
```

OUTPUT:

Enter number of steps: 10

1 1 2 3 5 8 13 21 34 55

Q.11. *Find is the given number is Prime or not.*

```
#include<stdio.h>
#include<conio.h>
```

```
void main()
{
int i, j, n, flag = 0;
clrscr();
printf("Enter Number: ");
scanf(%d", &n);
for(i = 2; i <= n/2; i++)
        {
        j = n%i;
        if (j == 0)
              {
              flag = 1;
              break;
              }
        }
if(flag == 1)
      print("The entered number is not prime");
else
      printf("The entered number is prime");
getch();
}
```

OUTPUT:

Enter Number: 7

The entered number is prime

Q.12. *Program to list prime numbers from 1 to 100.*

```
#include<stdio.h>
#include<conio.h>
void main()
{
int i, j, k, n flag = 0;
clrscr();
printf("Prime Numbers from 1 to 100 are:\n ");
for(n = 1; n <= 100; n++)
        {
        for(i = 2; i <= n /2; i++)
                {
                j = n%i;
                if (j == 0)
                   {
                   flag = 1;
                   break;
                   }
                }
        if(flag != 1)
                printf("%d\t", n);
```

```
                flag = 0;
                }
    getch();
    }
```

OUTPUT:

Prime Numbers from 1 to 100 are:

1	2	3	5	7	11	13	17	19	23
29	31	37	41	43	47	53	59	61	67
71	73	79	83	89	97				

Q.13. *Get value of sin(x) using library function.*

```
#include<stdio.h>
#include<conio.h>
#include<math.h>
void main()
{
float x, deg;
clrscr();
printf("Enter value in degree: ");
scanf("%df", &deg);
x = (deg * 3.14)/180;
printf("\n sin(x) = %f", sin(x));
getch();
}
```

OUTPUT:

Enter value in degree: 30

sin(x) = 0.499770

Q.14. (*a*) *Print the following pattern*

```
*   *   *   *   *
  *   *   *   *
    *   *   *
      *   *
        *
```

```
#include<stdio.h>
#include<conio.h>
void main()
{
int i, j, n, k = 1;
clrscr();
printf("How many lines do you want to enter :");
scanf("%d", &n);
for(i = n; i > 0; i--)
```

```
        {
        for(j = 1; j <= n - i; j++)
                printf("  ");
        for(j = 1; j <= i; j++)
                {
        printf("  *");
                k++;
                }
        printf("\n");
        }
getch();
}
```

OUTPUT:

How many lines do you want to enter : 5

```
*   *   *   *   *
  *   *   *   *
    *   *   *
      *   *
        *
```

Q.14. *(b) Print the following pattern*

```
#include<stdio.h>
#include<conio.h>
void main()
{
int i, j, n, k = 1;
clrscr();
printf("How many lines do you want to enter : ");
scanf("%d", &n);
for(i = n; i > 0; i--)
        {
        for(j = 1; j <= i; j++)
                {
                printf("*");
                k++;
                }
        printf("\n");
        }
getch();
}
```

OUTPUT:

How many lines do you want to enter : 5

```
*   *   *   *   *
  *   *   *   *
    *   *   *
      *   *
        *
```

Q.14. (*c*) *Print the following pattern.*

```
        *
      *   *
    *   *   *
  *   *   *   *
*   *   *   *   *
```

```
#include<stdio.h>
#include<conio.h>
void main()
{
int i, j, n, k = 1;
clrscr();
printf("How many lines do you want to enter : ");
scanf("%d", &n);
for(i = 0; i <= n; i++)
        {
        for(j = 1; j <= i; j++)
                {
                printf("*");
                k++;
                }
        printf("\n");
        }
getch();
}
```

OUTPUT:

How many lines do you want to enter : 5

```
        *
      *   *
    *   *   *
  *   *   *   *
*   *   *   *   *
```

Q.15. *Search a given number in an array*

```
#include<stdio.h>
#include<conio.h>
void main()
{
int a[10] = {1, 4, 7, 3, 6, 9, 2, 5, 8, 0);
int i, x, found = 0;
clrscr();
printf("Enter the number to be searched: ");
scanf("%d", &x);
for(i = 0; i < 10; i++)
        {
        if(x == a[i])
                {
                found = 1;
                break
                }
        }
if(found == 1)
        printf("\n Number %d found at position %d", x, i + 1);
else
        printf("\n Number not found");
getch();
}
```

OUTPUT:

Enter the number to be searched: 5

Number 5 found at position 8

Q.16. *Matrix-subtraction*

```
#include<stdio.h>
#include<conio.h>
void main()
{
int arr1[10][10], arr2[10][10], arr3[10][10] = {0};
int i, j, k, r1, c1, r2, c2;
clrscr();
printf("Matrix 1:\n");
printf("Enter the number of rows: ");
scanf("%d", &r1);
printf("Enter the number of cols :");
scanf("%d", &c1);
for(i = 0; i < r1; i++)
        {
        printf("\n Rows %d : ", i + 1);
        for(j = 0; j < c1; j++)
```

```
                {
                printf("\n Cols %d : ", j + 1);
                scanf("%d", &arr1[i][j]);
                }
        }
printf("----------------------------\n");
printf("Matrix 2:\n");
printf("Enter the number of rows :");
scanf("%d", &r2);
printf("Enter the number of cols :");
scanf("%d", &c2);
for(i = 0; i < r2; i++)
        {
        printf("\n Rows %d : ", i + 1);
        for(j = 0; j < c2; j++)
                {
                printf("\n Cols %d : ", j + 1);
                scanf("%d", &arr2[i][j]);
                }
        }
for(i = 0; i < r1; i++)
        {
        for(j = 0; j < c2; j++)
                {
                arr3[i][j] = arr3[i][j] + (arr1[i][j] - arr2[i][j]);
                }
        }
printf("----------------------------\n");
printf("Matrix 1:\n");
for(i = 0; i < r1; i++)
        {
        for(j = 0; j < c1; j++)
        printf("%d8d", arr1[i][j]);
   printf("\n");
   }
printf("----------------------------\n");
printf("Matrix 2:\n");
for(i = 0; i < r2; i++)
   {
   for(j = 0; j < c2; j++)
           printf("%8d", arr2[i][j]);
   printf("\n");
   }
```

```
printf("-----------------------------\n");
printf("Matrix after subtraction:\n");
for(i = 0; i < r1; i++)
   {
   for(j = 0; j < c1; j++)
            printf("%8d", arr3[i][j]);
   printf("\n");
   }
getch();
}
```

Q.17. *Matrix-multiplication*

```
#include<stdio.h>
#include<conio.h>
void main()
{
int arr1[10][10], arr2[10][10], arr3[10][10] = {0};
int i, j, k, r1, c1, r2, c2;
clrscr();
printf("Matrix 1:\n");
printf("Enter the number of rows :");
scanf("%d", &r1);
printf("Enter the number of cols :");
scanf("%d", &c1);
for(i = 0; i < r1; i++)
         {
         printf("\n Rows %d : ", i + 1);
         for(j = 0; j < c1; j++)
                  {
                  printf("\n Cols %d : ", j + 1);
                  scanf("%d", &arr1[i][j]);
                  }
         }
printf("-----------------------------\n");
printf("Matrix 2:\n");
printf("Enter the number of rows :");
scanf("%d", &r2);
printf("Enter the number of cols :");
scanf("%d", &c2);
for(i = 0; i < r2; i++)
         {
         printf("\n Rows %d : ", i + 1);
         for(j = 0; j < c2; j++)
```

```
                        {
                        printf("\n Cols %d : ", j + 1);
                        scanf("%d",  &arr2[i][j]);
                        }
                  }
      for(i = 0; i < r1; i++)
                  {
                  for(j = 0; j < c2; j++)
                     {
                     for(k = 0; k < r2; k++)
                        arr3[i][j] = arr3[i][j] + arr1[i][k] * arr2[k][j];
                     }
                  }
      printf("----------------------------\n");
      printf("Matrix 1:\n");
      for(i = 0; i < r1; i++);
                  {
                  for(j = 0; j < c1; j++)
                        printf("%8d",  arr1[i][j]);
                  printf("\n");
                  }
      printf("----------------------------\n");
      printf("Matrix 2:\n");
      for(i = 0; i < r2; i++)
                  {
    for(j = 0; j < c2; j++)
                  printf("%8d",  arr2[i][j]);
                  printf("\n");
                  }
      printf("----------------------------\n");
      printf("Matrix after multiplication:\n");
      for(i = 0; i < r1; i++)
                  {
                  for(j = 0; j < c1; j++)
                     printf("%8d",  arr3[i][j]);
                  printf("\n");
                  }
      getch();
      }
```

Q.18. *This program is for sorting in descending order of N numbers.*

```
#include<stdio.h>
#include<string.h>
void main()
{
```

```
    int arr[50];
    int i, p, c, n;
    clrscr();
    printf("\n Enter the number of values to be sorted :");
    scanf("%d", &n);
    for(i = 0; i < n; i++)
            {
            printf("\n Enter the number [%d] :", i + 1);
            scanf("%d", &arr[i]);
            }
for(p = 1; p < n; p++)
            {
               for(c = 0; c < n - p; c++)
                       {
                       if(arr[c] < arr[c + 1])
                          {
                                int temp = arr[c];
                                arr[c] = arr[c + 1];
                                arr[c + 1] = temp;
                          }
                       }
            }
printf("\n The sorted numbers in descending order :\n");
for(i = 0; i < n; i++)
        printf("\n The number [%d] : %d\n", i +1, arr[i]);
getch();
}
```

Q.19. *Program to implement Simple Merge.*

```
#include<stdio.h>
#include<conio.h>
void main()
{
int a[] = {11, 23, 42, 9, 25};
int i, j, l, FIRST, SECOND, THIRD;
int temp[5];
clrscr();
FIRST = 0;
SECOND = 3;
THIRD = 4;
i = FIRST;
j = SECOND;
l = 0;
while(i < SECOND&&J <= THIRD)
        {
        if(a[i] <= a[j])
```

```
                    {
                    temp[l] = a[i];
                    l++;
                    i++;
                    }
            else
                    {
                    temp[l] = a[j];
                    l++;
                    j++;
                    }
            }
    if(i >= SECOND)
            {
            while(j <= THIRD)
                    {
                    temp[l] = a[j];
                    l++;
                    j++;
                    }
            }
    else
            {
            while(i < SECOND)
                    {
                    temp[l] = a[j];
                    l++;
                    i++;
                    }
            }
    for(i = 0; i < l; i++)
            a[FIRST + i] = temp[i];
    printf("After Merging & Sorting: \n");
    for(i = 0; i < l; i++)
            printf("%d\t", a[i]);
    getch();
    }
```

Q.20. *WAP to perform search of a number.*

```
#include<stdio.h>
#include<conio.h>
void main()
{
   int n, a[50], I, num;
   clrscr();
   printf("\n How many numbers do you want to enter:");
```

```
    scanf("%d", &n);
    printf("\n Enter %d the numbers: \n", n);
    for(i = 0; i < n; i++)
            scanf("%d", &a[i]);
    printf("\n Enter the number you want to search: ");
    scanf("%d", &num);
    for(i = 0; i < n; i++)
    {
            if(num == a[i])
            {
               count = 1;
               printf("\n SEARCH SUCCESSFUL.");
               printf("\n %d is at position %d\r, ", num, i + 1);
            }
  }
  if(count != 1)
          printf("\n %d is not present in the array\n", num);
  getch();
  }
```

Q.21. *Structure of book consisting of author name, book name and price of the book.*

```
#include<stdio.h>
#include<conio.h>
struct book{
    char author_name[50];
    char book_name[50];
    int price;
    };
void main()
{
int i = 0;
struct book b;
printf("Enter book name\n"),
gets(b.book_name);
printf("Enter Author Name\n");
gets(b.author_name);
printf("Enter Price\n");
scanf("%d", b.price);
printf("Here is what you entered:\n");
printf("\n Book Name: %s", b.book_name);
printf("\n Author Name: %s", b.author_name);
printf("\n Price : %d", b.price);
getch();
}
```

Q.22(*a*). *This palindrome is for pallindrom (case sensitive).*

```
#include<stdio.h>
#include<conio.h>
void main()
{
char str[20];
int i, j;
clrscr();
printf("enter the string :");
gets(str);
for(i = 0; str[i]; i++);
for(i--, j = 0; j <= i&&str[i] == str[j]; j++, i--);
if(j > i)
printf("string is palindrome");
else
printf("string is not palindrome");
getch();
}
```

Q.22(*b*). *This palindrome is for palindrome (case insensitive).*

```
#include<stdio.h>
#include<conio.h>
void main()
{
char str[20];
int i, j;
clrscr();
printf("\n Enter the string :");
gets(str);
for(i = 0; str[i]; i++);
for(i--, j = 0; j <= i&&str[i] == str[j] || str[i] + 32 == str[j] ||
str[i] == str[j] + 32; u++, i--);
if(j > i)
printf("\n String is palindrome");
else
printf("\n String is not palindrome");
getch();
}
```

Q.23. *Read a line from file*

```
//Count loop & branch statements in a program
#include<stdio.h>
#include<conio.h>
#include<process.h>
void main()
{
char * line;
```

```
char ch;
int i = 0, j = 0;
clrscr();
FILE *fp;
fp = fopen("test.txt", "r");
if(fp == NULL)
        {
        printf("Can't open file");
        exit(0);
        }
while((ch = fgetch"(fp)) != EOF)
        {
        if(ch != '\n')
                line[i++] = ch;
        else
                {
                line[i] = '\0';
                j++;
                printf("%d th line is :%s\n", j, line);
                i = 0;
                }
        }
getch();
}
```

Q.24. *To find factorial using recursion*

```
#include<stdio.h>
#include<conio.h>
void main()
{
int n, i, fact;
clrscr();
printf("Enter number:\n");
scanf("%d", &n);
fact = factorial(n);
printf("\n Factorial = %d", fact);
getch();
}
int factorial(int a)
{
int f;
if(a == 0)
return 1;
else
   {
   f = a * factorial(a - 1);
   return f;
   }
}
```

Q.25. *Swap to numbers using pointers.*

```
#include<stdio.h>
#include<conio.h>
void swap(int*, int*);
void main()
{
int i = 2;
int j = 5;
clrscr();
swap (&I, &j);
printf("%d, %d", i, j);
getch();
}
void swap(int *x, int *y)
{
int *temp;
*temp = *x;
*x = *y;
*y = *temp;
}
```

WORM Write-Once Read Many

WYSIWYG What You See Is What You Get

WWW World Wide Web

X.400 Electronic Mial Protocol

X.500 Directory Server Protocol

XHTMLeXtensible Hyper Text Markup Language

XML extensible Markup Language

SUMMARY

An algorithm is a step-by-step description of how to arrive at the solution of the given problem

1. There are mainly three ways for represented the algorithms
   (*i*) As programs
   (*ii*) Flow charts
   (*iii*) As pseudo codes
2. C supports the use of pointers a very simple type of references that recodes, in effect, the address or location of an object or function in memory.
3. Array types in c are traditionally of a fixed, static size specified at compile time.
4. C does not have a special provision for declaring multidimensional array, *i.e.*, array of arrays.

APPENDIX-I

FREQUENTLY ASKED QUESTIONS (FAQs)

Declarations and Initializations

1. How should I decide which integer type to use ?
2. Why the sizes of the standard types aren't precisely defined ?
3. Are typedefs like int 16 and int 32 a good idea ?
4. What should the 64-bit type on new, 64-bit machines be ?
5. What's wrong with the declaration "char* pl, p2;"? I get errors when I try to use p2.
6. What's wrong with "char *p; *p = malloc (10) ;"?
7. What's the best way to declare and define global variables ?
8. What's the best way of implementing opaque (abstract) data types in C ?
9. How can I make a sort of "semiglobal" variable, that is, one that's private to a few functions spread across a few source files ?
10. Do all declarations for the same static function or variable have to include the storage class static ?
11. What does extern mean in a function declaration ?
12. What's the auto keyword good for ?
13. What's the difference between using a typedef or a preprocessor macro for a user-defined type ?
14. I can't seem to define a linked list node that contains a pointer to itself.
15. How can I define a pair of mutually referential structures ?
16. What's the difference between struct x {....} ; and typedef struct {....} x2; ?
17. What does "typedef int (*funfptr) ()"; mean ?
18. I have a typdef for char *, and it's not interacting with const the way I expect. Why not ?
19. Why can't I use const values in initializers and array dimensions ?
20. What's the difference between const char *p and char * const p ? Complex Declarations.
21. How I do declare an array of N pointers to functions returning pointers to functions returning pointers to characters, or figure out what similarly complicated declarations mean ?
22. How I can declare a function that returns a pointer to a function of its own type ?
23. Can I declare a local array (or parameter array) of a size matching a passed-in array, or set by another parameter ?
24. Why doesn't size of work on arrays declared extern ? Declaration Problems.
25. Why is compiler complaining about an invalid redeclaration of a function that I define and call only once ?
26. My compiler is complaining about mismatched function prototypes that look fine to me. Why ?
27. I'm getting strange syntax errors on the very first declaration in a file, but it looks fine. Why ?
28. Why isn't my compiler letting me declare a large array, such as double array [256] [256] ?
29. How can I determine which identifiers are safe for me to use and which are reserved ?
30. What can I safely assume about the initial values of variables that are not explicitly initialized ?
31. Why can't I initialize a local array with a string ?
32. What is the difference between char a [ ] = "string"; and char*p = "string" ?
33. Is char a [3] = "abc"; legal ?
34. How do I initialize a pointer to a function ?
35. Can I initialize unions ?

Structures, Unions, and Enumerations structure Declarations

36. What's the difference between struct x1 {...} ; and typedef struct {...} x2; ?
37. Why doesn't "struct x {...} ; x the struct"; work ?
38. Can a structure contain a pointer to itself ?
39. What's the best way of implementing opaque {abstract} data types in C ?
40. Why does the declaration "extern f (struct x*p)"; give me a warning message ?
41. I came across some code that declared a Structure with the last member an array of one element, and then did some tricky allocation to make it act as if the array bad several elements. Is this legal or portable ?
42. Can structures be assigned to variables and passed to and from functions ?
43. Why can't structures be compared using the built in == and != operations ?
44. How are structure passing and returning implemented ?
45. How can I create nameless, immediate, constant structure values ?
46. How can I read/write structures form/ to data files ?
47. How can I turn off structure padding ?
48. Why does size of report a larger size that I expect for a structure type ?
49. How can I determine the byte offset of a field within a structure ?
50. How can I access structure fields by name at run time ?
51. Does C have an equivalent to Pascal's with statement ?
52. If an array name acts like a pointer to the base of an array, why isn't the same thing true of a structure ?
53. I have a program that works correctly but dumps core after it finishes. Why ?
54. What's the difference between a structure and a union ?
55. Is there a way to initialize unions ?
56. Is there anautomatic way to keep track of which field of a union is in use ?
57. What is difference between an enumeration and set of preprocessor #defines ?
58. Are enumerations portable ?
59. Is there an easy way to print enumeration values symbolically ?
60. What do these colons and numbers mean in some structure declarations ?
61. Why do people use explicit masks and bit-twiddling code so much instead declaring bitfields ?

Expressions Evaluation Order

62. Why doesn't the code "a[i] = i++;" work ?
63. Under my compiler, the code "int i = 7; printf("%d\n", i++ *i++);l" prints 49. Regardless of the order of evaluation, shouldn't it print ?
64. How could the code "int i = 3; i = i++;" evergive 7 ?
65. Don't precedence and parentheses dictate order of evaluation ?
66. But what about the && and ¦¦ Operators ?
67. Is it safe to assume that the right-hand side of the && and ¦¦ operators won't be evaluated if the left-hand side determines the outcome ?
68. Why did "printf("%d %d", f1 (), f2 ()"; call f2 first ?
69. What is a "sequence point" ?
70. So if I write a [1] = i++; and don't care which cell of a [] gets written to, the code is fine, and I gets incremented by 1, right ?

71. I just tried some allegedly undefined code on an ANSI-conforming compiler and got the results I expected.
72. How can I avoid these undefined evaluation-order difficulties if I don't feel like learning the complicated rules ?
73. If I'm not using the value of the expression, should I use i++ or ++i to Increment a variable ?
74. Why doesn't "if (a < b < c)" work ?
75. Why doesn't the code "int a = 1000, long int c = a * b"; work ?
76. Why does the code degC = 5/9 * (degF-32);" keep giving me 0 ?
77. Can I use ? : on the left-hand side of an assignment expression ?
78. I have an expression "a ? b = c : d" that some compilers aren't accepting. Why ?

Pointers

79. What are pointers really good for, anyway ?
80. What's wrong with "char *p; *p = malloc(10) ;" ?
81. What Does *p++ increment: p or what it points to ?
82. I'm having problems using pointers to manipulate an array of ints.
83. I want to use a char * pointer to step over same ints. Why doesn't (int *)p) ++," work ?
84. Why can't I perform arithmetic on a void * pointer ?
85. I've got some code that's trying to unpack external structures, but it's crashing, with a message about an"unaligned access". What does this mean ?
86. I have a function that accepts, and is supposed to initialize, a pointer, but the pointer in the caller remains unchanged. Why ?
87. Can I pass a void * pointer "by reference" *i.e.*, as a void * * ?
88. I have a function that accepts a pointer to an int. How can I pass a constant like 5 to it ?
89. Does C even have "pass by reference" ?
90. What's the right way to call functions via pointers ?
91. What's the total generic pointer type for data function pointers ?
92. How are integers converted to and from pointers ?

Null Pointers

93. What is this infamous null pointer, anyway ?
94. How do I get a null pointer in my programs ?
95. Is the abbreviated pointer comparison "if (p)" to test for non-null pointers valid ?
96. What is NULL and how is it defined ?
97. How should NULL be defined on a machine that uses a nonzero bit pattern as the internal representation of a null pointer ?
98. If NULL were defined as ((char *) 0), wouldn't that make function calls that pass an uncast NULL work ?
99. My vendor provides header files that define NULL as OL. Why ?
100. Is NULL valid for pointers to functions ?
101. If NULL and O are equivalent as null pointer constants, which should I use ?
102. But wouldn't it be better to use NULL, in case the value of NULL changes ?
103. I once used a compiler that wouldn't work unless ~LL was used.
104. I use the preprocessor macro "#define Nullptr (type) (type*)0" help me build null pointers of the correct type.

105. This is strange: NULL is guaranteed to be 0, but the null pointer is not ?
106. Why is there so much confusion surroundings null pointers ?
107. Is there an easier way to understand all this null pointer stuff ?
108. Given all the confusion surrounding null pointers, wouldn't it be easier simply require them to be represented internally by zeroes?
109. Seriously, have any machines really used nonzero null pointers ?
110. Is a run-time integral value of 0, cast to a pointer, guaranteed to be a null pointer ?
111. How can I access an interrupt vector located at the machine's location 0 ?
112. What does a run-time "null pointer assignment" error mean ?

Arrays and Pointers

113. I had the definition char a [6] in one source file, and in another I declared extern char *a. Why didn't it work ?
114. But I heard that char a [] is identical to char *a. Is that true ?
115. So what is meant by the "equivalence of pointers and arrays" in C ?
116. Why are array and pointer declarations interchangeable as function formal parameters ?
117. Why can't I assign to arrays ?
118. Why can I assign to array parameters ?
119. How can an array be an value if I can't assign to it ?
120. What is the real difference between arrays and pointers ?
121. Someone explained to me that arrays are really just constant pointers. Is this accurate ?
122. Is a pointer a kind of array, or is an array a kind of pointer ?
123. What's the difference between array and &array ?
124. How do I declare a pointer to an array ?
125. How can I set an array's size at compile time ? How can ?
126. How can I declare local arrays of a size matching a passed-in array ?
127. How can I dynamically allocate a multidimensional array ?
128. Can I simulate a non-O-based array with a pointer ?
129. My compiler complained when I passed a two-dimensional array to a function Expecting a pointer to a pointer. Why ?
130. How can I use statically and dynamically allocated multidimensional arrays hangeably when passing them to functions ?
131. Why doesn't size of properly report the size of an array that is a parameter to a function ?
132. How can code in a file where an array is declared as extern determine the size of the array ?
133. How can I determine how many elements are in array, when sizeof yields the size in bytes?

Memory Allocation

134. Why doesn't the code "char *answer, gets (answer)", work ?
135. I can't get strcat to work. I tried "char *s3 = Strcat (s1, s2);" but I got strange results.
136. But the documentation for strcat says that it takes two char *'s as arguments. How am I supposed to know to allocate things ?
137. I'm using fgets to read lines from a file into an array of pointers. Why do all the lines end up containing copies of the last line ?
138. I have a function that is supposed to return a string, but when the function returns to its caller, the returned string is garbage. Why ?

139. Why am I getting "warning: assignment of pointer form integer lacks a cast" for calls to malloc ?
140. Why does some code carefully cast the values returned by malloc to the pointer type being allocated ?
141. Why does so much code leave out the multiplication by sizeof (char) when allocating strings ?
142. Why doesn't the little wrapper I wrote around malloc work ?
143. What's wrong with "char *p; *p = malloc (10)"; ?
144. How can I dynamically allocate arrays ?
145. How can I find out how much memory is available ?
146. What should malloc (0) do ?
147. I've heard that some operating systems don't allocate memory obtained via malloc until the program tries to use it. It this legal ?
148. Why is malloc returning crazy pointer values ? I'm sure I declared it correctly.
149. I'm allocating a large array for some numeric work, but malloc is acting strangely. Why ?
150. I've got 8 MB of memory in my PC. Why does malloc seem to allocate only 640K or so ?
151. My application depends heavily on dynamic allocation of nodes for data structures, and malloc/free overhead is becoming a bottleneck. What can I do ?
152. My program is crashing, apparently somewhere down inside malloc. Why ?
153. Dynamically allocated memory can't be used after freeing it, can it ?
154. Why isn't pointer null after calling free ?
155. When I call malloc to allocate memory for a local pointer, do I have to explicitly free it ?
156. When I free a dynamically allocated structure containing pointers, do I have to free each subsidiary pointer first ?
157. Must I free allocated memory before the program exits ?
158. Why doesn't my program's memory usage go down when I free memory ?
159. How does free ( ) know how many bytes to free ?
160. So can I query the malloc package to find out how big an allocated block is ?
161. Why doesn't size of tell me the size of the block of memory pointed to by a pointer ?
162. Having dynamically allocated an array, can I change its size ?
163. Is it legal to pass a null pointer as the first argument to realloc ?
164. What's the difference between calloc and malloc ?
165. What is alloca and why is its use discouraged ?

Characters and Strings

166. Why doesn't "strcat(string, '!');" work ?
167. Why won't the test if (string == "value") correctly compare string against the value ?
168. Why can't I assign strings to character arrays ?
169. Why can't I get streat to work ? I tried "char *s3 ; and char *p = "string"; ?
170. What is the difference between char a [ ] = "string"; and char *p = "string"; ?
171. How can I get the numeric valuc corresponding to a character ?
172. Does C have anything like the "substr" routine present in other languages ?
173. When my program reads strings typed by the use, why aren't sequences like \n handles properly ?
174. Why is sizeof ('a') not 1 ?
175. As the use of 16-bit, multinational character sets grows, won't a lot of code break when sizeof (char) becomes 2 ?

Boolean Expressions and Variables

176. What is the right type to use for Boolean values in C ?
177. What if a built-in logical or relational operator "returns" something other than 1 ?
178. Is if (pI, where p is a pointer, valid ?
179. Should I use symbolic names, such as TRUE and FALSE, for the Boolean constants or use plain 1 and 0 ?
180. A header file is defining its own TRUE and FALSE values incompatibly with my code. What can I do ?

The C Preprocessor

181. I'm trying to define a few simple little functions-like macros, but they're not always working.
182. I've got some cute preprocessor macros that let me with C code that looks more like Pascal.
183. How can I write a generic macro to swap two values ?
184. What's the best way to write a multistatement macro ?
185. What's the difference between using a typedef or a preprocessor macro for a user-defined type ?
186. What are .h files and what should I put in them ?
187. Is it acceptable for one header file to include another ?
188. Where are header ("#include") files searched for ?
189. Why am I getting strange syntax errors on the very first declaration in a file ?
190. I'm using header files that supply conflicting definitions for common macros such as TRUE and FALSE. What can I do ?
191. Where can I get a copy of a missing header file ?
192. How can I construct preprocessor #if directives ?
193. Does the sizeof operator work in preprocessor #if directives ?
194. Can I use #ifdef in a #define line to define something two different ways ?
195. Is there anything like #ifdef for typedef ?
196. How can I use a preprocessor #if expression to detect endianness ?
197. Why am I getting strange syntax errors inside lines I've used #ifdef to disable ?
198. How can I preprocess some code to remove selected conditional compilations, without preprocessing everything.
199. How can I list all of the predefined identifiers ?

ANSI/ISO Standard C The Standard

200. What is the "ANSI C Standard" ?
201. How can I get a copy of the Standard ?
202. Why does my ANSI compiler complain about prototype mismatches for parameters declared float ?
203. Is it possible to mix old-style and new-style functions syntax.
204. Why does the declaration "extern f (struct x *)" give me a warning message ?
205. Why don't function prototypes guard against mismatches in printf arguments ?
206. I heard that you have to include <stdio.h> before calling printf ?
207. Why can't I use const values in initializers and array dimensions ?
208. What's the difference between const char *p and char * const p ?
209. Why can't I pass a char * * to a function that expects a const char * * ?

210. I have a typdef for char *, and it's not interacting with const the way I expect. Why ?
211. Can I declare main as void, to shut off these warnings about main for returning a value ?
212. What about main's third argument, envp ?
213. I believe that declaring void main ( ) can't fail, since I'm calling exit instead of returning.
214. But why do all my books declare main as void ?
215. Is exit (status) tryly equivalent to returning the same status form main ?
216. How do I get the ANSI "stringizing" preprocessing operator '#' to stringize the macro's value instead of its name ?
217. What does the message "warning: macro replacement within a string literal" mean ?
218. Why am I getting strange errors inside lines I've used #ifdef to disable ?
219. What is the #pragma directive ?
220. What does "#pragma once" mean ?
221. Is char a [3] = "abc"; leagal ?
222. What's the difference between array and &array ?
223. Why can't I perform arithmetic on a void * pointer ?
224. What's the difference between memcpy and memmove ?
225. What should malloc (0) do ?
226. Why does the ANSI standard not guarantee more than six case-insensitive characters of external identifier significance ?
227. Whatever happened to noalias ?
228. Why is my complex rejecting the simplest possible test programs, with all kinds of syntax errors ?
229. Why are some ANSI/ISO C Standard library functions showing up as undefined, even though I've got an ANSI complier ?
230. Does anyone have a tool for converting old-style C programs to ANSI C or for automatically generating prototypes ?
231. Why won't my C compiler, which claims to be ANSI compliant, accept this code ?
232. What's the difference between implementation, defined, unspecified, and undefined behavior ?
233. I'm applied that the ANSI standard leaves so man issues undefined. Isn't a standard supposed to standardize things ?
234. I just tired some allegedly-undefined code on an ANSI-conforming compiler, and got the results I expected

The Standard I/O Library

235. What's wrong with "char c ; while ((c = getcgar()) != EOF) ...." ?
236. Why won't the simple line-copying loop "while (!feof(infp)) { fgets(buf, MAXLINE, infp); fputs (buf, outfp);}" work ?
237. I'm using fgets to read lines form a file into an array of pointers. Why do all the lines end up containing copies of the last line ?
238. My program's prompts and intermediate output don't always show up on the screen.
239. How can I read one character at a time, without waiting for the Return key ? Printf Formats.
240. How can I print a' % 'character with printf ?
241. Why doesn't "long int n = 123456; printf("%d\n",n)" ; work ?
242. Aren't ANSI function prototypes supposed to guard against argument type mismatches ?
243. How can printf use % for type double, if scanf requires %lf?

244. How can I implement a variable field width with printf?
245. How can I print numbers with commas separating the thousands ?
246. Why doesn't the call "scanf("%d", i)" work ?
247. Why doesn't the code "double d; scanf("%f", &d);" work ?
248. Why doesn't the code "short int s; scanf("%d", &s);" work ?
249. How can I specify a variable width in a scanf format string ?
250. How can I read data from data files width particular formats ? How can I read an arbitrary number of fields from a line into an array ?
251. When I read numbers from the keyboard with scanf"%d\n", it seems to hand until I type one extra line of input. Why ?
252. I'm reading a number with scanf%d and then a strong with gets ( ), but the compiler seems to be skipping the call to gets ( ) ! Why ?

APPENDIX-II

ANSI C HEADER FILES

Functions	Data type	Task Returned
<ctype.h>		
isalnum(c)	int	Determine if argument is alphanumeric. –Return non zero value if true; 0 otherwise
isalpha(c)	int	Determine if argument is alphabetic. Return nonzero value if true; 0 otherwise
isascii(c)	int	Determine if argument is an ASCII character. Return non-zero value if true; 0 otherwise
iscntrl(c)	int	Determine if argument is an ASCII control character. Return nonzero value if true; 0 otherwise
isdigit(c)	int	Determine if argument is a decimal digit. Return nonzero value if true; 0 otherwise
isgraph(c)	int	Determine if argument is a graphic printing ASCII character. Return nonzero value if true; 0 otherwise
islower(c)	int	Determine if argument is lowercase. Return nonzero value if true; 0 otherwise
isodigit(c)	int	Determine if argument is an octal digit. Return nonzero value if true; 0 otherwise
isprint(c)	int	Determine if argument is a printing ASCII character. Return nonzero value if true; 0 otherwise
ispunct(c)	int	Determine if argument is punctuation character. Return non-zero value if true; 0 otherwise
isspace(c)	int	Determine if argument is a whitespace character. Return nonzero value if true; 0 otherwise
isupper(c)	int	Determine if argument is uppercase. Return nonzero value if true; 0 otherwise
isxdigit(c)	int	Determine if argument is hexadecimal digit. Return nonzero value if true; 0 otherwise
toascii(c)	int	Convert value of argument to ASCII.
tolower(c)	int	Convert letter to lowercase.
toupper(c)	int	Convert letter to uppercase.
<math.h>		
acos (d)	double	Return the are cosine of d.
asin(d)	double	Return the are sine of d.
atan(d)	double	Return the are tangent of d.
atan2 (d1,d2)	double	Return the are tangent of d1/d2.
ceil(d)	double	Return a value rounded up to the next higher integer.
cos(d)	double	Return the cosine of d.
cosh(d)	double	Return the hyperbolic cosine of d.
exp(d)	double	Raise a to the power d.
fabs(d)	double	Return the absolute value of d.

	floor(d)	double	Return a-value rounded down to the next lower integer.
	fmod(d1,d2)	double	Return the remainder of d1/d2 (with same sign as d1).
	labs(1)	long int	Return the absolute value of 1
	log (d)	double	Return the natural logarithm of d.
	log10(d)	double	Return the logarithm (base 10) of d.
	pow (d1,d2)	double	Return d1 raised to the d2 power.
	sin(d)	double	Return the sine of d.
	sinh(d)	double	Return the hyperbolic sine of d.
	sqrt(d)	double	Return the square root of d.
	tan(d)	double	Return the tangent of d.
	tanh(d)	double	Return the hyperbolic tangent of d.
<stdio.h>			
	fclose(f)	int	Close file f. Return 0 if file is successfully closed.
	feof(f)	int	Determine if an. end-of-file condition has been reached. If so, return a nonzero value; otherwise; return 0.
	fgetc(f)	int	Enter a single character form file f.
	fgets(s, i, f)	chat*	Enter string s, containing i. Characters, form file f.
	fopenls1,s2j	file*	Open a file named s1 of type s2. Return a pointer to the file.
	fprintf(f,)	int	Send data items to file f.
	fputc(c,f)	int	Send a single character to file f.
	fputs(s,f)	int	Send string s to file f.
	freads(s,i1,i2,f)	int	Enter i2 data items, each of size i1 bytes, from file f to string s.
	fscanf(f)	int	Enter data items from file f.
	fseek(f,1,i)	int	Move the pointer for file f a distance 1 bytes from location i.
	ftell(f)	long int	Return the current pointer within file f.
	fwrite (s,i1,i2,f)	int	Send i2 data items, each of size i1 bytes from string s to file f.
	getchar(void)	int	Enter a single character from the standard input device.
	gets(s)	char*	Enter string s form the standard input device.
	printf( )	int	Send data items to the standard output device.
	putc(c,f)	int	Send a single character to file f.
	putchar(c)	int	Send a single character to the standard output device.
	puts(s)	int	Send string s to the standard output device.
	rewind(f)	void	Move the pointer to the beginning of file f.
	scan(f)	int	Enter data items from the standard input device.
<stdlib.h>			
	abs(i)	int	Return the absolute value of i.
	atof(s)	double	Convert string s to a adouble-precision quantity.
	atoi(s)	int	Convert string s to an integer.
	atolls)	long	Convert string s to a longer integer.
	calloc(u1,u2)	void*	Allocate memory for an array having u1 elements, each of length u2 bytes. Return a pointer to the beginning of the allocated space.
	exit(u)	void	Close all files buffers, and terminate the program. (Value of u is assigned by the function, to indicate termination status).

APPENDIX-III

FREQUENTLY USED ABBREVIATIONS

4FGL	:	Fourth Generation Language
ALU	:	Arithmetic and Logic Unit
ANSI	:	American National Standards Institute
ASCII	:	American Standard Code for Information Interchange
BCD	:	Binary Coded Decimal
CD	:	Compact Disk
CD-ROM	:	Compact Disk Read Only Memory
CISC	:	Complex Instruction Set Computing
CPU	:	Central Processing Unit
CRT	:	Cathode Ray Tube
CU	:	Control Unit
DMP	:	Dot Matrix Printer
EBCDIC	:	Extended Binary Coded Decimal Interchange Code
EOF	:	End of File
FTP	:	File Transfer Protocol
GIGO	:	Garbage In Garbage Out
HLL	:	High Level Language
HTML	:	Hyper Text Markup Language
HTTP	:	Hyper Text Transfer Protocol
OCR	:	Optical Character Recognition
OMR	:	Optical Mark Recognition
OS	:	Operating System
OSI	:	Open System Interconnection
PC	:	Personal Computer
PROM	:	Programmable Read Only Memory
PVM	:	Parallel Virtual Machine
RAM	:	Random Access Memory
RISC	:	Reduced Introduction Set Computing
VDU	:	Visual Display Unit
WWW	:	World Wide Web

APPENDIX-IV

REVIEW

- # : Compiler directive used to search and define files and value
- &&, ||, ! : Boolean operators
- () : Always used in a function to give function parameters
- *.bak : Source file saved twice
- *.c : Source file
- *.exe : Executable file which gives output
- *.obj : Compiled source file
- ; : Statement termination
- { : Used to initiate a set of statements
- } : Used to close the block of statements
- " " : To include files outside the compiler
- " " : Used to say the compiler parts in an input output statement
- +,-,*,/,% : Arithmetic operators
- <,>, ==, !=, =<, >= : Logical operators
- < > : To include file inside the compiler
- <<, >>, &, | : Bitwise operators
- Actual parameters : Values used during definition of function
- Address operator (&) : The operator used with the pointer to point or assign the value of a variable
- Alt+F9 : Use to "COMPILE" a C program
- Append mode(a) : File opened in mode so that data can be appended in the file
- Arithmetic statement : Which show instruction to evaluate an expression
- Arrays : A collection of similar type of data.
- Assignment statement : Which shows instruction to assign a value to a variable
- Break condition is : To terminate the execution of the block of statements if satisfied
- Call by name : Giving variable value as formal parameters
- Call by reference : Giving address value as formal parameters
- Call by value : Giving constant value as formal parameter
- Char : To Alphabetic type data
- Character set : Symbols permitted by the compiler
- Column major : Scanning of multidimensional array in columns first and row later
- Comment : No executable statement put in
- Compiler : A computer program used to generate the machine code from a source program
- Conditional : Which control the sequence or flow of a program with the use of a function
- Constant : A label with given value and remaining unchanged till execution
- Continue : To continue the execution in a loop but don't allows rest to the block above which it appears
- Control statement : Which controls the sequence or flow of a program

Ctrl+F9	: Used to "RUN" a C program
Data types	: Type of data supported by C compiler
Decrement operator	: Operator used to decrement the value of a variable
Default	: The case is not having any values
Define	: Used to define constants
Deliminator	: Symbols used for syntactic meanings
Do while	: It is loop working once with default condition & then checks condition also called exit loop
Dynamic memory allocation	: Memory allocation to a variable during execution as per requirement
Escape sequence	: A character combination with ("\")
Exit	: Statement used to terminate execution of a program at any incidence
File	: Data type used to declare a file
Files	: Space to store data
Float	: To Real type data
For	: Mainly used for known no of times, the loop to be executed called counter loop
Formal parameters	: Labels used during definition of function
Parameter passing	: Operation to pass values to given function
Parameters	: Values used to execute function
Pointer	: Variables used to find address of a given variable
Printf & scanf	: Used to input and output variable data
Random access files	: Can be accessed in any sequence
Read mode (r)	: File opened in mode so that data can be read
Recursion	: A function calling itself is called recursion
Reproducing	: Accessing a variable through its address or any other label
Row major	: The scanning of multidimensional array first in row than in column
Sequential file	: Can be accessed only in a sequence
Statement	: Assign a value variable they are of four types
String	: Set of characters
Structure	: Collection of different types of data under common name
Subprogram	: A function which may or may not return a value.
Swapping	: Process to interchange values of two variable in a program
Switch case of a data	: Used to generate different options for different possible values of a data
Type conversion	: Conversion of a value of an expression to a particular type
Type conversion	: Automation type conversion
Union	: A structure with the size same as the component of a structure with maximum memory size
Variable execution	: A label used in a program whose value can be changed during execution
Void	: Independent to use any type of data
While	: Entry loop since condition is checked at the beginning of loop. It works for any condition
Write mode	: File opened in mode so that data can be edited in the file.

GLOSSARY

The purpose of this glossary is to present definitions of some of the terms that are often used in the field of computers and data processing.

A

Access control.	Deals with the policies and mechanisms to prohibit a user/ process from accessing those resources/information, which he/she/ it is not authorized to access.
Access time.	The time interval between the instant at which data is called for from a storage device and the instant delivery begins.
Accumulator Register (A).	A register, which holds the initial data to be operated upon, the intermediate results, and also the final results of processing operations.
Activity ratio.	The ration of the total number of records in transaction file and the total number of records in master file.
Adder.	A logic circuit capable of forming the sum of two or more quantities.
Address.	An identification, represented in the form of a name, label, or number, for designating a particular location in storage area.
Address register.	A local storage register, which contains the address of the next instruction to be executed.
Algorithm.	A sequence of precise and unambiguous instructions for solving a problem in a finite number of operations.
Alphabetic.	Pertaining to a character set, which contains the letter A to Z and the blank character.
Alphanumeric.	Pertaining to a character set, which contains letters, digits, and usually other special characters, such as comma, dollar sign, plus sign etc.
American National Standards Institute (ANSI).	A U.S. based national organization, which establishes uniform standards in several fields.
American Standard Code for Information Interchange (ASCII).	A standard coding system for computers. ASCII-7 is a 7-bit code, and its extended version, ASCII-8, is an 8-bit code.
Analog computer.	A computer, which operators on data, which is in the form of continuously variable physical quantities, such as electrical current.
Anonymous ftp site.	On the internet, a computer, which allows a user to log in with a username of anonymous and then a password, which is the user's e-mail address.

Antivirus utility.	A program used to cure a computer from virus infection.
Application programmer.	A programmer who prepares application software.
Application software.	A set of one or more programs designed to solve a specific problem or do a specific a task, such as pay calculation, processing of examination results, stores accounting and inventory control etc.
Architecture.	The organization and interconnection of the various components of a computer system.
Archiving.	The process of storing old data files on separate disks or tapes to make room for new files on the hard disk of a computer.
Arithmetic Logic Unit (ALU).	The unit of a computing system, which performs all mathematical and logical operations. It is one of the components of the central processing unit (CPU) of the computer.
Artificial intelligence.	A computer program, which translates an assembly language program to its machine language equivalent.
Assembly language.	A programming language, which allows instructions and storage location to be represented by letter and symbols instead of numbers. Also known as symbolic language.
Assembly program.	A program written in an assembly language. Also known as symbolic program.
Asynchronous communication.	Data transmission mode in which the sender can send data at any convenient time and the receiver will accept it.
Automated tape library.	A mass storage device, which uses a set of magnetic tapes and tape drives with a controller mounted in a single unit. All the tapes of an automated tape library form a single large storage unit. They are typically used for data archiving and as an online data backup device for automated backup.
Automatic Teller Machine (ATM).	An unattended machine used in banks, which allows a customer to deposit or withdraw cash by the use of an electronic card without the need to interact with a bank employee.
Auxiliary memory.	A storage, which supplements the main memory of a computer. Often referred to as secondary storage, this section of the computer's memory is non-volatile and has low cost per bit stored, but it generally has an operating speed far slower than that of the primary storage.

B

Backbone.	The main trunk lines of a computer network, which facilitates the interconnection of other computers and computer networks on the same network.
Background processing.	The automatic execution of lower-priority (background) computer programs, when higher-priority (foreground) programs are not using the system resources.

Backup.	Alternate facilities of programs, data files, hardware equipment, etc. which are used in case the original one is destroyed, lost, or fails to operate.
Backup file.	A copy of a file, created as a safety precaution against loss of data caused due to corruption, or inadvertent deletion of the original file.
Band printers.	See chain printers.
Bandwidth.	The range of frequencies available for data transmission. The wider the bandwidth of a communications system, the more than data it can transmit in a given period of time.
Bar codes.	Representation of alphanumeric data by a combination of adjacent vertical lines (called bars) by varying their width and the spacing between them. A barcode reader is a scanner, which is used for reading (decoding) bar-coded data.
Base.	The total number of digits (symbols) available to represent numbers in a positional number system.
Batch processing.	The running of several computer programs one after another without the need of a human operator to run each program individually.
Baud.	A unit for measuring data transmission speed. It is used to describe the capacity of a carrier. In general usage, a buad is identical to bits per second.
Beginners All-Purpose Symbolic Instruction Code (BASIC).	An easy-to-learn, high-level, interactive programming language, which is frequently used with personal computers, and in timesharing environments.
Bernoulli disk.	A magentic disk-based storage medium in which a single hard disk platter is encased in a plastic cartridge.
Beta testing.	The use of beta version of a software by a selected set of users for identifying errors, which might have been overlooked during the regular testing phase.
Beta version.	The version of a software, which is released to a selected set of users for testing, before its actual release.
Binary.	A characteristic or property involving a selection, choice, or condition, in which there are two possibilities.
Binary Coded Decimal (BCD).	One of the early coding systems, which is based on the idea of converting each digit of a decimal number into its binary equivalent, rather than converting the entire decimal value into a pure binary form. For example, the decimal number 42 is represented by 0100 0010 in 8-4-2-1 BCD notation.
Binary number system.	A number system with a base of two. It consists of two digits : 0 and 1
Biometric device.	A device used for user authentication, which verifies some physical characteristic of a user, such as the person's appearance, fingerprints, hand geometry, voice, or signature.
Bit.	Acronym for binary digit, which stands for one binary piece of information. This can be either 0 and 1.

Bitamp.	A method of displaying graphic images on a monitor by altering the color (or turning on or off) of individual dots (pixels) on the coordinate system.
Block.	A group of related items (records, characters, etc.) handled as a unit during input and output. A section of program code treated as a unit.
Blocking factor.	The process of grouping two or more records together to form a block, and the number of records put together in each block is called a blocking factor.
Boolean algebra.	An algebra, which deal with logical propositions, which are either true or false. This algebra is suitable for use with binary number system, and is very useful in designing logic circuits, which are used by the processors of computer systems.
Boolean function.	A mathematical function in Boolean algebra. For example, $w = x + y . z$
Boolean variable.	A variable used in Boolean algebra. It can assume a value true or false.
Booting.	The process of automatic loading of the operating system to primary storage, and readying a computer system for use.
Branch instruction.	An instruction, which transfers program control to a non-consecutive instruction.
Bridge.	An internetworking tool, which is used to connect networks that use the same communication protocols above the data-link layer, but may not use the same protocols at the physical and data-link layers.
Broadband channel.	Communication channels, which are capable of data transfer rates of 1 million baud (bits/second) or more. They are used to handle high volumes of data, and for high-speed computer to computer communication, or for simultaneous transmission of data to several different devices.
Browser.	A software tool, which provides several navigation facilities to help users do internet surfing easily and effectively.
Buffer.	A small storage area used to store information on a temporary basis for compensating the difference in rates of flow of data between various computer device. For example, when data flows from an I/O device to the CPU, it passes through a buffer.
Bug.	An error in a computer program.
Built-in-functions.	Subprograms, which are provided with the language so that the programmer need only call them in a program to have them automatically invoked. Also known as intrinsic subprograms.
Bundled.	The inclusion of software with the hardware of a computer system as part of system's total price.
Byte.	A fixed number of adjacent bits, which represent a particular character or symbol. Normally a byte consists of eight bits.

C

C.	A programming language, which was designed to have the virtues of high-level programming languages (mainly machine independence) with the efficiency of an assembly language.
C++.	A programming language, which contains all the elements of the basic C language, but has been expanded to include numerous object-oriented programming features.
Cache memory.	A small high speed memory, which is used to increase the speed of processing by making current programs and data available to the CPU at a rapid rate.
Call statement.	A program statement, which transfers program control to a subroutine.
Canonical form.	A Boolean function whose terms contain all variables (or their complements). This is the unreduced form of the Boolean function in minterm or maxterm form.
Carrier.	Any device, which is used to transmit data from one location to another.
Cathode Ray Tube (CRT).	An electronic tube with a TV like screen upon which information may be displayed.
C-band transmission.	The use of 4 GHz band of frequencies for transmission and retransmission of microwave signals in a satellite communication system.
CD-ROM jukebox.	A mass storage device, which use a set of CD-ROM disks, disk drives, and a controller mounted in a single unit. All the CD-ROM disks of a CD-ROM jukebox form a single large storage unit. They are typically used for archiving read-only data.
Cell.	The intersection of a row and column in a spreadsheet. A user enters text, number, or formula in a cell.
Central Processing Unit (CPU).	The control unit and the arithmetic logic unit of a computer system are jointly known as the CPU. It is the brain of any computer system in which all calculations and comparisons performed by a computer are carried out. The CPU is also responsible for activating, and controlling operations of other units of a computer system.
Chain printers.	Line printers, which print characters by striking a set of hammers on an inked ribbon and paper placed against a metallic chain on which all the characters of the character set supported by the printer are embossed.
Channel.	(1) A path for carrying signal between a source and a destination. (2) A track on a magnetic tape, or a band on a magnetic drum.
Character addressable storage.	A storage device, in which each character as one unique location with its own address. Another name for character addressable storage is variable-word-length storage.

Character printer. A printer with a print mechanism, which prints one character at a time.

Charge-Coupled Device (CCD). A completely electronic storage device fabricated on semiconductor chips. It stores data as pockets of charge in a semiconductor.

Chip. A thin wafer of silicon on which integrated electronic components are deposited.

Circuit switching. The simplest method of data communication in which a dedicated physical path is established between the sending and the receiving stations through the nodes of the network for the complete duration of information exchange.

Client computer. In a client-server computing environment, a computer, which is used by an end user to interact with the server computer. It runs client processes, which send service requests to the server.

Client-server computing a network of computers, which consists of a server computer (such as, file server, database server, print server, name server), and multiple client computers, which share programs and data from the server.

Clip art library. A collection of graphic images stored on disk, which can be readily used in word processing or desktop publishing documents, or in presentation graphics, or for other purposes.

Clock speed. The number of times the built-in electronic clock of a computer system pulses in one second.

Coaxial cable. A cable made up of a single wire in the center of an insulator wrapped in mesh. It is often used as a medium to transmit data between computers, and between computers and peripheral devices.

Code generator. A very high-level programming language in which programmers specify through an interactive dialog with the system, the design specifications of a system (which tasks are to be performed), and it automatically generates (produces) the program source code for the system.

Coding. The process of writing computer instructions in a programming language.

Collate. To combine items from two or more sequenced files into a single one.

Collating sequence. An ordering assigned to the characters of a character set to be used for sequencing purposes. A commonly encountered collating sequence involves the special characters, letters, and digits, in that order.

Combinational circuit A group of logic gates interconnected to form a logic circuit.

Command interpreter. The part of an operating system, which serves as an interface for the user to communicate with the computer via its operating system.

Command-line interface. A textual user interface in which the user gives instructing to the computer by typing commands using the keyboard.

Comment. An entry in a computer program for the purpose of documentation or explanation. Comments are used within a program to assist anyone reading the source program listing. They do not contain any program logic, and are ignored (not translated) by the language processor.

Common Business Oriented Language (COBOL). A high-level programming language developed for business data processing applications.

Common carriers. Data transmission service providers.

Communication protocol. A set of rules and procedures established to interconnect and communicate between computers. It provides a method for orderly and efficient exchange of data by establishing rules for the proper interpretation of controls and data transmitted as raw bits and bytes.

Communications processor. A processing unit, which coordinates networks and data communications. Within a computer network, it ensures that data flows to and from different computer systems correctly and efficiently.

Communications satellite a microwave relay station precisely positioned 36000 kms. Above the equator with an orbit speed that exactly matches the earth's rotation speed. It is use for data transmission between any two randomly chosen points in a very-very large area.

Communications software. Software that enables transfer of data and programs from one computer system to another in a network of computers.

Compact Disk-Read-Only Memory (CD-ROM). A shiny, silver color metal disk of 5¼-inch (12 cm) diameter having a storage capacity of about 650 Megabytes. It is so called, because of its enormous storage capacity on a compact-size disk, and because it is a read-only storage medium.

Compile. To translate a program written a high-level language into its equivalent machine language program. Usually a single source statement yields more than one machine instruction.

Compiler. A translator program (software package), which translates a high-levels language program into its equivalent machine language program.

Complement. For a number, which has n digits in it, a complement is defined as the difference between the number and the base raised to the nth power minus one. For example, complement of $37_{10} = 10^2 - 1 - 37 = 62_{10}$. In Boolean algebra, the complement of a variable is the reverse (NOT) of its value. For example, complement of A is $\overline{A}$.

Completely connected network. A network in which there is a separate physical link for connecting each node to any other node in the network.

Complex Instruction Set Computer (CISC) Architecture. An architecture of CPUs with large instruction set, variable-length instructions, and a variety of addressing modes.

Computer.	An electronic device, which can automatically accept and store input data, process them, and produce output results by interpreting and executing programmed instructions.
Computer Aided Design (CAD).	Use of computers to automate design and drafting operations.
Computer Aided Manufacturing (CAM).	Use of computers of automate manufacturing operations.
Computer animation.	The area of computer science, which does with the generation, sequencing, and display (at a specified rate) of a set of images (called frames) to create an effect of visual change or motion, similar to a movie film (video). Animation is commonly used in those instances where videography is not possible, or animation can better illustrate the concept than video.
Computer audio.	The area of computer science, which deals with synthesizing, recording, and playback of audio or sound with the aid of a computer.
Computer graphics.	The area of computer science, which deals with the generation, representation, manipulation and display of pictures (lines drawings and images) with the aid of a computer.
Computer literacy.	Having sufficient computer knowledge, so that an individual can work and live in a computerized society.
Computer network.	A distributed data processing system in which multiple computers are linked together for the purpose of data communication and resource sharing.
Computer system.	The various components (input and output devices, storage, CPU) of a computer integrated together to perform the steps called for in the program being executed.
Computer video.	The area of computer science, which deals with the recording and display of a sequence of images at a reasonable speed to create an impression of movement.
Computer-Based Training (CBT).	Using computer technologies for training and education. The use of computer helps in making touring programs, which are tailored to the student's level of subject mastery, and can provide immediate feedback.
Conference on Data Systems Languages (CODASYL).	A committee of computer users, manufacturers and the United States government, which helps to establish programming standards for various programming languages.
Console.	In a mainframe system,the terminal, which is directly connected to the host (main-computer), and is mainly used by the system administrators to monitor the health of the system, or to perform some system administration activities.
Constant.	A value, written into a program instruction, which does not change during the execution of the program.
Control program.	An operating system program, which control the operations and management of resources of a computer system.

	The control program's major functions are job scheduling, input/output scheduling, and program monitoring.
Control unit.	The unit of a compute system, which manages and coordinates the operations of all the other components of the central processing unit (CPU) of the computer.
Counter.	A device, register or storage location for storing integers, which is suitably incremented or decremented to represent the number of occurrences of an event.
CPU scheduler.	The part of an operating system, which is connected with deciding which of the ready jobs should be allotted the CPU for execution.
CPU-bound jobs.	Jobs which heavily utilize the CPU operations during the course of their processing.
Crash.	A hardware or software failure that causes a computer system to stop functioning.
Cryptography.	A means of protecting private information against unauthorized access in those situations where it is difficult to ensure access control. The basic idea behind this security technique is that, if it is not possible to ensure access control, it is better to prevent comprehension of information.
Cursor.	A highlight on the screen of a monitor, which indicates the location of the next keyed-in character on the display screen. It can appear as a small rectangular object, line, arrow, or I-beam pointer, or in a spreadsheet, as a large block covering an entire cell.
Cybernatics.	The use of computers coupled with automatic machinery to carry out complex operations.
Cyberspace.	The world-wide network of computers.
Cycle time.	The time interval between the instant at which a read/write command is given to a memory, and the instant when the next such instruction can be issued to the memory (also known as memory cycle time).
Cylinder.	In a disk pack, a set of corresponding tracks on all the surfaces is called a cylinder. All tracks of a cylinder are accessible by a single movement of the access mechanism.

D

Daisy wheel printer.	A letter-quality printer, which uses a printing head with the appearance of daisy and/or a wheel. Each petal of the daisy wheel has a character embossed on it.
Data.	A collection of facts in raw form, which become information after proper organization or processing.
Data Base Management System (DBMS).	A set of programs provided to facilitate the users in organizing, creating, deleting, updating, and manipulating their data in a database.

Data Definition Language (DDL).	A language used to define the structure of a database.
Data dependence.	Dependency of data on the application.
Data dictionary.	A document, which maintains the data definitions of a database. It is automatically created/updated by the DDL as the database schema is defined or changed.
Data element.	A meaningful collection of related characters. Also called a field or data item.
Data entry.	The conversion of human readable data into a form, which a computer system can interpret. This is also called data preparation.
Data integrity.	Consistency of data in all files.
Data Manipulation Language (DML).	A language used to enter and manipulate the data in a database.
Data processing.	See processing.
Data processing system.	A system that accomplishes data processing. It includes the necessary resources,which are people, procedures and devices needed to process the data.
Data redundancy.	Repetition of the same data items in more than one file.
Data storage hierarchy.	In data processing, organization of data into growing hierarchy for easy manageability. A typical data storage hierarchy consists of bits, characters, fields, records, files and database.
Data transfer rate.	The speed at which data is transferred from main memory to another medium on which data are recorded. For magnetic tape, the data transfer rate is equal to the product of the tape speed and recording density. In a network environment, it refers to the speed of transfer of data from one computer to another on the network.
Database.	A collection of data files integrated and organized into a single comprehensive file system, which is arranged to minimize duplication of data, and to provide convenient access to information within that system to satisfy a wide variety of user needs.
Database administrator.	One who is responsible for defining, updating, and controlling access to a data base.
Database model.	The manner in which the various files of a database are linked together. The four commonly used database models are hierarchical, network, relational, and object-oriented.
Database schema.	The database structure definition.
Database software.	A set of programs, which enables users to create a database, maintain it (add, delete and update its records), organize its data in desired fashion, and to selectively retrieve useful information from it.
De Morgan's theorem.	A theorem in Boolean algebra. Which states how to complement a Boolean expression.

Debugger.	A software tool, which helps the programmer in debugging the logic of a program by allowing him/her to follow the program's execution step-by-step, and to display intermediate calculation results and field values whenever desired.
Debugging.	The process of finding and correcting program errors (bugs).
Decimal number system.	A number system with a base of 10. The ten allowable digits are 0, 1, 2, 3, 4, 5, 6, 7, 8 and 9. It is used in our day-to-day life.
Decision logic.	A selection logic.
Decoder.	The part of CPU, which has the necessary circuitry to decode and interpret the meaning of every instruction supported by the CPU.
Dedicated line.	See leased line.
Design phase.	A phase in the life-cycle of software system during which the detailed design of the system selected in the study phase occurs.
Desktop Publishing (DTP).	An application software package, which allows a user to perform design, typesetting, and paste-up functions, and to produce high-quality, camera-ready printed pages of the documents so prepared on a high-quality printer.
Development phase.	A phase in the life-cycle of a software during which a system is constructed to meet the requirements specified in the design phase.
Diagnostic routines.	Programs used to print error messages by a computer to indicate system problems, and improper instructions.
Dial-up line.	A data transmission service, which operates in a manner similar to a telephone call. Also known as switched line.
Digital Computer.	A computer, which works with discrete quantities. It uses numbers to simulate real-time processes. Compare with analog computer.
Digitizer.	An input device used for converting (digitizing) pictures, maps and drawings into digital form for storage in computers. This enables re-creation of the drawing form the stored information whenever required, and easy incorporation of changes in the drawing as and when required.
Direct file.	A file organization in which the desired record (piece of information) can be directly located by its key field value without having to search through a sequence of other records. Also known as random file.
Direct/leased-line connection.	A method of connecting a computer to the Internet by using a dedicated (leased) telephone line.
Directory.	A mapping table, which is used by operating systems to map file names to their corresponding file attributes and file data, and also to provide greater flexibility to users in file naming.
Disk.	A flat, circular plate coated with a magnetic material on which data can be stored by magnetization or portions of the flat surface.

Disk array.	A mass storage device, which uses a set of hard disks, hard disk drives, and a controller mounted in a single box. All the disks of a disk array form a single large storage unit. Also known as Redundant Array of Inexpensive Disks (RAID).
Disk drive.	A device used for storage and retrieval of data stored on disk.
Disk pack.	A removable direct-access storage medium containing multiple magnetic disks mounted vertically on a single shaft.
Diskette.	At low-cost, thin, flexible magnetic disk storage device used on small computer systems. Also called a floppy disk.
Distributed computing system.	A computer system consisting of interconnected, multiple computers.
Distributed database.	Seamless integration of multiple databases located on different computers. A distributed database management system functions in a manner that the multiple distributed databases managed by it appear as a single, centralized database to the end users.
Documentation.	Documentation of a software system involves collecting, organizing, storing, and maintaining a complete historical record of programs, and other documents used or prepared during the different phases of the system.
Dot-matrix printers.	Character printers, which form characters and all kinds of images as a pattern of dots.
Dots Per Inch (DPI).	A measurement of the quality for printed output. It refers to the number of dots, which can be printed per linear inch, horizontally or vertically.
Downloading.	Moving a file from a remote computer to ones own computer in a netrwork environment.
Downtime.	The period during which a computer is malfunctioning or not operating correctly due to machine failures.
Drum printers.	Line printers, which print characters by striking a set of hammers on and inked ribbon and paper placed against a solid cylindrical drum with character embossed on its surface in the form of circular bands.
Dum terminal.	A terminal, which has no local processing capability.
Dynamic Data Exchange (DDE).	A technique for linking applications, which allows a user to move data from one application into another, such as from a spreadsheet into a word-processor. Changes made in one application are automatically reflected in linked applications.
Dynamic RAM (DRAM).	A type of RAM, which uses an extenal circuitry to periodically "regenerate" or refresh the storage charge to retain the stored data.

E

Edit.	To modify the form or format of the data by inserting or deleting characters where needed.
Editor.	A software used to interactively review and modify text materials and other program instructions.
Education software.	Software, which allows computer systems to be used as a teaching and learning tool.
Electrically EPROM (EPROM).	An EPROM chip in which the stored information is erased by using high voltage electric pulses. Also known as flash memory.
Electronic card.	A small plastic card having encoded data appropriate for the application for which it is used. An electronic card reader, which is normally connected to a computer, is used to read the data encoded on an electronic card, and transfer it to the computer for further processing.
Electronic Data Interchange (EDI).	The use of computers and data communications to transit data electronically between companies.
Electronic Data Processing (EDP).	Pertaining to data processing equipment, which is predominantly electronic, such as an electronic digital computer.
Electronic Funds Transfer (EFT).	A general term referring to a cashless approach used to pay for goods and services. Electronic signals between computers are often used to adjust the accounts of the parties involved in a transaction.
Electronic mail.	A service on the Internet, which allows an Internet user to send a mail (message) to another Internet user in any part of the world in a near-real-time manner.
Electronic pen.	An input device, which serves as an effective point-and-draw device.
Electrostatic printer.	A high-speed printer, which uses charged pins to form character matrices on chemically treated paper.
Electrothermal printer.	A high-speed printer, which uses heated elements to create characters as matrices of small dots on heat-sensitive paper.
Elementary data item.	A data item, which is not broken down into smaller units.
E-mail.	See electronic mail.
Emulator.	A program, which permits one computer to execute the machine-language instructions of another computer of different make.
Encryption.	The process of transforming an intelligible information into an unintelligible form.
End user.	Any individual who uses the information generated by a compute based system.
End-to-end solutions.	A computerized solution offered to a user in which a single vendor takes the responsibility of supplying all the hardware and software components of the solution.
Entertainment software.	Software, which allows computer system to be used as an entertainment tool.

Erasable Programmable Read Only Memory (EPROM).	A memory chip in case of which it is possible to erase information stored in it, and the chip can be reprogrammed to store new information.
Ethernet.	The most widely used LAN technology.
Execution time.	The total time required to execute a program on a particular system is called its execution time for that computer system.
Explicitly Parallel Instruction Computing (EPIC).	A technology, which is fast emerging as the technology for next-generation processors. The three key features used in this technology for improved processor performance are explicit parallelism, predication and speculation.

F

Fascimile (FAX).	Transmission of pictures, texts, maps, graphs, etc., over transmission lines, phone lines, and other carriers between geographically separated points. An image is scanned at a transmitting point, and duplicated at a receiving point.
Feasibility study.	A study to determine whether the proposed solution is technically and economically feasible in all respect.
Field.	In a record, a meaningful collection of one or more related characters treated as a unit.
Fifth-generation computers.	Computers built since 1989 till now. They use ultra large-scale integrated circuits, very fast and large main memory and disk storage, and very powerful programming languages and operating systems.
File.	A collection of related information.
File Management System (FMS).	A set of programs provided to facilitate the users in organizing, creating, deleting, updating, and manipulating their files.
File Transfer Protocol (FTP).	An application level protocol, which allows a user to move a file from one computer to another in a network environment.
File utilities.	A set of routines, which perform a variety of generalized operations (such as, sorting, searching, merging, copying, printing and maintenance) on data files.
Firewall.	A software, which usually runs on the proxy server of an organization, and controls the flow of incoming and outgoing messages from within an organization for providing better security to the organization.
Firmware.	A sequence of instruction (software), which is substituted for hardware, and stored in Read Only Memory (ROM).
First-generation computers.	Computers built between 1942 and 1955, which used vacuum tubes, and were programmed in assembly language. Few examples are ENIAC, EDVAC and EDSAC.

Fixed-wireless system.	A wireless computing system, which supports little or no mobility of the computing equipment associated with the wireless network.
Fixed-head magnetic disk.	A magnetic disk system, which that eliminates the use of an access mechanism by distributing all the read/write heads over the disk surfaces.
Flash memory.	See Electrically EPROM (EPROM).
Flip-flop.	A electronic circuit, which can be placed in one out of two stable states. Each state may be used to represent a binary digit.
Floating-point numbers.	Signed numbers held in a fraction-exponent format. For example, 3216 would be represented as 0.3216×10^4 in floating-point notation.
Floppy disk.	See diskette.
Flowchart.	A pictorial representation, which uses predefined symbols to describe either the logic of a computer program (program flowchart), or the data flow and processing steps of a system (system flowchart).
Flowcharting.	The process of drawing a flowchart for an algorithm.
Font.	A complete set of characters with the same style and size.
Foreground processing.	Automatic execution of high priority (foreground) jobs by preempting resources held by low-priority (background) jobs. Contrast with background processing.
FORmula TRANslation (FORTRAN).	A high-level, programming languages used for scientific and engineering applications.
Fourth-generation computers.	Computers built between 1975 and 1989. They used large-scale integrated circuits, semiconductor memories, and powerful high-level languages and operating systems.
Frequency Division Multiplexing (FDM).	A method used to concurrently transmit data between several transmitters and receivers over a single transmission medium. The available bandwidth of a physical medium is divided into smaller, disjoint, logical bandwidths, and each of the component bandwidths is used as a separate communications line (channel).
Front-end processor.	A processor designed specifically to handle the communications processing task. Its main purpose is to off-load communications processing task from the host computer, thereby the host computer can be dedicated for applications and data processing jobs.
Full adder.	An adder, which adds three binary digits and outputs a result bit and a carry bit.
Full duplex.	A data transmission mode in which data signals can be transmitted between a source and a destination in both directions simultaneously.
Function.	A subprogram, which returns a single value.

G

Garbage-In-Garbage-Out (GIGO).	Refers to computer errors caused due to incorrect input data, on unreliable programs.
Gateway.	(1) A computer, which is connected to the Internet by using a dedicated (leased) telephone line, and is used to provide Internet connectivity to other computers via it. (2) An inter-networking tool, which is used to interconnect dissimilar networks that use different communication protocols.
Generation.	In computer talks, it is a step in technology. It provides a framework for the growth of the computer industry.
Gigabytes (GB).	Memory storage equal to 1,073,741,824 (2^{30}) bytes in a computer.
Gigaflop.	10^9 floating-point arithmetic operations per second.
Graphical User Interface (GUI).	An interface for computer users, which users can select with a mouse for telling the computer what they want it to do for them.
Graphics software.	Software, which enables users to use computer system for creating, editing, viewing, storing retrieving and printing designs, drawings, pictures, graphs, and anything else, which can be drawn in a traditional manner.
Gray scales.	The number of shades of a color that can be presented on a monochrome (black and white) monitor's screen, or on a monochrome printer's output.
Groupware.	See Computer Supported Co-operative Working (CSCW).

H

Hacker.	A computer enthusiast who uses the computer as a source of recreation by pushing its capabilities to its limits (performance, security, storage etc.)
Half adder.	An adder, which adds two binary digits, and outputs a result bit and a carry bit (if any).
Half duplex.	A communication system in which data can be transmitted between a source and a destination in both directions, but only in one direction at a time.
Hard disk.	A magnetic disk storage device, which uses disks made of rigid metal (frequently aluminium). The hard disk platters come in many sizes ranging from 1 to 14-inch diameter.
Hard-copy output.	A computer output, which is permanent in nature and can be kept in paper files, when the person is not using the computer. For example, output produced by printers or plotters on paper.
Hardware.	The physical components of a computer system, such as electronic, magnetic, and mechanical devices.
Hashing.	The process of using an address generating function (called hashing algorithm) to map a record's key field value to its storage address.

Hertz.	One cycle per second.
Hexadecimal number system.	A number system with a base of 16. Its digits range from 0 to F. It is commonly used as a shortcut notation for groups of four binary digits.
Hierarchical database.	A database model in which the data elements are linked in the form of an inverted tree structure with the root at the top and the branches formed below.
Hierarchical network.	A communications network in which computers or processors are connected in a tree like structure.
High-level language.	A programming language whose structure is application oriented, and is independent of the structure of the computer. Each statement of such a language is translated into many language statements.
Hotlist.	A personal list of favorite URL addresses, which an Internet user is likely to frequently visit in future. A user's hotlist is automatically created and stored an his/her local web client computer by a browser.
Hybrid printers.	A network, which is a combination of two more different network topologies.
Hydra printers.	Multifunctional devices, which perform the functions of two or more of the following office equipment-printer, fax machine, copy machine and scanner.
Hypertext.	Documents that are prepared by using special linking facility for easier electronic access and manipulation.
Hypertext Markup Language (HTML).	A powerful language used for creating hypertext documents.
Hypertext Transport Protocol (HTTP).	An Internet Protocol for interaction between the computers on the Internet.

I

I/O ports.	Sockets used to plug-in I/O devices to a compute system.
I/O-bound jobs.	Jobs whose CPU utilization is very low. They mostly perform I/O operating during the course of their processing.
Icon.	A graphical object displayed on a visual display screen, which is used in place of words or phrases to allow users to select program options, when selected with a mouse or other pointing device.
Impact printer.	A printer, which prints characters by causing hammers to strike against the paper on which information is to be printed.
Indexed Sequential Access Method (ISAM).	See Indexed sequential file.

Indexed sequential file.	A file organization in which an index (directory) file is used to have both sequential and random access to the records of the file. Also known as the Indexed Sequential Access Method (ISAM).
Information.	Processed data obtained as the output of data processing. It is used by people to enhance understanding and to achieve specific purpose.
Inkjet printers.	Character printers, which form characters and all kinds of images by spraying small drops of ink on to the paper.
Input.	Data and instructions entered into a computer for processing purposes.
Input device.	A device used to enter data and instructions into a compute. Examples are keyboard, mouse, trackball, joystick, scanner, digitizer, voice recognition system, and vision input system.
Input/Output (I/O).	Pertaining to the techniques, media, and devices used for man-machine interaction.
Input/Output Register (I/O).	A register, which is used to communicate with the input/output devices.
Instruction.	A command or order given to a computer. It normally consists of a code to indicate the operation to be performed, and address(es) in memory where the operand(s) would be found.
Instruction register.	(I) A register, which holds the current instruction that is being executed.
Instruction set.	A set of machine instructions that the CPU has built-in ability to execute.
Integrated Circuits (ICs).	Circuits consisting of several electronic components like transistors, resistors and capacitors grown on a single chip of silicon, eliminating wired interconnection between components.
Integrated Services Digital Network (ISDN).	A telephonic system, which provides digital (not analog) telephone and data services.
Intelligent terminal.	A terminal having extensive local processing capability. It has a built-in microcomputer, which can be programmed by users.
Inter Block Gap (IBG).	When several records are in one block, these gaps separate the blocks of records on magnetic tape.
Inter Record Gap (IRG).	Blank space between two consecutive records on tape.
Interface.	Electronic circuit used to interconnect I/O devices to a computer's CPU or memory.
Internal storage.	The addressable storage in a digital computer, which is directly under the control of the CPU.
Internet.	A network of computer's which links many different types of computers all over the world.

Internet search engine.	An application available on the WWW, which helps users locate the web sites containing useful information and references to such information.
Internal Service Provider (ISP).	An organization, which maintains one or more gateway computers, and provides Interent access facility to other users by allowing them to connect their computers to its own gateway computer(s) by using a modem.
Internet surfing.	The process of navigating the Internet to search for useful information.
Internetworking.	Interconnecting of two or more networks to form a single network. The resulting network is called an internetwork.
Interpreter.	A language processor, which translates a statement of a high-level language, and immediately executes it before translating the next source language statement. It is the most common language processor for BASIC.
Iteration logic.	A program construct, which is used to produce loops in program logic, when one or more instructions may be executed several times depending on some condition. Also known as looping logic.

J

Java.	A programming language, which was designed to have machine-independent compiled code. It is primarily used for Internet-based applications.
Job.	See process.
Job Control Language (JCL).	A special purpose language, which is used to describe to a computer's operating system the resource requirements of a job fed to the computer for processing.
Joystick.	An input device, which serves as an effective pointing device for applications, such as video games, flight simulators, training simulators, and for controlling industrial robots.
Jumps instruction.	An instruction or signal, which conditionally or unconditionally, specifies the location of the next instruction, and directs the computer to that instruction. A jump instruction is used to alter the normal sequence of control of the computer.
Justification.	The alignment of text at the left margin, the right margin, or both margins.

K

Kernel.	The central controlling part of an operating system, which implements the most primitive of the system's functions. It is the only part of an operating system, which a user cannot replace or modify.
Key field.	A unique field in a record, which is used to distinguish one record from another.

Keyboard.	An input device, which enables data entry into a computer by pressing a set of keys (labelled buttons), which are neatly mounted on a keyboard connected to the computer system.
Key-to-tape.	A device used to enter data onto a magnetic tape.
Kilobytes (KB).	Memory storage equal to 1024 (2^{10}) bytes in a computer.
Kiosk.	An unattended system, which is used to store information of public interest, and allows common people to access the stored information as per their requirement.
K u-band transmission.	The use of 11 GHz to 14 GHz band of frequencies for transmission and retransmission of microwave signals in a satellite communication system.

L

Label.	One or more characters used to identify a statement, an instruction, or a data field in a computer program.
Label record.	A machine-readable record, which is used to identify a data file. It is the first record of the file.
Landscape mode.	A mode of printing in which the printed lines are parallel to the longer edge of the paper.
Language processor.	A software used to convert source program instruction to object or machine language instructions. Few examples are assembler, compiler and interpreter.
Large Scale Integration (LSI).	Integration of over 30,000 electronic components on a single chip.
Laser disk.	See optical disk.
Laser printers.	Page printers, which produce very high quality output by forming characters and all kinds of images with very tiny ink particles. They use a combination of laser-beam and electrophotographic techniques to create printed outputs.
Latency.	In case of disk storage, the relational delay time for the desired data (sector) to come under the read/write head positioned over that track. Maximum latency time equals the time taken by disk to rotate once.
Leased line.	A data transmission service in which a special conditioned telephone line directly and permanently connects two computers. A leased line can be used for both voice and data transmission. Also known as private line or dedicated line.
Library routine.	A tested routine maintained in a library of programs.
Light pen.	A pen shaped device, which is used as an input device to input data into computers by writing or sketching on the screen of a cathode ray tube.
Linker.	A program, which is used to properly combine all the object program files (modules) of a software, and to convert them into the software's final executable form.

Linux. — An open-source operating system enhanced and backed by thousands of programmers world-wide. It is a multi-tasking operating system, which was originally designed to be used on personal computers.

LISt Processing (LISP). — A programming language suitable for manipulating non-numeric data, such as symbols and strings of text. It is used in the areas of pattern recognition, artificial intelligence, and for simulation of games.

Load module. — The final executable form of a software produced by a linker.

Local Area Network (LAN). — A computer network, which interconnects computers and other peripheral devices within a limited geographical area of a few kilometers.

Logic circuit. — See combinational circuit.

Logic error. — An error, which occurs when the actual logic of a program is different from the desired logic. Such errors cause the program to produce incorrect output.

Logic gate. — An electronic circuit, which operates on one or more input signals to produce standard output signals. For example, AND, OR and NOT gates. Logic gates are the building blocks of all the circuits in a computer.

Logical operators. — Symbols used to show a logical relationship between two data items. Examples in FORTRAN are .EQ. for equal, and G.T. for greater than.

Logo. — An easy-to-learn programming language, which is commonly used to teach problem-solving skills to children.

Loop. — A sequence of instructions, which is executed repeatedly, until a terminal condition occurs.

Looping logic. — See iteration logic.

Low-level languages. — Programming languages, which normally translate from one source instruction to one object instruction. These languages are machine dependent.

M

Machine language. — A low-level language, which is directly understandable by the computer system. Each model of a computer has a unique machine language.

Macro. — A sequence of frequently used operations, or keystrokes bundled together as a single command, or keystroke by software, so that the invocation of the single command or keystroke leads to the invocation of all the operations/keystrokes in the specified sequence. This helps speed user interaction with the system.

Macro flowchart. — A flowchart, which outlines the main segments of a program, or shows less detail.

Macro instruction.	An instruction in a source language, which is equivalent to a specified sequence of machine.
Magnetic core.	Tiny rings made of magnetic material, which can be polarized to represent a binary 1 or 0.
Magnetic disk.	See disk.
Magnetic Ink Character Recognition (MICR).	A technology used by the banking industry for faster processing of the large volume of cheques. This technology also ensures accuracy of data entry, because most of the information is pre-printed on the cheque and is directly fed to the computer.
Magnetic storage.	Storage device such as disks, drums tapes, cores, etc., which utilize the magnetic properties of materials to store data.
Magnetic tape.	A secondary storage device, which uses a long plastic strip coated with a magnetic material as a recording medium.
Magneto-optical disk.	A storage disk, which integrates optical and magnetic disk technologies to enable rewritable storage with laser-beam technology.
Main memory.	See primary storage.
Mainframe system.	A computer system, which is mainly used for handling the bulk of data and information processing of such organizations as banks, insurance companies, hospitals, railways, etc. They are also used in such environments where a large number of users need to share a common computing facility, such as in research groups, educational institutions, engineering firms, etc.
Management Information System (MIS).	An organized collection of people, procedures, and devices used to provide the right information to the right person at the right time for proper decision-making.
Manufacturer-programmed ROM.	A ROM in which data is burnt in by the manufacturer of the electronic equipment in which it is used.
Mass storage.	Storage systems, which provide access to several terabytes of stored data. They use multiple units of storage media (such as multiple disks, multiple tapes, multiple CD-ROMs) as a single secondary device.
Massively Parallel Processing (MPP).	An approach to designing supercomputers in which thousands of processors are integrated within a single computer, so that the supercomputer can perform thousands of tasks simultaneously.
Master file.	A file containing relatively permanent data. This file is often updated by records in a transaction file.
Maxterm.	A Boolean quantity consisting of all terms (in its normal form or complement form) Ored together. Any combination (2^n for n variables) of terms and complements is permissible, provided all are included in the term.

Medium Scale Integration (MSI). A circuit with about 100 transistors fabricated on a single chip.

Megabytes (MB). Memory storage equal to 1,048,576 (2^{20}) bytes in a computer.

Memory Address Register (MAR). A register, which holds the address of the active memory location and loaded form the program control register when an instruction is read from memory.

Memory Buffer Register (MBR). A register, which holds the contents of the memory word read from or written in, memory.

Memory dump. Contents of memory duplicated on another storage device or printed on a printer.

Memory partition. In a multiprogramming system, the area occupied by each job residing simultaneously in the main memory.

Menu. A list of processing choices displayed on the screen from which a user may select.

Menu bar. A menu in which the options are displayed on a horizontal bar (usually at the top of the display screen) displayed across the screen.

Merging. The combining of records from two or more ordered files into a single ordered file.

Message switching. A data communications method in which the data (message) to be sent is first appended with the destination address, and then sent across the network to its destination.

Metropolitan Area Network (MAN). Networks, which share some of the characteristics of both LANs and WANs. They usually interconnect computers spread over a geographical area of about 50 kilometers.

Micro flowchart. A flowchart with more details. It is also called a detailed flowchart.

Microcode. The very basic* directions, which tell the CPU how to execute an instruction ; located in the control unit.

Microcomputer. The smallest category of computer fabricated using a microprocessor, and other integrated circuits, namely a ROM, RAM, and I/O interface fashion.

Microprocessor. An IC chip, which contains all the circuits needed to perform arithmetic, logic and control functions, the core activities of all computers, on a single chip.

Microprogram. Firmware programs residing in Read-Only Memory (ROM). They deal with low-level machine functions, and are essential substitutes for additional hardware.

Microsecond. One-millionth of a second.

Millisecond. One-thousand of a second.

Minterm. A Boolean quantity consisting of all terms (in its normal form or complement form) ANDed together. Any combination (2^n for n variables) of terms and complements is permissible, provided all are included in the term.

MIPS. Millions of Instructions Per Second.

Mnemonic.	Any kind of mental trick we use to help us remember. For example, a computer may be designed to interpret the machine code of 1111 (binary) as the subtract operation, but it is easier for a human being to remember it is SUB.
Mobile computing.	A wireless computing system, which supports mobility of the computing equipment, which the users use to access the resources associated with the wireless network. It allows mobile users to access information from anywhere and at anytime. Also known as nomadic computing.
Modulation.	The technique by which a digital signal is converted to its analog form for transmission over an analog facility.
Modulator-DEModulator (Modem).	Devices used to convert digital signals (to be communicated over an analog channel, such as telephone line) to analog form at the sending end, and back to digital form at the receiving end.
Monitor.	A popular output device used for producing soft-copy output. It displays the output on a television like screen.
Motherboard.	The main circuit board of a computer system. It has the CPU chip, RAM chips, ROM chips, I/O handling chips, etc., mounted on it. Also known as system board.
Mouse.	A small, hand-held input device, which serves as an effective point-and-draw device in today's computers.
MS-DOS.	Stands for Microsoft Disk Operating System. A single-user operating system, which was popularly used for personal computers in the 1980s.
Multi-access bus network.	A network in which a single transmission medium is shared by all nodes.
Multimedia.	Use of more than one media (such as text, graphics, animation, audio and video) for information presentation.
Multimedia computer system.	A computer system, which has the capability to integrate two or more types of media (text, graphics, animation, audio and video) for the purpose or generation, storage, representation, manipulation and access of multimedia information.
Multiplexing.	The method of dividing a physical channel into many logical channels, so that a number of independent signals may be simultaneously transmitted on it.
Multiprocessing.	A term used to describe interconnected computer configurations, or computers with two or more independent CPUs, which have the ability to simultaneously execute several programs.
Multiprocessor.	A computer system consisting of two or more CPUs monitor under a common control.
Multiprogramming.	Interleaved execution of two or more different and independent program by the same computer.
Multitasking.	Concurrent execution of multiple jobs (often referred to as tasks of same user) in a single-user.

N

Nanosecond.	One-billionth (10^{-9}) of a second.
Narrowband channel.	Communication channels, which handle low volumes of data, typically from 45 to 300 baud. They are used mainly for telegraph lines and low speed terminals.
Netiquette.	Deals with the rules of framing messages while interacting with order Internet users.
Network.	See computers network.
Network database.	A database model in which the data elements are organized in the form of parent-child relationships.
Network Interface Card (NIC).	A hardware device, which allows a computer to be connected to a network, both functionally and physically.
Network topology.	The structure of interconnection of nodes of a computer network.
Newsgroup.	A group of Internet/Intranet users, who use the usenet facility of the Internet to exchange their views/ideas/information on some common topic, which is of interest to all the group members.
Node.	An end point of a branch in a network, or a common junction of two or more network branches.
Nomadic computing.	See mobile computing.
Nonimpact printer.	A printer, which performs some type of operation to the paper, instead of physically striking it (as in the case of an impact printer). To print characters with nonimpact printers, the paper can be sprayed with ink, magnetized, electrically charged, heated, placed under pressure, or struck by laser beams.
Non-positional number system.	A number system in which each symbol represents the same value, regardless of its position in the number, and the symbols are simply added to find out the value of a particular number. It is very difficult to perform arithmetic with such a number system.
Non-volatile storage.	A storage medium, which retains its contents when the power is turned off or interrupted.
Notebook computer.	A small, portable computer mainly for use by people who need computing power wherever they go.
Numeric.	Pertaining to a character set, which contains the number 0 to 9.

O

Object Linking and Embedding (OLE).	A feature found in application software packages, which allows joining of documents in different applications, so that changes in either document are reflected in the other document.

Object program.	A fully compiled or assembled program, which is ready to be loaded into the computer. It results from the translation of a source program by a language processor.
Object-oriented database.	A database model, which captures object-oriented concepts, such as class hierarchy, inheritance, and methods.
Object-oriented programming (OOP).	A programming methodology, which deals with solving problems by identifying the real-world objects of the problem and the processing required of those objects, and then creating simulations of those objects, their processes, and the required communications between the objects.
Object-oriented programming languages.	Programming languages, which encapsulate data and sequences of operations into abstract entities called objects, providing a stronger encapsulation mechanism than procedure. Hence, object-oriented programming provides a more powerful modeling tool than procedure-oriented programming.
Octal number system.	A number system with a base of 8. The octal digits range from 0 to 7. It is commonly used as a shortcut notation for groups of three binary digits.
Off-line.	A device or system not directly under the control of a computer system.
Off-line data entry devices.	Input devices through which data is recorded on some media, such as floppies or tapes, and then entered later into the computer from the media for processing.
On-line.	A device or system directly connected to and under the control of a computer system.
On-line data entry devices.	Input devices, which are connected directly to the computer on which the entered data is processed.
Operand.	The part of a machine level instruction, which tells the central processor the location of the data to be manipulated.
Operating system.	An integrated set of programs, which controls the resources of a computer system, and provides its users with an interface or virtual machine, which is more convenient to use than the bare machine.
Operation code (op code).	The part of a machine level instruction which tells the central processor what has to be done.
Operation phase.	The life-cycle phase during which the system constructed in the development phase is used.
Optical bar-code reader.	An input devices, which is able to interpret combinations of marks (bars), which represent data.
Optical Character Recognition (OCR) Device.	An input device (a scanner) equipped with a character recognition software. It is used for inputting text documents, and store them in a form suitable for doing word processing of the documents.

Optical disk. A storage medium, which consists of a rotating disk, which is coated with a thin metal or some other material that is highly reflective. Laser beam technology is used for recording/reading of data on the disk. Also known as laser disks.

Optical fibre. Hair-thin threads of glass or plastic used as a data transmission medium. They use light signals for data transmission.

Optical Mark Reader (OMR). An input device (a scanner), which is capable of recognizing a pre-specified type of mark made by pencil or pen. Any input data, which is of a choice or selection nature can be recorded for OMR input.

OSI protocol. A communication protocol to interconnect geographically dispersed heterogeneous computers. This protocol has been standardized by the International Standards Organization (ISO).

Output. The information generated as a result of processing by a system.

Output device. A device used in a computer system to supply information and results of computation of the outside world. Examples are monitor, printer, plotter, screen image projector, and voice response system.

P

Packed decimal format. A modified form of zoned decimal number, which places two decimal digits into each byte of the field with the exception of the rightmost byte, which contains one digit and the sign of the field.

Packet switching. A data communication method in which the data (message) to be sent is first split up into packets of fixed size; each packet is then appended with source and destination addresses, as some control information; and then the packets are sent across the network to their destination. At the receiver end, the packets are reassembled to recreate the message.

Page. A program segment, which is loaded into the main memory only when it is needed for execution.

Page printer. A high-speed printer with a mechanism, which appears to print an entire page at one time.

Palmtop computer. A battery-operated computer with personal assistance tools. It is small-enough to fit in ones pocket, and operated by keeping it on ones palm.

Parallel binary adder. An adder in which all the bits of the two binary numbers are added simultaneously.

Parallel processing. A technology in which a multiprocessor system is used to solve complex problems faster by breaking the problem into sub-problems, and allowing different sub-problems to be processed simultaneously by different processors of the multi-processor system.

Parity bit.	An extra bit added to a string of bits, which enables the computer to detect internal errors in the transmission of binary data.
Pascal.	A high-level programming language named after Blaise Pascal, which facilitates the use of structured programming techniques.
Password.	A code by which a user gains access to a computer system. It is used for security purposes.
Patch.	A modifications of a software carried out between its two released versions. A patch (modification) is created to fix a newly discovered bug. All the patches are incorporated in a new release version of the software.
Peripherals.	The various input/output devices and auxiliary storage units of a computer system.
Personal assistance software.	Software, which enables users to use personal computers for storing and retrieving personal information, and planning and managing personal schedules, contracts, finance, and inventory of important items.
Personal Computer (PC).	A small and inexpensive computer used by individuals for carrying out personal jobs, or for applications, such as entertainment, home management, and hobbies.
Personal Digital Assistant (PDA).	A pocked-sized computer having facilities, such as calendar, calculator, notepad, etc.
Phase modulation.	A form of modulation in which two binary values of digital data are represented by the shift in phase of the carrier signal. That is, a sine wave with phase = 0° represents a digital 1, and a sine wave with phase = 180° represents a digital 0.
Picosecond.	One trillionth of second.
Pixel.	A picture element. It is use to represent one point in a raster scan display device.
Plotter.	An ideal output device, which is often used by architects, engineers, city planners, and others who need to routinely generate high-precision, hard-copy, graphic output of widely varying sizes.
Point-and-draw devices.	Input devices, which can be used to rapidly point to, and select a particular graphic icon, or menu item from the multiple options displayed on the screen. Many of these devices can also be very effectively used to create graphic elements on the screen, such as lines, curves and freehand shapes. Some of the commonly used point-and-draw devices are mouse, trackball, joystick, electronic pen and touch screen.
Point-Of-Sale (POS) Device.	An I/O device capable of immediately updating sales and inventory records at a central CPU, and producing a printed sales transaction receipt.
Portrait mode.	A mode of printing in which the printed lines are parallel to the shorter edge of the paper.

Positional number system. A number system in which there are only a few symbols called digits, and these symbols represent different values, depending on the position they occupy in the number. The value of each digit in such a number is determined by the digit itself, the position of the digit in the number, and the base of the number system.

Preview. A feature of a word-processing package, which permits the users to see what the document will look like (almost, if not exactly) when it is printed.

Primary storage. A temporary storage area, which is built into the computer hardware, and in which instructions and data of a program reside mainly when the program is being executed by the CPU.

Printer. An output device used to produce hard-copy output.

Private line. See leased line.

Procedure. A subprogram, which performs an action but returns no value.

Process. A program in execution. Also known as a job.

Processing. Performing a series of actions, or operation on data to convert them into useful information.

Processor. A unit of a computer system, which interprets instructions and executes them.

Program. A set of sequenced instructions (written in a language that can be understood by a computer) used to direct and control the operations of the computer to solve a problem, or to performs a particular task.

Program Control (PC) Register. A register, which holds the address of the next instruction to be executed.

Program Design Language (PDL). See pseudocode.

Program library. A collections of complete programs, subroutines, and program modules, which have already been developed, tested, and documented, usually as a result of other programming projects.

Programmable Read-Only Memory (PROM). Similar to read only memory with the exception that these chips can be reprogrammed by using special external equipment.

Programmer. One who designs, writes, tests, and maintains computer programs.

Programming language. A language used to express algorithms in a computer understandable form.

Protocol. See communication protocol.

Prototyping. The process of developing a small working model of a final operational system to demonstrate the concepts, look, and feel of the final system.

Pseudocode. — A programming analysis tool, which is used for planning program logic. It is an imitation of actual computer instructions written in a natural language, such as English. Also known as Program Design Language (PDL).

Public-domain software. — A software, which is available free, or for a nominal charge from the bulletin boards, or user-group libraries on the Internet. Also known as shareware or user-supported software.

Q

Quantum. — See time slice.

Query By Example (QBE). — A software tool, which enables database users to specify search criteria by providing a front end for the query language, which collects the facts about a query from the use, and composes query language statements internally.

Query language. — A language, which enables users to define their requirements for extracting the desired information from the database in the form of queries.

R

Radix — Same as base. See base.

Random Access Memory (RAM). — A memory in which the time to retrieve stored information is independent of the address where it is stored.

Random file. — See direct file.

Random/direct0\-access storage device. — A storage device in which access to any stored information is direct, and approximately equal access time is required for accessing any information irrespective of its location. Magnetic, optical and magneto-optical disks are typical examples of such a storage device.

Raster graphics. — Graphic objects composed of patterns of dots called pixels.

Read-Only Memory (ROM). — A non-volatile memory chip in which data are stored permanently, and cannot by the programmer.

Record. — A collection of related items of data treated as a unit.

Record length. — A measure of the size of a record, usually specified in units, such as characters.

Reduced Instruction Set Computer (RISC). — Architecture. An Architecture of CPUs with a small instruction set, fixed-length instructions, and reduced references to memory to retrieve operands.

Redundant Array of Inexpensive Disks (RAID). — See disk array.

Registers. — Small, high-speed storage units, which are used to hold the information on a temporary basis when there is an interpretation and execution of instructions by the CPU. Data stored in a specific register have a special meaning to the CPU.

Relational database. — A database model in which the data elements are organized in the form of multiple tables, and the data in one table is related to data in another table through the use of a common field.

Remote access. — Accessing a computer from a distant station using communication facilities.

Report file. — A file, which holds a copy of a report generated by a data processing application in computer-accessible form, until it is convenient to print it.

Report generator. — A software, which enables the users of a database to design the layout of report, so that it can be presented in the desired format.

Report Program Generator (RPG). — A business oriented, general purpose programming language designed to generate the output reports resulting from the processing of common business applications.

Response time. — The elapsed time between submission of a job to the system for processing, and the first response produced by the system for the job.

Ring network. — A computer network in which there is no host computer for controlling other computers, and each computer in the network has communicating subordinates.

Router. — An internetworking tool, which is use to interconnect those networks, which use the same high-level protocols above the network layer.

Routing. — The selection of actual path to be used to transmit a message in a wide-area network environment.

RS-232-C interface. — A standard interface used for interconnecting user terminals to computers. It was defined by the Electronics Industrial Association (USA).

Run time. — The time required to complete a single, continuous, execution of an object program.

S

Scanner. — An input device used for direct data entry into the computer system from source documents.

Schema builder. — A software tool, which enables a user to define a database schema interactively by prompting the user to enter the field name, field type, field size, and so on for each field.

Screen image projector. — An output device, which is used to project information from a computer on to a large screen (such as a cloth screen or a wall), so that can be simultaneously viewed by a large group of people.

Scrolling.	Using program-specified ways (by the use of keys or mouse) to move the items displayed in a window up or down, or left or right to see parts of the file that extend past the bottom or top or sides of the window.
Second-generation computers.	Computers built during the period 1955 and 1964. They used transistors in CPU, and magnetic cores for main memory. On software front, they used "high-level languages like FORTRAN and COBOL for programming, and batch operating systems.
Secondary storage.	See auxiliary memory.
Sector.	The smallest unit with which any disk can work. Disk drivers are designed to access only whole sectors at a time.
Security.	Policies and mechanisms, which deal with protecting the various resources and information of a computer system against destruction and unauthorized access.
Seek time.	In a disk system, the time required for a read/write head to move to the track where the data to be read or written is stored. Maximum seek time equals the time taken for the head to move from the outermost track to the innermost track.
Selection logic.	A program construct, which is used for selecting the proper path out of two or more alternative paths in the program logic. Also known as decision logic.
Self-documenting languages.	Programming languages, which do not require much explanation to be understood by someone reading the program instruction. For example, COBOL language.
Semiconductor storage.	A storage device whose storage elements are formed as solid-state electronic components on an integrated circuit chip.
Sequence logic.	A program construct, which is used for performing instructions one after another in sequence.
Sequential file.	A file in which records are stored one after another in an ascending or descending order determined by the value of the key field of the records.
Sequential processing.	A technique in which a number of similar items or transactions to be processed are grouped together and processed in a designated sequence.
Sequential-access storage device.	A storage device in which information can only be retrieved in the same sequence in which it is stored. Magnetic tape is a typical example of such storage device.
Server computer.	In a client-server computing environment, a computer, which manages a shared resource and provides a set of shared user services to the clients. It runs the server process, which services client requests for use of the resource managed by the server.
Shareware.	See public-domain software.
Simplex.	A data transmission mode in which data can flow only in one direction.

Simulation. To represent and analyze properties or behavior of a physical or hypothetical system by the behavior of a system model.

Single In-line Memory Module (SIMM). A memory board with memory with memory chips on it. Memory chips can be added on the board to increase the computer's main memory capacity.

Small Scale Integration (SSI). Integration of only about ten to twenty electronic components on a single chip.

Smart card. An electronic card having a built-in microprocessor chip. Data to be encoded on the card is permanently stored in the memory of the chip.

Smart terminal. A terminal having local data editing capability, and the ability to consolidate input data, before sending them to the main computer. It has a microprocessor, some internal storage, and I/O capabilities.

Soft-copy output. A computer output, which is temporary in nature, and vanishes after use. For example, output displayed on a terminal screen, or spoken out by a voice response system.

Software. A set of computer programs, procedures, and associated documents (flowcharts, manuals, etc.) related to the effective operations of a computer system.

Software Package. A group of programs, which solve a specific problem, or perform a specific type of a job. For example, a word-processing package.

Software piracy. The illegal copying or use of software.

Solid state. Electronic components, whose operation depends on the control of electric or magnetic phenomena in solids, such as transistors and diodes.

Sort. The process of arranging data into a desired sequence.

Source program. A program written in a symbolic or high-level language, such a assembly language, COBOL, BASIC, etc.

Special character. A graphic character, which is neither a letter, a digit, nor a space character. For example, the dollar sign, comma, period, etc.

Special purpose computer. A computer, which is meant for doing only a particular type of jobs.

Speech synthesizer. A voice response system, which converts text information into spoken sentences.

Spreadsheet. A numeric data analysis tool (software package), which allows users to create a kind of computerized ledger.

SQL. A standard query language for relational databases.

Stack. A memory in which information, which is stored last is on top, and is retrieved first. Also known as LIFO (Last-in-first-out) storage.

Stand-alone. In a distributed data processing system, it refers to a computer system, which has an independent (from a central-site computer) processing and storage capability.

Star network.	A network in which multiple computers are connected to a central host compute. These computers are not linked directly to each other, and can communicate only via the host computer.
Statement.	In programming, an expression or generalized instruction in a source language.
Storage.	See memory.
Storage hierarchy.	A hierarchy of storage technologies (such as cache memory, main memory, secondary storage and mass storage) used in a computer system. This is usually done because a single type of storage is not superior in speed of access, capacity, and cost.
Stored program computer.	A computer where the program to solve a problem, and the necessary data are stored in its memory.
Structured design.	A system design approach in which a difficult problem is broken into smaller problems, which is small enough to manage, but independent enough to solve separately.
Structured programming.	An organized approach to programming involving the use of the three basic control structures-sequences, selection, and iteration, and the use of top-down concepts to decompose main functions into lower-level components for modular coding purposes.
Study phase.	A system life-cycle phase during which a problem is identified, alternative solutions are studied, and the most feasible solution is selected.
Subprocedure.	See subroutine.
Subroutine.	A standardized program written in a manner that it can be used as part of another program whenever necessary. A subroutine is normally invoked through other programs by these of CALL statements. Also known as subprogram and subprocedure.
Supercomputer.	Compute system characterized by their very high processing speeds. They are generally used for complex scientific applications.
Swapping.	Storing programs on disk, and then transferring these programs into main storage as and when they are needed. The technique is used to process large programs, or several programs with limited memory.
Symbolic language.	See assembly language.
Symbolic program.	See assembly program.
Synchronous communication.	Data transmission mode in which the sender and receiver must synchronize with each other to get ready for data transmission, before it takes place.
Syntax.	A set of rules of a programming language, which define the pattern or structure of the word order and punctuation of an instruction. It is analogous to rules of grammar in English language.

Syntax errors.	Errors in computers programs, which typically involve incorrect punctuation, incorrect word sequence, undefined terms, or misuse of terms. These errors are automatically detected, and pointed out by language processors.
Systems.	A group of integrated parts (people, methods, machines, and materials), which have a common purpose of achieving some objective(s).
System analysis.	A detailed step-by-step investigation of related procedures to see what must be done, and the best way of doing it.
System analyst.	The individual responsible for planning a computer data processing system. He/she utilizes tools, such as flowcharts, decision tables, program design language, etc. These plans are then passed to the computer programmer.
System commands.	Commands used to communicate with the operating system of the computer.
System programmer.	A programmer who prepares system software.
System software.	A set of one or more programs designed to control the operation, and extend the processing capability of a computer system.

T

Tape density.	The amount of data, which can be placed over a given length of tape. The density is usually expressed in bytes or characters per inch.
Tape drive.	A device used for storage and retrieval of data stored on magnetic tape medium.
Telecommunications.	Transmissions of data between computer system and/or terminals at different locations through telephone facilities.
Telnet.	An application level protocol, which allows a user to log in to another computer from his/her current computer in a network environment.
Template.	A standard format used to quickly create new documents in the same format.
Terabytes (TB).	Memory storage equal to about one trillion (10^{12}) bytes.
Teraflop.	10^{12} floating-point arithmetic operations per second.
Terminal.	See Video Display Terminal (VDT)
Testing.	The process of making sure that the program performs the intended task.
Thermal printer.	A printing device, which utilizes paper that is sensitive to heat.
Third-generation computers.	Computers built between 1964 and 1975, which used integrated circuits in CPU, high speed magnetic core main memories, powerful high-level languages, and time sharing operating system.

Throughput. The total amount of useful processing carried out by a computer system within a given time period. It is measured as the number of processes, which are completed by the system per unit time.

Time division multiplexing. A method of sharing a communication channel in which the total time available in the channel is divided between several users and each user of the channel is allotted a time slice during which he/she may transmit a message. The channel capacity is fully utilized by interleaving a number of data streams belonging to different users into one data stream.

Time log. A log documentation automatically maintained by many computer systems, which describes in detail how the computer system was used during the day.

Time slice. The short period of the during which a user process gets the attention of the CPU in a time-sharing system. Also known as time slot or quantum.

Time slot. See time slice.

Time-sharing. A mechanism to provide simultaneous, interactive use of a computer system by many users in a manner that each user is given the impression that he/she has his/her own computer. It uses multiprogramming with a special CPU scheduling algorithm to achieve this.

Top-down approach. A disciplined approach to system design or program design in which top-level functions are decomposed into a hierarchy of understandable lower-level modules for better management and easy handling.

Touch screen. A simple, intuitive, and easy to learn input device, which enables the users to choose from available options by simple touching with their finger the desired icon or menu item displayed on the computer's screen.

Track. In case of magnetic disk, one of many circular concentric rings used for storing data. In case of magnetic tape, a horizontal strip, or channel, running the full length of the tape, and used for recording data.

Trackball. An input device, which serves as an effective pointing device.

Transaction file. A file in which current data are stored for subsequent processing usually in combination with a master file.

Transducer. A device capable of changing signals from analog form to digital form, or vice versa.

Transistor. A controlled electronic switch fabricated using a semiconductor. It is extensively used in the design of various electronic equipment.

Transponder. A device mounted on a communication satellite, which receives, amplifies and retransmits signals from each stations.

Truth table.	A table, which gives the output values for the varies input combination in case of a logical expression.
Tuple.	A group of related fields (a row of a table) in a relational databases.
Turnaround time.	The elapsed time between the submission of a job to a computer system for processing, and the completion of the job.
Turnkey solution.	See end-to-end solution.
Twisted-pair cable.	A simple, inexpensive, and slow wired transmission medium.

U

Ultra Large Scale Integration (ULSI).	Integration of about ten million electronic components on to a single chip.
Ultra Violet EPROM (UVEPROM).	An EPROM chip in which the stored information is erased by exposing the chip for sometime to ultraviolet light.
Unbundled.	A term, which means that the application software is priced separately from the computer hardware.
Unconditional transfer.	A program instruction, which causes the program control to flow out of normal sequence unconditionally.
Uniform Resource Locator (URL).	An addressing scheme used by WWW browsers to locate clean and continuous power even during power failures.
Universal gate.	A logic gate, which is alone sufficient to implement and Boolean function. For example, NAND and NOR gates.
Universal Product Code (UPC).	A universal or standardized optical bar code, which normally appears on retail packages, and which is read by a laser beam scanner.
Unix.	A multi-user, time-sharing operating system. It is a very popular operating system, and can be used on a wide variety of a computers, ranging from notebook computers supercomputers.
Uploading.	Moving a file from ones own computer to a remote computer in a network environment.
Uptime.	The time duration when the computer system is in operation.
Upward compatible.	The ability of hardware or software to function with all the same equipment and software with which is predecessors could function.
Usenet.	A service on the Internet, which allows a group of Internet users to exchange their views/ideas/information on some common topic, which is of interest to all the members belonging to the group.
User authentication.	Deals with the problem of verifying the identity of a user (person or program), before permitting access to the requested resource.

User-friendly.	A program or computer system designed in a manner that even individual who lack computer experience can easily use the system without much training.
User-programmed ROM.	A PROM in which the user can load and store "read-only" programs and data.
User-supported software.	See public-domain software.
Utilities.	A set of programs, which help users in performing system maintenance and other tasks of routine nature.

V

Value Added Network (VAN).	Enhanced data transmission service provided by doing value addition to the standard service of the common carriers. Added value may include features, such as electronic mail, data encryption/decryption, access to commercial databases, and code conversion for communication between incompatible computers.
Variable name.	In a program, the name assigned to a data field, which can assume any of a given set of values.
Vector graphics.	Graphic objects composed of patterns of lines, points, circles, arcs and other geometric shares (vectors), which can be easily represented by few geometric parameters.
Very Large Scale Integration (VLSI).	An electronic circuit with about 10,000 transistors fabricated in a single silicon chip.
Very Small Aperture Terminals (VSATs).	Smaller disk antennas having lower power transmitters and receivers, which can be installed at user's sites. It enables a large number of users to benefit from satellite communication.
Video conferencing.	A system in which persons sitting at CRT screens see and talk to each other via computer communications network. It saves travelling cost and the valuable time of executives.
Video Display Terminal (VDT).	A monitor and a keyboard used together as both an input and an output device. Also known as terminal.
Virtual machine.	The concept of adding the operating system layer on top of the bare hardware to manage all parts of the system, and present the users with an interface, which is easier to program and use.
Virtual memory.	A memory management scheme, which allows the execution of processes, which might not be completely loaded in the main memory. The three basic concepts used for the realization of virtual memory are on-line secondary storage, swapping and demand paging.
Virus.	A computer virus is a piece of code attached a legitimate program, which, when executed, infects other programs in the system by replicating effect, a virus normally does some other damage to the system, such as corrupting/ersasing time.

Vision input system.	An input device, which allows a computer to accept input by seeing on object. The input data in this case is normally an object's shape and features in the from all an image.
Visualization.	Deals with exploring data and information graphically for better comprehension.
Voice recognition device.	An input device, which allows a person to input data to a computer by speaking to it.
Voice reproduction system.	A voice response system, which produces audio output by selecting appropriate audio output from a set of pre-recorded audio responses.
Voice response system.	An output device, which enables a compute to talk to its users.
Voiceband.	Data communications system, which handles moderate volumes of data, typically from 300 to 9600 bauds. Phone lines, which we use to talk to other people is an example.
Volatile storage.	A storage medium, which loses its contents when power fails, or when power is switched off.

W

Web client.	Any computer on the Internet, which can access web servers.
Web page.	A hypertext document on the Internet.
Web server.	Any computer on the Internet, which uses the HTTP protocol.
Wide Area Network (WAN).	A computer network, which interconnects computers spread over a large geographical area. It may also enable LAN's to communicate with each other. This type of network may be developed to operate nationwide or worldwide, and the transmission medium used are normally public systems, such as telephone lines, microwave and satellite links.
Wildcard (character).	A special character, usually a ? or an *, which is used in software commands as a generic reference to any character, or any combination of characters, respectively.
Winchester disk.	Medium-sized, non-interchangeable metal disks permanently housed in sealed, contamination free containers, with built-in read/write heads.
Window.	A rectangular portion of a computer screen, which is dedicated to specific activity or application. The display screen can be separated into several windows to simultaneously show the status of the different applications at any instance of time.
Windows.	An operating system developed by Microsoft for use on personal computers. Its various release versions are Windows 3.0, Windows 95, Windows 98, Windows 2000 and Windows XP.

Windows NT.	A multi-user, timesharing operating system developed by Microsoft, which has Unix-like features. It is designed to be used for powerful workstations, and network and database servers.
Wireless computing system.	A computer network, which uses wireless communication technologies. It enhances the functionality of computing equipment by freeing communication from the location constraints of the wired computing systems.
Word.	A group of bits or characters considered as an entity, and capable of being stored in one storage location. Also fixed-size storage areas, which form the primary memory of a computer system.
Word length.	A measure of the size of a word, usually specified in units, such as characters or bits. Each location of a computer system can store a fixed number of characters or bits, called its word length.
Word processing.	The use of computers to create, view, edit, format, store, retrieve, and print text materials.
Word wrap.	A word processing feature, which automatically moves words down to the beginning of the next line, if they extend beyond the right margin.
Word-addressable storage.	Storage designed to store a fixed number of characters (equal to its word-length in bytes). For such a storage device, storage space is always allocated in multiples of word-length. Its another name is fixed-word-length storage.
Workstation.	A powerful desktop computer designed to meet the computing needs of engineers, architects, and other professionals, who need greater processing power, larger storage, and better graphics display facility than what PCs provide.
World Wide Web (WWW or W3).	Network of computers across the world interconnected together on the Internet, and using the concept of hypertext to link Internet sites and information on the Internet.
Worm.	A computer virus designed to erase/alter the data/program from a computer system's memory/disk.
Write-Once, Read-Many (WORM) Disk.	An optical disk, which looks like a standard CD-ROM disk, but allows the user to record his/her own information on it by using a CD-Recordable (CD-R) drive.
WYSIWYG.	Stands for What You See Is What You Get. This feature of a word-processing package allows the users to display a document on the screen in a form, which closely resembles what the printed document will look like.

Z

Zip disk.	See Bernoulli disk.
Zoned decimal number.	Any numeric character coded in the Extended Binary Coded Decimal Interchange Code (EBCDIC). Each decimal digit occupies one byte of storage.

INDEX